ISSUES IN INDUSTRIAL ECONOMICS

In loving memory of my father

Issues in Industrial Economics

SATYA R. CHAKRAVARTY
Indian Statistical Institute, Calcutta

Avebury
Aldershot · Brookfield USA · Hong Kong · Singapore · Sydney

© Satya R. Chakravarty 1995

All rights reserved. No part of this publication may be reproduced, stored in a retrieval system, or transmitted in any form or by any means, electronic, mechanical, photocopying or otherwise without the prior permission of the publisher.

Published by
Avebury
Ashgate Publishing Limited
Gower House
Croft Road
Aldershot
Hants GU11 3HR
England

Ashgate Publishing Company
Old Post Road
Brookfield
Vermont 05036
USA

British Library Cataloguing in Publication Data

Chakravarty, Satya R.
 Issues in Industrial Economics
 I. Title
 338

ISBN 1 85972 018 8

Library of Congress Catalog Card Number: 94-73471

Printed and bound by Athenæum Press Ltd.,
Gateshead, Tyne & Wear.

Reprinted 1996

Contents

Figures	vii
Preface	viii

1 On the measurement of concentration — 1
   Some definitional problems — 3
   Properties for an index of concentration — 5
   Indices of concentration — 15
   Concentration and diversification — 21
   Concentration : some theoretical implications — 25
   Determinants of concentration — 28
   Dynamic issues in concentration measurement — 28
   Concluding remarks — 34

2 Market power in oligopolistic models — 37
   Standard market structures and monopoly power — 38
   Properties for an industrial market power function — 47
   A general form of industrial market power — 48
   Industrial market power and diversification — 53
   Game theory : a brief discussion — 57
   Power to monopolize the market : a game theoretic approach — 61
   Welfare consequences of market power — 66
   Concluding remarks — 73

3 Measuring efficiency — 76
   Properties for an index of efficiency — 77
   Indices of efficiency — 82
   Concluding remarks — 88

4	**Merger, efficiency and concentration**	89
	Merger activity : reasons and some historical evidences	90
	Measuring efficiency of merger	92
	Efficiency of merger and concentration	94
	Price effects of horizontal mergers	96
	Welfare effects of horizontal mergers	100
	Concluding remarks	105
5	**On structure performance relationships**	106
	Measures of performance	107
	Alternative measures of performance and industry structure	110
	Some additional issues	122
	Structure performance relationship : an evaluation from Chicago School's viewpoint	127
	Concluding remarks	132
6	**The size distribution of firms**	136
	The stochastic models	137
	Managerial efficiency and the size distribution of firms	142
	An alternative formulation	145
	Concluding remarks	150
	Extended bibliography	152
	Index	171

Figures

Figure 1.1	Concentration curves	11
Figure 2.1	Determination of the monopoly price	42
Figure 2.2	Cournot equilibrium	43
Figure 2.3	Stackelberg equilibrium	44
Figure 2.4	Price leadership oligopoly	46
Figure 3.1	Allocative and technical efficiencies	85
Figure 4.1	Efficiency of merger	94
Figure 6.1	Average cost	149
Figure 6.2	Optimal density	150

Preface

This book deals with firm behavior and market performance. The central topic of the book is market power of firms, their control over price and capacity to exclude competitors.

Chapter 1 provides a rigorous analysis of concentration. A formal discussion on market power, its explanation and consequences are presented in Chapter 2.

Chapter 3 presents efficiency in an axiomatic framework. Chapter 4 analyzes merger in terms of efficiency, concentration, price and welfare effects.

Chapter 5 examines structure performance relationships from different perspectives. Finally, Chapter 6 offers a synthesis of alternative approaches to the size distribution of firms.

I wish to express sincere gratitude to Alexis Jacquemin for his suggestions at various stages of this work. I have benefited from generous comments made by Dennis W. Carlton, Roger Clarke, Rolf Färe and Tony Shorrocks, and to them too I am grateful. I thank Nachiketa Chattopadhyay, Amita Majumder and Tandra Rao for their advice and help in using word processor. The first draft of the manuscript was typed by Gita Ghosh. Buddhadev Ghosh did the painstacking job of arranging the extended bibliography alphabetically. I am thankful to both of them for their cooperation. I offer special thanks to Dibyendu Bose who spent many hours on the word processor and prepared the final draft of the book. Thanks are also due to the Indian Statistical Institute for partial financial support. Finally, since this work has been completed at the cost of neglecting my family for quite sometime, acknowledgement is due to my son, Ananyo, and to my wife, Sumita, for their patience during the period.

1 On the measurement of concentration

An index of concentration of firms in an industry is a measure of the extent to which economic activity is controlled by large firms. A distribution of business firms by size has often been noted to possess a single mode and a highly skewed upper tail. Thus, loosely speaking, a measure of industrial concentration is a summary statistic reflecting the distribution of firms in the industry. In the words of Scitovsky (1955, p. 109) 'Measures of concentration try to express the number and size distribution of competitors in terms of a one-parameter index, which could then be regarded as a direct measure of the degree of oligopoly'. A highly concentrated industry will take on a higher value for the index and is expected to be closer to the monopoly end of the monopoly to competition spectrum than an industry with a low value for the index.

There are many reasons for being interested in concentration. In this introductory discussion we mention only a few. Concentration has been regarded as one of the significant dimensions of market structure because it is believed to have played an important role in determining market power and hence business behavior and performance. In a seminal article, Lerner (1934) suggested the use of the ratio between the profit margin (price minus marginal cost) and the price as a direct measure of departure from competitive ideal for a single firm. It is a measure of market power of a firm in the sense that it determines the firm's ability to set price above the competitive level. Alternative aggregation procedures of individual Lerner indices in an industry have been employed to show that various concentration indices can be related to the market power for the industry as a whole. These results are somewhat similar to the Stigler (1964) theory of collusion which stresses the importance of concentration in explaining the market outcome. The relationship between aggregate market power and concentration indices shows that concentration may be helpful in assessing market performance which is judged by comparing the results of market conduct to the perfectly competitive set up. Following Bain's (1951, 1956) pioneering contributions on structure performance relationships, models of oligopoly that permit evaluation along this line have made substantial progress. These issues are explored in greater detail in Chapters 2 and 5.

A second application of concentration concerns the gain in efficiency realized from horizontal merger of firms. There are several economic reasons for two firms to consolidate into one. For instance, horizontal merger of firms producing some good may lead to an increase in productive efficiency. It has been argued that the Debreu (1951) – Farrell (1957) measure to calculate the efficiency gain resulting from combining two or more firms producing a homogeneous good can be related to a concentration formula. We take up this issue more explicitly in Chapter 4.

Another application of concentration arises in the context of diversification of different firms' activities. A firm's activity need not be restricted to one particular sector. It may be profitable for a firm to produce more than one good. Thus, it becomes a member of more than one industry. Concentration indices have been employed to study diversification by explicitly taking into account the role of intersector linkages and total scale of firms operating in multiple sectors. (See Gort (1962), Amey (1964), Berry (1971, 1975), Rhoades (1973, 1974), Sutton (1973), Gorecki (1974, 1975), Grant (1974), Prais (1981a), Hassid (1977), Utton (1977, 1979), Jacquemin and Berry (1979), Clarke and Davies (1983, 1984), Encaoua, Jacquemin and Moreaux (1986) and Hay and Morris (1991) for matters relating to diversification.)

High concentration in an industry may be regarded as one of the factors that facilitate the formation of a cartel, an association of firms which agrees to coordinate the activities (production and pricing) of its members to increase the joint and individual profits by restricting output. More precisely, if in an industry most of the output is produced by a few large firms, then they may coordinate their activities by forming a cartel and may raise price without involving the small firms in the industry. Among other interesting applications of concentration are its role in explaining size distribution of firms and its link with welfare.

In this chapter we are concerned with measurement of concentration. More precisely, the purpose of this chapter is to discuss indices of concentration, their properties, determinants of concentration and some of their applications including diversification. A rigorous definition of a concentration index will require explanation of the unit in which the economic activity of different firms is measured. Below we present this explanation and clearly define the concepts of an industry and a market. We then look at the properties for an index of concentration and their implications. These properties will enable us to combine our observations on economic activity of firms into a single summary measure of industrial structure. This is followed by an examination of concentration indices that have been proposed in the literature. Next, we deal with some applications and theoretical implications of concentration. Determinants of concentration and the dynamic aspects of concentration measurement are analyzed after this. Some extensions and remarks are presented in a conclusion.

Some definitional problems

Since concentration refers to the degree of control of economic activity of large firms, we need to present a rigorous definition of the unit in which economic activity is measured. One possible measure of economic power of a firm is its assets. This is a natural measure of economic influence, but proper valuation of assets involves many factors including accounting conventions (see Chapter 5). Furthermore, the accounting conventions may vary over firms. Asset is a quite appropriate unit if we are interested in looking at the degree of command exercised by the ownership of assets. Employment can also be regarded as a size variable. In fact, it is the unit of economic activities if we wish to look at the concentration of employees in industries. Generally, large firms are more capital intensive than small ones. This means that while asset measures tend to emphasize the importance of large firms, employments tend to diminish it. Therefore, both employment and assets have their own systematic biases.

Another measure of the importance of a firm's activities is its value added, the sales revenue less the input costs of the firm. Evidently, this measure takes some account of both capital and labor. Its principal disadvantage is the lack of information about it. We need to know the sales by each firm in final markets. In case of various stages of production, identification of a product at each stage is necessary. That is, at each stage of production, price of the semi-processed product is to be calculated, though actually no price is paid for it. However, chance of getting such information is very low. We can also consider the use of gross output or sales as a size measure. Since there may be interfirm sales, a seller of the output in the final market need not be its manufacturer. Thus, the concentration measure based on sales will overstate the importance of firms engaged in distribution as opposed to manufacture. However, for analysis of firms within the same market or for average concentration across markets a sales measure is appropriate. It has been shown by Blair (1972) that various size measures are often highly correlated. This means that interchangeability of the size measures is allowable. Smyth et al. (1975) and Shalit and Sankar (1977) argued that we require stronger conditions than correlations for interchangeability of the size variables.

The next problem is regarding the definition of industries and markets, which are often used interchangeably. Two criteria are generally employed to define an industry: the product being produced (market criterion) and the methods of production (technological criterion). According to the first criterion, which is also referred to as the demand side approach, an industry is defined as a group of firms producing similar but not necessarily identical products for which cross elasticities of demand and cross elasticities of supply are significant. That is, the firms produce all those products that are good substitutes on the demand and supply sides. A product A is a demand side substitute for a product B if an increase in the price of B causes consumers to use more of A. Product A is a supply side substitute for product B if firms producing B switch some of their production facilities to the production of A as a result of increase in the price of B. But it is difficult to estimate cross elasticities numerically. Furthermore, judging the level of significance of cross elasticities to justify whether two products are close substitutes is also quite difficult. For identifying good substitutes for a particular product, an obvious way will be to interview producers and customers. Another way is to examine price correlations among different products. If two goods are substitutes, their prices should move together. However, price correlations should be interpreted cautiously. For instance, dissimilar products made from similar inputs may have quite high price correlation. Analogously, low price correlation need not always indicate that the two products are not in the same market.

According to the second criterion firms are grouped into an industry by similarity of technological process or raw materials used. It should be noted that the technological criterion for defining an industry need not coincide with the market criterion. This becomes clear if we consider two consumer products which are close substitutes but are made from different materials. For census purposes it is not the firms but the establishments that are grouped together. The technological, that is, the supply side characteristics get main importance in the process of allocation of establishments to different groups.

Although industrial classifications differ from country to country, basic principles behind them are more or less similar. A certain range of numbers is allocated to a broad category of industry (e.g. food). Then successive subdivisions will produce finer details (e.g. soft drinks). In the U.S.A., the process involves a series of numbers so that people can talk about four digit level etc. Two digit numbers will identify broad areas of manufacturing. (For example, Standard Industrial Classification 38 stands for 'Instruments and Related Products' Industries.) The classification then goes down to the very finely divided seven digit level. However, it has been argued that the four digit industries come closest to the markets in economic sense. In the U.K. there is a dual classification scheme:the Standard Industrial Classification order (Roman numbers) and the minimum list heading (a three digit number), which shows the main level of disaggregation. The international scheme is, however, similar conceptually to the American system. In India four digit level classifications are followed. One digit level figures describe the sections, and there are ten such sections with a special section X for the activities not adequately defined in sections 0-9. For example, section 1 represents mining and quarrying. Two digit level figures define the divisions. For instance, division 12 represents mining of iron ore. Three and four digit level figures will indicate finer subdivisions. International comparability criterion of data is also suggested. (See 'The Revised National Industrial Classification of All Economic Activities:1987', issued by the Central Statistical Organization, New Delhi, for further details.)

It is important to note that in all classification systems, establishments producing more than one output are classified according to their major activities. This means that there may be underestimation of the number of establishments producing some goods. Another point that needs to be mentioned is the geographical extent of market. Given that details are collected from domestic establishments only, the size of a market defined as the total domestic sales of domestic establishments, may not be estimated correctly in the case of open economies. Next, concentration indices are based on industry data, where industry boundaries are defined mainly by supply side characteristics. Apart from its own classification problems, this procedure may neglect important characteristics of an economic market, that is, demand side characteristics. In order for industry concentration to be a meaningful concept, it must be true that the industry comprises a relevant economic market. The use of unadjusted concentration indices may give us quite erratic results if industry and markets are substantially different. Therefore, classifications should be adjusted to ensure that the establishment groupings are suited to reflect the specific objective in mind. Sometimes we become interested in aggregate concentration rather than concentration in particular industries. In such a case the domain of definition of a concentration index is the entire economy or a sector of the economy. Consequently, some of the problems enlisted above will not be relevant here. (The discussion of this section has been based mainly on Hannah and Kay (1977), Curry and George (1983), Waterson (1984), Schmalensee (1989) and Carlton and Perloff (1990). For further enquiry, see the references cited in these works.)

Properties for an index of concentration

The number of firms in an industry is indexed by $n \in N$, where N is the set of natural numbers; $N = \{1, 2, \ldots, \}$. We suppose that a firm's size is measured by its output; the formal analysis applies equally well to any scalar measure of a firm's size. Unless specified explicitly, it will be assumed that all the firms in the industry produce a homogeneous good. For a fixed $n \in N$ be the set of possible output distributions is D^n, with a typical element $x = (x_1, x_2, \ldots x_n)$, where D^n is the nonnegative orthant of the Euclidean n-space R^n with the origin deleted. That is, for any $x \in D^n$, $x_i \geq 0$ is the output of firm i, $i = 1, 2, \ldots, n$. (We have $x_i > 0$ for at least one i, $1 \leq i \leq n$.) Thus, in this formulation, an industry consisting of n firms can include some firms that exist but are currently producing no output. The set of all output distributions is $D = \cup_{n \in N} D^n$.

We will adopt the following notation. For any function $H : D \to R^1$, we denote the restriction of H on D^n by H^n. For all $n \in N$, $x \in D^n$, $X = \sum_{i=1}^n x_i$, the sum of outputs of different firms in the industry; $\lambda(x) = X/n$, the average output of the firms; $s = (s_1, s_2, \ldots s_n) = x/X$, the vector of output shares of the firms in the industry and x^o is that permutation of x such that $x_1^o \geq x_2^o \geq \ldots \geq x_n^o$. For all $n \in N$, we write a(n) for the number of active firms in the industry under consideration. (A firm will be called active if it has a positive output.) For all $n \in N$, 1^n will stand for the n-coordinated vector of ones. Given that the firms in the industry produce the same good; X, $\lambda(x)$ and x^o are well defined. Since $X > 0$, s is also well defined.

An index of concentration in an n-firm industry is real valued function defined on D^n. We will now present some important properties for an arbitrary concentration index $I : D \to R^1$. Discussion along this line has been made by Rosenbluth (1955), Blair (1956), Stigler (1964), Hall and Tideman (1967), Hart (1971), Hannah and Kay (1977), Hause (1977), Davies (1979), Encaoua and Jacquemin (1980), Blackorby, Donaldson and Weymark (1982), Curry and George (1983), Waterson (1984), Jacquemin (1987), Chakravarty and Weymark (1988), Gehrig (1988), Schmalensee (1989), Chakravarty and Eichhorn (1991), Hay and Morris (1991), and many others. We begin our presentation with the normalization principle.

Normalization (NOM):For all $n \in N$, for any scalar $\theta > 0$, $I^n(\theta 1^n) = \frac{1}{n}$.
Postulate NOM, which is concerned with the cardinality properties of a concentration index, says that the index value should be $1/n$ when all the n firms in the industry have identical output. This seems intuitively reasonable; if output is equally distributed across firms, no firm enjoys a dominant position in the industry, consequently, concentration should depend only on the number of firms in this case. Since an increase in the number of firms n here will increase competition, concentration should be inversely related to n. Note that the formulation shows that a concentration index will achieve the value 1 in the case of complete concentration (that is, when the industry is monopolized by a single firm). We provide a rationale for the axiom NOM afterwards.

The next postulate we consider also deals with cardinality properties of concentration. This property, which we call the replication principle, requires the value of an index to decrease under firm by firm replication of the industry. If an industry is replicated several times, the shares of large firms reduce. Consequently, the dominance of large firms, that is, concentration should decrease. The reduction in concentration under such a change is described by the following formulation:

Replication Principle (REP):For all $m, n \in N$, for all $x \in D^n$, $I^{mn}(y) = \frac{1}{m} I^n(x)$, where $y = (x, x, \ldots, x)$ is an m-fold replication of x.

The third property means that the concentration index should depend only on output shares, not on absolute output levels. Thus, the index is independent of the unit in which outputs are measured. Formally, we require the concentration index to be homogeneous of degree zero.

Homogeneity (HOM):For all $n \in N$, for all $x \in D^n$, for all scalars $\theta > 0$, $I^n(x) = I^n(\theta x)$.

In measuring concentration we need to be concerned only with the sizes of the firms. All irrelevant characteristics, for instance, the names of the firms, should be ignored. This means symmetry of the concentration index in its arguments. That is, the concentration index should not alter under any permutation of output levels.

Symmetry (SYM): For all $n \in N$, for all $x \in D^n$, $I^n(y) = I^n(x)$, where y is any permutation of x.

An implication of symmetry is that the concentration index can be defined directly on ordered distributions.

It should be evident that concentration should decrease if the size of a small firm increases at the expense of the size of a large firm. We formalize this argument as

Output Transfers Principle (OTP): For all $n \in N$, $x \in D^n$, if y is obtained from x by a transformation of the form:

$$y_i = x_i + \delta < y_j \qquad (1.1)$$
$$y_j = x_j - \delta,$$

where $\delta > 0$, $y_k = x_k$ for all $k \neq i, j$; then $I^n(y) < I^n(x)$.

The output transfers principle requires concentration to decrease if some output is transferred from a large firm to a small firm (without reversing their ranking). Symmetrically, concentration will increase under a transfer from a small firm to a large firm. If the index satisfies symmetry then we allow only those transfers that do not alter the rank orders of the firms.

Measures of concentration are concerned with the dominance of firms of significant size. In contrast, inequality measures compare the output levels of small firms with those of large firms. Even if there are some similarities between indices of concentration and inequality, they do not reflect the same features of the distribution. To understand the distinction explicitly, let us consider an industry 'dominated by a small number of giants of similar size. Now suppose many small firms enter, but enjoy little success, so that even in the aggregate their market share is very low. Then concentration has not been significantly affected, but degree of inequality in firms' sizes has greatly increased' (Hannah and Kay (1977, p. 50)). Now, a firm entering the industry is certainly small enough if it is not larger than the smallest of the existing firms. So we say that a concentration index satisfies the 'small-firms property', if the addition of a firm with output not larger than that of the smallest of the existing firms, all other firms' outputs constant, does not increase its value.

Small-Firms Property (SFP): For all $n \in N$, for all $x \in D^n$, $I^{n+1}(t, x) = I^{n+1}(x_1, t, x_2, \ldots x_n) = \ldots = I^{n+1}(x, t) \leq I^n(x)$, where $t \geq 0$ is a scalar such that $t \leq \min_i x_i$.

SFP, which was suggested by Blackorby, Donaldson and Weymark (1982), is stronger than a property considered by Hannah and Kay (1977, p. 49) under the assumption of postulate HOM. According to the Hannah-Kay property the entry of new firms with output shares below some arbitrary significant level should reduce concentration.

If the output of a firm added to the industry is zero, the significance of large firms does not get affected at all, though inequality increases. Consequently, we have

Zero output Independence (ZOI): For all $n \in N$, for all $x \in D^n$, $I^n(x) = I^{n+1}(0,x) = I^{n+1}(x_1, 0, x_2, \ldots, x_n = \ldots = I^{n+1}(x, 0)$.

Analogously, the deletion of a firm with zero output does not change the level of concentration.

Entry and exit change the number of firms in an industry. Another property that generates this type of change is merger. Under merger a new firm is created by combining two or more firms. Mergers can occur between competitors (horizontal mergers), between firms where one produces for another (vertical merger) and between firms in unrelated business (conglomerate mergers). Thus, the recent merger between the Punjab National Bank and the New Bank in India will be an example of horizontal merger (Business Standard, Calcutta, 24 July 1993). Merger of a steel firm with a firm producing pig iron is an example of vertical merger. We examine the reasons for merger and some historical evidences in Chapter 4.

In the present context we are concerned only with horizontal merger. We formally state the merger condition as:

Merger Principle (MEP): For all $n \in N$, $n \geq 2$, $x \in D^n$,
$I^n(x_1, x_2, \ldots, x_n)$
$< I^{n-1}(x_1, \ldots, x_{i-1}, x_i + x_j, x_{i+1}, \ldots, x_{j-1}, x_{j+1}, \ldots, x_n)$
$= I^{n-1}(x_1, \ldots, x_{i-1}, x_{i+1}, \ldots, x_{j-1}, x_i + x_j, x_{j+1}, \ldots, x_n)$,
where $i, j \in \{1, 2, \ldots, n\}$ and both x_i and x_j are positive.

MEP requires concentration to increase if two firms merge and receive their pre-merger combined total output, all other firms' outputs remaining fixed. Hannah and Kay (1977, p. 50) noted that a merger can be regarded as a two-stage procedure: first, the entire output of the smaller firm is transferred to the large firm and then the small firm quits the industry.

'Outside the United States, mergers have been an important source of increases in seller concentration' (Schmalensee (1989, p. 995)). In the United States until recently there has been strict antimerger policy, particularly against horizontal and vertical mergers; and the role of merger as an explanatory factor of concentration increase has been relatively unimportant.

Stigler (1950) and Hart (1975) argued that a merger between firms of intermediate size may give rise to an increased competition for large firms in an industry. Thus, the dominance of large firms may reduce; however, the reduction in the number of firms because of merger may reduce overall competition. The resultant effect of a merger of the type considered will be determined by the relative strengths of these two forces. This is one possible outcome. Another outcome can be a more cohesive oligopoly group. Since mergers involve reshuffling of property interests among the existing firms in the industry, the actual outcome will be determined by a number of factors, including, the number and size distribution of firms, the cost structure, the type of the product etc. Concentration is a many-faceted phenomenon. Therefore, it is not reasonable to expect that every concentration index will capture all aspects of firms' behavior. Curry and George (1983) argued that the output transfers principle extended to include the merger effects will be an useful property.

Assuming homogeneity postulate for a concentration index $K : D \to R^1$, Gehrig (1983) considers the following formulation of the merger principle:

$$K^{n-1}(s_1 + s_2, s_3, \ldots, s_n) = K^n(s_1, s_2, \ldots, s_n) + (s_1 + s_2)K^2(\frac{s_1}{s_1 + s_2}, \frac{s_2}{s_1 + s_2})$$

with the convention that $0K^2(0/0, 0/0) = 0$. The above formulation shows the increase in concentration resulting from merger between firms 1 and 2. To understand this more explicitly, note that in an n-firm industry with output share vector $(s_1, s_2, \ldots, s_n)$ if the first two firms amalgamate, then we have an $(n-1)-$ firm industry with output share vector $(s_1 + s_2, s_3, \ldots, s_n)$. In view of MEP, we must have $K^{n-1}(s_1 + s_2, s_3, \ldots, s_n) > K^n(s_1, s_2, \ldots, s_n)$. Note also that this function eliminates inner concentration between firms 1 and 2, that is, $K^2(s_1/(s_1 + s_2), s_2/(s_1 + s_2))$. Simply because of this it is argued that the concentration of the new situation is equal to the sum of the concentration before merger and the internal concentration between the amalgamated firms weighted by sum of their output shares $(s_1 + s_2)$. This formula is in fact a reinterpretation of a property considered by Aczél and Daróczy (1975) in information theory. If in addition to this particular formulation of the merger principle, the concentration index satisfies symmetry, then it will meet zero output independence (Aczél and Daróczy (1975, p. 59)).

A common problem is obtaining accurate data on firms' outputs. It is therefore desirable that small errors in the measurement of output should have little impact on the value of a concentration index. Demanding that, for each n∈ N, a concentration index be continuous achieves this objective.
Continuity (CON):For all n∈ N, I^n is a continuous function.
Combined with zero output independence, continuity also ensures that the value of a concentration index is not over sensitive to the omission/addition of very small firms in the industry. As Adelman (1969) pointed out this becomes quite important if the determination of the exact industry size turns out to be difficult because of presence of firms whose outputs are very small compared to the rest of the industry.

We now discuss some implications of the above properties. Let us begin with the following observation:The output transfers principle implies that a concentration index takes on the minimum value when all the firms in the industry have identical output (Encaoua and Jacquemin (1980)). Further, for any concentration index satisfying NOM and OTP, $I^n(x) > 1/n$, where $x \in D^n$ is unequal and arbitrary and $n \in N$, $n > 1$, is also arbitrary. Also note that if a concentration index I^n fulfills OTP, SYM and HOM, then it is bounded, where the bounds are given respectively by $I^n(1^n/n)$ and $I^n(1,0,\ldots,0)$. That is, in this case for all $x \in D^n$, $I^n(1^n/n) \leq I^n(x) \leq I^n(1,0,\ldots 0)$.

The next implication is concerning the small-firms property. Formally,

Theorem 1.1: If a concentration index $I : D \to R^1$ satisfies SYM, HOM, OTP, and ZOI, then it meets SFP.

Proof: For any $x \in D^n$, consider the addition of a firm to the industry with output t, where $t \leq min_i x_i$. If $min_i x_i = 0$, then by ZOI, the value of the concentration index will not alter under addition of the new firm. Now, suppose $min_i x_i > 0$ and assume also the positivity of t. Since I is symmetric, SFP requires to show that $I^n(x^o) \geq I^{n+1}(x^o, t)$.

We can now reallocate the new firm's output to all of the other firms in proportion of their outputs. The resulting output distribution is $(x_1^o + \epsilon_1, x_2^o + \epsilon_2, \ldots, x_n^o + \epsilon_n)$, where $\epsilon_i = tx_i^o/X$. By OTP, we have $I^{n+1}(x_1^o + \epsilon_1, \ldots, x_n^o + \epsilon_n, 0) > I^{n+1}(x^o, t)$. In view of ZOI, $I^{n+1}(x_1^o + \epsilon_1, \ldots, x_n^o + \epsilon_n, 0) = I^n(x_1^0 + \epsilon_1, \ldots, x_n^0 + \epsilon_n)$. Since I verifies HOM, $I^n(x_1^o + \epsilon_1, \ldots, x_n^o + \epsilon_n) = I^n(\theta x^0) = I^n(x^0)$, where $\theta = 1 + t/X$. We therefore have $I^n(x^0) > I^{n+1}(x^0, t)$. □

To study some additional implications, let us consider a concentration curve, a plot of the cumulative output shares against the cumulative number of firms, with firms ranked from the largest to the smallest. Formally, the concentration curve $CN(x, i)$ of any output vector $x \in D^n$ is obtained by plotting $\sum_{j=0}^{i} x_j^o/n\lambda(x)$ against i, where $i = 0, 1, \ldots, n$. We assume that $CN(x, 0) = 0$. The extension $CN(x, 0) = 0$ ensures that the concentration curve is a closed graph. Clearly, $CN(x, i)$ increases as i increases from 0 to n. The curve is concave also. These two properties of a concentration curve can be demonstrated using arguments similar to that employed for proving that a Lorenz curve is increasing and convex. The Lorenz curve for any output vector $x \in D^n$ indicates the share of the total output X produced/marketed by the smallest t proportion ($0 \leq t \leq 1$) of the firms. (See Kakwani (1980) and Chakravarty (1990) for rigorous derivation of the properties of a Lorenz curve.) In the case of minimal concentration when output is equally distributed, the curve coincides with the no-concentration line (line OB in the figure below). If there is complete concentration, the curve will be of the shape OAB in Figure 1.1. Clearly, OA =1 .

Given any two output vectors x, $y \in D^n$, we say that the concentration curve of x dominates that of y ($x >_{=c} y$, for short) if the former lies nowhere below and at some places (at least) above the latter. Formally, $x >_{=c} y$ means that $\sum_{j=0}^{i} x_j^o/n\lambda(x) \geq \sum_{j=0}^{i} y_j^o/n\lambda(y)$ for all $i = 0, 1, \ldots, n$, with strict inequality for at least i, $1 \leq i < n$. For defining the dominance criterion in the case when $x \in D^m$, $y \in D^n$, where $m < n (m > n)$, add n-m (m-n) new firms to the m(n)-firm industry, each producing zero output. By construction the concentration curve is insensitive to the addition/deletion of firms with zero output. Given that the number of firms in the two industries are now the same, the dominance relation becomes well defined. In Figure 1.1 two concentration curves are depicted; the dashed line is a concentration curve for a four-firm industry and the solid line is a concentration curve for a two-firm industry. In this case we have $x >_{=c} y$, where $x(y)$ is the output distribution for the two (four) - firm industry.

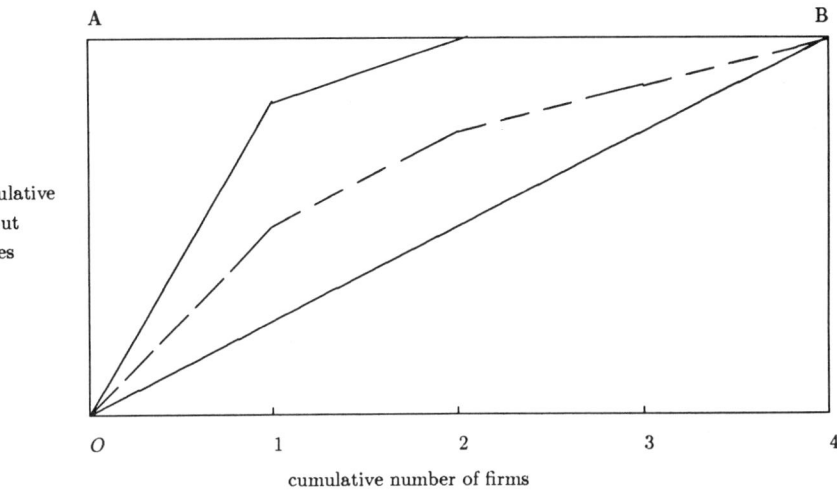

Figure 1.1 Concentration curves

It should be evident that if $x \in D^m$, $y \in D^n$ and $x >_{=c} y$ holds, then we must have $a(m) \le a(n)$. This necessary condition is, however, far from being sufficient. Note also that the ordering induced by the relation $>_{=c}$ is a quasiordering: it is transitive (for any x, y, z, $\in D$, if $x >_{=c} y$ and $y >_{=c} z$ hold, then we have $x >_{=c} z$), but not complete (if the concentration curves of x and y cross then neither $x >_{=c} y$ nor $y >_{=c} z$ holds).

The following result identifies the class of concentration indices that implies and is implied by the concentration curve dominance criterion. It is based on Hannah and Kay (1977), Encaoua and Jacquemin (1980), Blackorby, Donaldson and Weymark (1982) and Chakravarty and Eichhorn (1991).
Theorem 1.2: Let $x, y \in D$ be arbitrary. Then the following statements are equivalent:
(a) $x >_{=c} y$.
(b) $I(x) > I(y)$ for all concentration indices $I : D \to R^1$ that satisfy HOM, SYM, OTP and ZOI.
Proof: $(a) \Rightarrow (b)$. Let $x \in D^m$ and $y \in D^n$. Clearly, $m \lessgtr n$. Suppose $m < n$. Add $(n - m)$ firms each producing zero output to the industry whose output vector is x. Denote the new output vector by x^1, so that $x^1, y \in D^n$. Since a concentration curve satisfies zero output independence, $CN(x,i) = CN(x^1,i)$. Now, let $\alpha = Y/X^1 = Y/X$. Define $x^2 = \alpha x^1$. By homogeneity of the concentration curve in the industry output vector we have $CN(x^1,i) = CN(x^2,i)$.

11

Thus, x^2 and y are two distributions of the same total output Y over the same number of firms n and $x^2 >_{=c} y$. From this we can conclude that y Lorenz dominates x^2, that is, the Lorenz curve for y lies nowhere below and somewhere strictly above the Lorenz curve for x^2. This in turn implies that $\bar{y}$ can be obtained from $\bar{x}^2$ through a finite sequence of transformations transferring outputs from large firms to small firms (Kolm (1969), Atkinson (1970), Dasgupta, Sen and Starrett (1973) and Encaoua and Jacquemin (1980)), where for any $z \in D^n$, $\bar{z} = (\bar{z}_1, \bar{z}_2, \ldots, \bar{z}_n)$ stands for that permutation of $z = (z_1, z_2, \ldots, z_n)$ such that $\bar{z}_1 \leq \bar{z}_2 \leq \ldots \leq \bar{z}_n$. Since I satisfies OTP, we have $I^n(\bar{y}) < I^n(\bar{x}^2)$. But I is also symmetric. Therefore, $I^n(x^2) > I^n(y)$. Homogeneity of I ensures that $I^n(x^2) = I^n(x^1)$. Finally, using ZOI, $I^n(x^1) = I^m(x)$. Hence $I^m(x) > I^n(y)$.

$(b) \Rightarrow (a)$. Since a concentration curve itself is a concentration index satisfying HOM, SYM, OTP, and ZOI, this part of the theorem also follows. □

Theorem 1.2 shows that an unambiguous ranking of output distributions by concentration indices can be obtained through the pairwise comparison of the concentration curves of distributions. The total outputs as well as the number of firms in the industries concerned need not be the same for this general result to hold. However, if two curves cross then no unambiguous ranking can be made. That is, if the concentration curves of x and y cross then we can get two concentration indices I_1 and I_2 satisfying HOM, SYM, OTP and ZOI such that $I_1(x) < I_1(y)$ but $I_2(x) > I_2(y)$. Since we have already mentioned that concentration is a many-faceted phenomenon, this quasiordering of output distributions should not be taken as a shortcoming of the criterion $>_{=c}$. A concentration index $I: D \to R^1$ will be called consistent with the criterion $>_{=c}$ if for any $x, y \in D, I(x) > I(y)$ is implied by $x >_{=c} y$.

Clearly, theorem 1.2 holds for a fixed number of firms and also for a fixed industry output. More precisely, the following results drop out as interesting corollaries of theorem 1.1.

Corollary 1.3: Let $x, y \in D^n$ be arbitrary. Then the following statements are equivalent:

(a) $x >_{=c} y$.

(b) $I^n(x) > I^n(y)$ for all concentration indices $I^n: D^n \to R^1$ that satisfy HOM, SYM and OTP.

Corollary 1.4: Let $x, y \in D_\theta$ be arbitrary, where $D_\theta = \{x \in D \mid \lambda(x) = \theta\}$. That is, D_θ contains all those output distributions over industries with arbitrary number of firms such that the fixed mean output is θ. Then the following statements are equivalent:

(a) $x >_{=c} y$.

(b) $I(x) > I(y)$ for all concentration indices $I: D_\theta \to R^1$ satisfying SYM, OTP and ZOI.

An interesting application of this latter result is as follows. Suppose that a policy maker who has an objective of minimizing concentration is required to distribute a fixed amount of output among firms in one of two competing industries. Thus, the policy maker has direct control over distribution of output but not over the aggregate output. It is evident in such a situation the policy maker will favor the output distribution with a lower concentration curve. We employ the same objective in Chapter 6 under the additional constraint that the resources available to the industry are fixed to generate the most favored size distribution of firms of all those feasible.

Proof of theorem 1.2 shows that Lorenz domination and concentration curve domination are related as follows:

Theorem 1.5 (Blackorby, Donaldson and Weymark, 1982) : A concentration index I : D $\rightarrow R^1$ is consistent with the concentration curve dominance rule if and only if it is consistent with the Lorenz dominance criterion and satisfies zero output independence.

When both the number of firms and the total output are fixed, concentration indices can be characterized as strictly S-convex functions. (A numerical function F^n defined on D^n is S-convex if for all $x \in D^n$ and for all bistochastic matrices B of order n, $F^n(Bx) \leq F^n(x)$. A square matrix B of order n is a bistochastic matrix if all of its entries are nonnegative and each of its rows and columns sums to one. F^n is strictly S-convex if $F^n(Bx) < F^n(x)$ whenever Bx is not a permutation of x. All S-convex functions are symmetric (see Berge (1961)[1]). The characterization theorem is formally stated as:

Theorem 1.6 (Hannah and Kay, 1977) : Let $x, y \in D^n$, where $X = Y$, be arbitrary. Then the following statements are equivalent :

(a) $x >_{=c} y$.
(b) $I^n(x) > I^n(y)$ for all concentration indices $I^n : D^n \rightarrow R^1$ that satisfy strict S-convexity.
(c) If y^o is not a permutation of x^o, then there exists a bistochastic matrix B such that $y^o = Bx^o$.
(d) y^o can be obtained from x^o by a finite sequence of transformations transferring output from large firms to small firms.

Theorem 1.6 is a reinterpretation of a theorem of Dasgupta, Sen and Starrett (1973). (See also Kolm (1969).) We have already noted the equivalence between conditions (a) and (d). Hannah and Kay (1977) interpret conditions (c) as the requirement that random brand switching by customers should reduce concentration. If we allow customers' allegiance to particular firms to change in a random fashion, it is likely that large firms will lose customers and small firms will gain. This in turn implies reduction of concentration. Condition (b) puts some structure on the concentration index. This condition, in view of its equivalence with (a) (and (d)), means that all concentration indices satisfying symmetry and the output transfers principle are strictly S-convex. Furthermore, the converse is also true.

Hall and Tideman (1967), Theil (1967) and Encaoua and Jacquemin (1980) stated that one property of a concentration index is that in case of industries composed of firms of equal size, the measure of concentration should decrease with an increase in the number of firms. However, this property follows from stated that one property of a concentration index is that in case of industries composed of firms of equal size, the measure of concentration should decrease with an increase in the number of firms. However, this property follows from some primitive axioms. This was observed by Encaoua and Jacquemin (1980), Gehrig (1988) and Chakravarty and Eichhorn (1991).

Theorem 1.7: If a concentration index I:D $\to R^1$ satisfies HOM, ZOI and OTP, then $I^n(\theta.1^n)$ is decreasing in n, where $\theta > 0$ is arbitrary.

Proof: by hom,

$$I^n(\theta.1^n) = I^n(1^n/n) = I^{n+1}(1^n/n, 0), by ZOI. \tag{1.2}$$

Using OTP, we can demonstrate that $I^{n+1}(1^n/n, 0) > I^{n+1}(1^{n+1}/(n+1))$, from which the result follows. □

Clearly, the above theorem provides a rationale for the normalization axiom and it is quite reasonable intuitively.

The next theorem specifies some properties for a particular formulation of a measure of concentration. Suppose that the concentration index defined on the output share distributions is of the form $\sum_{i=1}^{n} s_i h(s_i)$, where h:[0,1] $\to R^1$. Thus, the concentration index is a share weighted average of the functional values $h(s_1), \ldots, h(s_n)$. Define also the real valued function f:[0,1] $\to R^1$ by f(t) = th(t).

Theorem 1.8 (Encaoua and Jacquemin, 1980):
(a) If the function f is strictly convex, then the measure $\sum_{i=1}^{n} s_i h(s_i)$ satisfies OTP.
(b) If the function h is increasing, then the measure $\sum_{i=1}^{n} s_i h(s_i)$ satisfies MEP.

Proof: (a) Strict convexity of f implies strict convexity of $\sum_{i=1}^{n} s_i h(s_i)$. We also note that $\sum_{i=1}^{n} s_i h(s_i)$ is symmetric. All strictly convex, symmetric functions are strictly S-convex. Hence the given form of concentration index is strictly S-convex. Therefore, in view of theorem 1.6 the required result now follows.
(b) In the case of merger of firms i and j, giving the output share $(s_i + s_j)$ to the resulting firm and leaving all other output shares unchanged, the difference of concentration between two size distributions, after and before merger, may be written as $s_i[h(s_i + s_j) - h(s_i)] + s_j[h(s_i + s_j) - h(s_j)]$. If the function h is increasing, the above difference becomes positive and MEP follows.□

Theorem 1.8 is quite appealing. We will see that many concentration indices can be expressed in the form $\sum_{i=1}^{n} s_i h(s_i)$. An index of this form is easy to compute and the effects of alternative properties on the index can be examined easily.

It may be worthwhile to note that properties HOM, OTP, ZOI, SYM, CON and MEP are independent, that is, any five of them can be satisfied by a function that does not fulfill the remaining property. We state this formally as

Theorem 1.9: Properties HOM, OTP, ZOI, SYM, CON and MEP are independent.

Proof: The following functions satisfy all of them but one:
(i) $K_1^n(x) = \sum_{i=1}^n x_i^2$, (not HOM),
(ii) $K_2^n(x) = \sum_{i=1}^n s_i(1 - e^{-s_i})$, (not OTP),
(iii) $K_3^n(x) = \sum_{i=1}^n s_i^2 - 1/n$, (not ZOI),
(iv) $K_4^n(x) = \sum_{i=1}^n s_i^2 + s_1^2$ if $s = (1, 0, \ldots 0)$
$\qquad = \sum_{i=1}^n s_i^2$ otherwise, (not SYM),
(v) $K_5^n(x) = \sum_{i=1}^n s_i^2$ if $s_i > 0$ for all $i = 1, 2, \ldots n$,
$\qquad = \alpha \sum_{i=1}^n s_i^2$ if $s_i = 0$ for some i, where $\alpha > 0, \alpha \neq 1$, is a constant,
(not CON),
(vi) $K_6^n(x) = \sum_{i=1}^n s_i e^{-s_i}$, (not MEP). □

It will now be interesting to look at independence among members of the other sets of properties that include in addition to the above six, both or one of NOM and REP. We conclude this discussion by mentioning that axioms HOM, SYM, OTP, ZOI (hence SFP), MEP, NOM and REP are consistent in the sense that there exist functions that fulfil them. Examples of such functions are presented below.

Indices of concentration

The concentration curve can be utilized to derive some simple measures of concentration. Two such measures relate to a single point on the curve. The first measure is the k-firm concentration ratio, the sum of output shares attributable to the k top firms in the industry. Formally, the k-firm concentration ratio is defined as

$$I_k^n(x) = \sum_{i=1}^k s_i^o, \qquad (1.3)$$

where $n \in N$ and $x \in D^n$ are arbitrary. This measure is very easy to calculate and has wide empirical applications. (In fact, government statistical sources in many countries provide k firm concentration ratios for 3 digit industries. For instance, for the U.K. 5-firm ratio, for Germany 3-firm ratio and for the U.S. a wide range including 4, 8 and 20-firm ratios are available.) But the choice of k in (1.3) is quite arbitrary. The second measure is the number of firms that comprises a given percentage of industry output (e.g. 60 per cent). The k firm concentration ratio is insensitive to interfirm output transfers outside the k largest firms. Even an output transfer among the largest k firms does not alter I_k^n. The same criticisms also apply to the second measure we have considered. Another criticism is that these measures do not take direct account of the number of firms in the industry[2]. In terms of the formulation of the concentration index considered in theorem 1.8, I_k^n can be written as $\sum_{i=1}^n s_i^o h(s_i^o)$, where $h(s_i^o) = 1$ if $i = 1, 2, \ldots, k$ and $h(s_i^o) = 0$ if i=k+1, ..., n. We however note here discontinuity of the function h.

Linda (1976) suggested an index which is based on the concentration ratio but allow for inequalities between large firms. The Linda index for the largest k firms is

$$I_{L_k}^n(x) = \frac{1}{k(k-1)} \sum_{i=1}^{k-1} \frac{\sum_{j=1}^{i} s_j^o / i}{\sum_{j=i+1}^{k} s_j^o / (k-i)}. \tag{1.4}$$

Evidently, I_{L_k}, which is based on the ratio between the average share of the top i firms and the average share of the remaining (k-i) firms, is designed to measure inequality between shares of output accounted for by various subsamples of firms. Note that if all firms upto the k largest have the same output, then $I_{L_k}^n = 1/k$. Note also that if the output of the (k+1)th firm is much smaller than its predecessors', then $I_{L_{k+1}}^n$ will be much larger than $I_{L_k}^n$. It has, therefore, been argued that 'oligopolistic arena' should be defined by the number of firms for which a minimum value of I_{L_k} is reached. The measure is quite popular in European community studies of industry structure. It has the obvious shortcoming of being insensitive to output transfers. Further, its designation as a measure of inequality shows its disadvantages.

Another concentration curve based measure is the Rosenbluth (1955) index $I_R : D \to R^1$, where for all $n \in N, x \in D^n$,

$$I_R^n(x) = \frac{1}{\sum_{i=1}^{n}(2i-1)s_i^o}. \tag{1.5}$$

It was later independently proposed by Hall and Tideman (1967) and Finkelstein and Friedberg (1967). Rosenbluth (1955) noted that $I_R^n(x)$ is simply the inverse of twice the area above the concentration curve corresponding to x. This index verifies all the desirable properties for a concentration formula.

A parametric generalization of the Rosenbluth index was suggested by Blackorby, Donaldson and Weymark (1982). This generalized index is given by $I_\delta : D \to R^1$, where for all $n \in N, x \in D^n$,

$$I_\delta^n(x) = \frac{1}{(\sum_{i=1}^{n}[i^\delta - (i-1)^\delta]s_i^o)^{1/(\delta-1)}}, \tag{1.6}$$

with $\delta > 1$ being a parameter. I_R drops out as a special case of I_δ when $\delta = 2$. As the flexibility parameter δ varies we have a class of concentration indices, with each member of the class satisfying all the properties we have considered earlier. Having the power to choose δ means that the class is large enough to incorporate a wide variety of views about concentration. In fact, as δ increases larger firms get more and more weight in the aggregation rule.

Another summary measure that satisfies all of our desirable properties is the Herfindahl (1950) index $I_H : D \to R^1$, where for all $n \in N, x \in D^n$,

$$I_H^n(x) = \sum_{i=1}^{n} s_i^2. \tag{1.7}$$

Hirschman (1945) used earlier the square root of I_H. Since the two indices are ordinally equivalent, we will refer to I_H as the Herfindahl-Hirschman index. Squaring of output shares in (1.7) implies that the smaller firms contribute less than proportionately to the index. I_H^n is in fact a share weighted average of the form $\sum_{i=1}^{n} s_i h(s_i)$, with the specification that $h(s_i) = s_i$. Clearly, this function is continuous. The Herfindahl-Hirschman index has many interesting applications. (See Chapter 2.) Also see next two parts of this chapter. A more complex index of the Herfindahl-Hirschman type was developed by Horvath (1970). The 'comprehensive concentration index' suggested by Horvath is defined as

$$I_v^n(x) = s_1^o + \sum_{i=2}^{n} (s_i^o)^2 (2 - s_i^o), \qquad (1.8)$$

where $n \in N$ and $x \in D^n$ are arbitrary. I_v and I_H are related as $I_v^n(x) = 2I_H^n(x) - \sum_{i=1}^{n} s_i^3 + s_1^o(1 - 2s_1^o + (s_1^o)^2)$. The index was intended to reflect both the relative size of the largest firm and the dispersion of the size distribution of firms. Horowitz (1972) pointed out that I_v may not satisfy the output transfers principle.

Sometimes it becomes convenient to use a numbers equivalent index of concentration. A numbers equivalent (or an equivalent number of equal sized firms) index requires that if all the n firms in the industry have the same output, then the index value is given by the actual number of firms n (Adelman (1969)). In response to a question like 'how concentrated is the industry', we can say 'it is as if there are k firms of roughly equal size', if we use a concentration index normalized in the numbers equivalent fashion. While an answer like this is a quite meaningful description of concentration, an answer like 'there are now n firms' is not very appropriate.

Numbers equivalents are inverse measures of concentration; an increase in the value of a numbers equivalent corresponds to a reduction in concentration. (See Blackorby, Donaldson and Weymark (1982) for a rigorous discussion on numbers equivalents.)

Hannah and Kay (1977) suggested a one-parameter class of numbers equivalent indices $I_\alpha : D \to R^1$ defined by

$$I_\alpha^n(x) = (\sum_{i=1}^{n} s_i^\alpha)^{\frac{1}{(1-\alpha)}}, \ \alpha > 0, \alpha \geq 1 \qquad (1.9)$$

$$= \pi_{i=1}^{n} s_i^{-s_i}, \ \alpha = 1 \qquad (1.10)$$

for all $n \in N$, $x \in D^n$ with the convention that $0^0 = 1$. I_α is a satisfactory measure of inverse concentration for all $\alpha > 0$. When $\alpha = 2$, this index is the Herfindahl-Hirschman measure expressed as a numbers equivalent. As $\alpha \to 0, I_\alpha^n \to n$ and as $\alpha \to \infty, I_\alpha^n \to 1/max_i s_i$. A transfer of output from a small firm to a large firm decreases I_α by a larger amount the higher is

α. The parameter α thus represents different perceptions of concentration. The choice of a value for the parameter α is a subjective one. Choosing $\alpha = 2$ implies that in measuring concentration we wish to give proportionally higher weights to large firms, whereas choosing $\alpha = 1$ means that we wish to decrease the importance of large firms. In fact, as α increases, in measuring concentration large firms get more and more weights. Choice of α may be dictated by economic policy considerations. 'For instance, in measuring the existing degree of concentration in a given industry, a government might give a low weight to the market shares of public enterprises while assuming a higher weight for subsidiaries of foreign multinationals' (Jacquemin (1987, p. 53)).

The class of indices obtained by subjecting the Hannah-Kay measures to a logarithmic transformation is known in the information theory literature as the Rényi (1961) entropy formula of order α. Formally, the Rényi entropy function of order α is defined by $E_\alpha : D \to R^1$, where for all $n \in N$, $x \in D^n$,

$$E_\alpha^n(x) = \frac{1}{1-\alpha} \log \sum_{i=1}^{n} s_i^\alpha, \alpha > 0, \alpha > 1 \qquad (1.11)$$

$$= -\sum_{i=1}^{n} s_i \log s_i, \alpha = 1. \qquad (1.12)$$

For $\alpha = 1$, E_α is the Shannon (1948) entropy function. It was popularized by Theil (1967) as an inverse concentration measure. The base of logarithm in (1.11) and (1.12) is 2 and this base has its origin in Shannon and Rényi's works. Of course, changing the base merely results in an index proportional to E_α. Since E_α and I_α are ordinally equivalent, E_α is also an inverse measure of concentration. In information theory entropy is considered as measure of uncertainty represented by a probability distribution. It takes on the maximum value for a uniform distribution, since in this case the information content of the probability distribution is zero. On the other hand, the minimum value is attained when the system is in a particular state with certainty (that is, with probability 1). Correspondingly, in our context E_α gives the maximum value $\log n$ for all $\alpha > 0$ when output is equally distributed. It takes on the minimum value zero in a situation of monopoly. It may be noted that $-E_\alpha$ is a direct measure of concentration. For the particular case $\alpha = 1$, $-E_\alpha$ can be written as $\sum_{i=1}^{n} s_i h(s_i)$ under the continuous specification $h(s_i) = \log s_i$.

An interesting property of E_α when $\alpha = 1$ is additive decomposability. According to additive decomposability the industry is partitioned into some disjoint subgroups, such as on the basis of control exerted on the firms—public, private, national, international etc., and the researcher becomes interested in examining how the overall degree of concentration can be appropriately resolved into contributions due to (i) concentration within each of the groups, and (ii) concentration between groups, that is, due to variations in average levels of the size variable (here output) across these groups. To see that the Shannon entropy measure can be disaggregated in such a fashion, let us suppose that an n-firm industry has been subdivided into k groups, with n_i firms in group i, $\sum_{i=1}^{k} n_i = n$. Let $S_i = (s_{i1}, s_{i2}, \ldots, s_{in_i})$ be the vector of output shares in group i and $S_i^a = \sum_{j=1}^{n_i} s_{ij}$ be this group's market share.

Clearly, $\sum_{i=1}^{k} S_i^a = \sum_{i=1}^{k} \sum_{j=1}^{n_i} s_{ij} = 1$. The Shannon entropy index E_1 can then be written as

$$E_1(S) = E_1(S_1^a, S_2^a, \ldots, S_k^a) + \sum_{i=1}^{k} S_i^a E_1(S_i), \tag{1.13}$$

where S stands for the vector $(S_1, S_2, \ldots, S_k)$. Note that since the index E_1 is homogeneous of degree zero in outputs, in (1.13) we have defined it directly on output shares. The first term on the right hand side of (1.13) is the between group measure of concentration and the second term is a weighted average of within group concentrations, where the weights add upto one. Jacquemin and Kumps (1971) made an extremely interesting application of the decomposability formula (1.13). In examining the level of industrial concentration within the European Economic Community (EEC), they considered two subgroups comprised respectively of British firms and firms within the rest of the EEC. It may be interesting to note that the numbers equivalent form corresponding to E_1 satisfies a multiplicative decomposability criterion, where the aggregate concentration can be written as the product of the between group concentration and a geometric average of within group concentrations (see Chakravarty and Weymark (1988)).

We already talked about inappropriateness of an inequality index as an index of concentration. However, an inequality index combined with some other industry structure may be an appropriate concentration index. Davies (1979) supposed that an inverse concentration measure could be written as a function of the number of firms(n) and a measure of inequality (J). He studied the properties of isoconcentration curves, which show all combinations of (n, J) yielding a given value for inverse concentration. Following Davies (1979) and Blackorby, Donaldson and Weymark (1982) we write a numbers equivalent n_e for an n-firm industry as

$$n_e(x) = f(n, J^n(x)), \tag{1.14}$$

where $x \in D^n$ and $n \in N$, $n > 1$. (Note that for $n = 1$ an inequality index is not defined. However, a concentration index is well defined even if n=1.) The function f is increasing in n and decreasing in J. As an example, we observe that the numbers equivalent form of I_δ^n in (1.6) can be written as $n[1 - J_\delta^n(x)]^{1/(\delta-1)}$, where

$$J_\delta^n(x) = 1 - \frac{1}{n^\delta \lambda(x)} \sum_{i=1}^{n} [i^\delta - (i-1)^\delta] x_i^o, \tag{1.15}$$

the Donaldson-Weymark (1980) single-parameter generalized Gini inequality index. If $\delta = 2$, J_δ in (1.15) is the Gini coefficient and we can thus have a relation of the Gini measure with the Rosenbluth index in (1.5). As a second example, we note that the Herfindahl-Hirschman numbers equivalent can be written as $n[(v^n(x))^2 + 1]^{-1}$, where for all $n \in N$, $x \in D^n$,

$$v^n(x) = \sqrt{\frac{1}{n}\sum_{i=1}^{n}(x_i - \lambda(x))^2/\lambda(x)}, \tag{1.16}$$

the coefficient of variation. The numerator in (1.16) is the standard deviation, the positive square root of the variance. The coefficient of variation is also a quite popular index of inequality. (See Adelman (1969) and Kelly (1981) for further discussions.)

Hannah and Kay (1977) considered indices of absolute concentration. Such a measure will be a function, not of shares of individual firms, but of their actual sizes. While in the earlier case a numbers equivalent gives us the equivalent number of equal sized firms, in this case the measure will be the size of such a firm. It will be derived simply by dividing the total output of the industry by the numbers equivalent. This is referred to as the 'effective average size of a firm'. This effective average size is an absolute concentration measure and it has the same unit in which we measure the size of a firm. For the particular case $\alpha = 2$, the effective average size corresponding to I_α in (1.9) was suggested by Niehans (1958) as an absolute concentration measure. It turns out to be

$$I_N^n(x) = X.I_H^n(x), \tag{1.17}$$

where $n \in N$ and $x \in D^n$ are arbitrary. Note that if a concentration index satisfies the replication principle, then the corresponding effective average size is replication invariant.

Many studies have found alternative concentration measures to be highly correlated. It has therefore been argued sometimes that empirical investigations using concentration indices will show similar results regardless of the choice of index. But the choice among even highly correlated concentration measures can affect the results obtained. Sleuwaegen and Dehandschutter (1986) showed that for highly concentrated industries the Herfindahl-Hirschman index and the k-firm concentration ratio cannot be substituted for each other. Kwoka (1981) demonstrates that the choice of concentration ratios can matter a great deal. He claims incompleteness of the argument that dismisses the choice as unimportant. (See also Nelson (1963), Kilpatrick (1967), Bailey and Boyle (1971), Aaronovitch and Sawyer (1975), Schmalensee (1977, 1989), Hause (1977) and Donsimoni, Geroski and Jacquemin (1984). We take up this issue in greater detail in Chapter 5.)

In fact, the choice of an index should be guided by the specific objective we have in mind. For instance, if we are interested in ranking of distributions, then any index consistent with the concentration curve ranking criterion will do (see theorem 1.2, its corollaries and theorem 1.5). For decomposability of concentration, the entropy index is a proper choice. One important basis for choice is axiomatic foundation for an index. That is, we look for a set of sufficient (strictly speaking, necessary also) conditions that will be satisfied by an index. For example, Gehrig (1983) showed that the Shannon (1948) entropy index is the only function that satisfies OTP, SYM and an additive decomposability postulate. (See Chakravarty and Weymark (1988) for an analogous characterization of the corresponding numbers equivalent form by a multiplicative decomposability property.) Gehrig (1983) axiomatized the negative of the Shannon entropy function by OTP, SYM and his formulation of the merger principle discussed earlier. Chakravarty and Eichhorn (1991) suggested an axiomatic characterization of the Hannah-Kay indices by the replication principle. Another important criterion can be economic theory—measures of concentration should be derived from oligopoly theory (see Chapter 2). We have indicated only a few criteria. There can be many more. This will become clear as we proceed for more elaborate analysis.

Concentration and diversification

Industrial diversification is a well known feature in many countries and some studies show that for a number of countries there is a clear indication of a rapid increase in diversification. For instance, in the case of the U.S.A. there is an increasing tendency by firms to choose new product lines outsides the primary two digit sectors (see Gort (1962), Jacquemin and Berry (1979) and Hay and Morris (1991)). A similar picture has been observed for the U.K. also - large enterprises tended to grow more by diversification than within sectors (Prais (1981a) and Hay and Morris (1991)). In India many industries are becoming more and more diversified. For example, the Indian Tobacco Company, which is known as a cigarette producer, has diversified its activities to many other product lines, such as, edible oil and hotels.

According to Sutton (1973) and Grant (1974) managerial motivation is the key element behind diversification. They identify three reasons for managerial motivation. The first is the low and/or falling growth rates of existing products. In this case the organization will try to find new and fast growing product lines (see also Gort (1962) and Amey (1964)). It may be the case that internally generated funds from low growth profitable organizations are substantially larger than those required to maintain the position in the areas of specialization. In this case there may be a tendency towards diversification (see Penrose (1959) and Caves et al. (1980)). If firms incur expenditure on innovation, new product lines with high potentiality may be identified by Research and Development. As a result firms may be interested in diversification even though the existing product is quite satisfactory. Therefore, this may be one reason that motivates a firm to introduce variety in production. Finally, diversification may take place with a view to reducing market risks. (See Hay and Morris (1991) for further discussions.)

According to Berry (1975) diversification that gave rise to fast rates of corporate growth generally has not been to markets where the entering firm is a potential competitor. It has rather been to a greater extent to 'markets that are related to – and potentially if not actively competitive with-those in which the entering firm will frequently share whatever market power already exists' (op cit., p. 74). Hilke and Nelson (1988) argued that under reasonable conditions large diversified firms that are about to enter an industry may be more likely to exit in the face of unexpected lower returns or higher risks (predation) than are small nondiversified firms. In predatory pricing a firm initially reduces its price to drive out rivals and frighten potential entrants of risks. When rivals disappear, the firm will increase its price. From an entrant's view point predation will lower expected profit since the existing firms' aggression may signal competitive disadvantage which may reduce expected revenues. Therefore, a large diversified firm may be more likely to exit than a less diversified firm under the reasonable assumption that large diversified firms face lower marginal costs in moving resources to other sectors/markets not affected by predation.

Utton (1977) defined a diversification curve for a firm as a plot of the cumulative shares of employment levels of different industries in which the firm operates against the cumulative number of industries, where the industries are ranked in nonincreasing order (by their employment). He considers the area above the curve as a diversification index. It is given by

$$d_U = \sum_{i=1}^{k}(2i-1)l_i, \qquad (1.18)$$

where l_i is the proportion of employment in industry i and $l_1 \geq l_2 \geq \ldots \geq l_k$. d_U takes on the minimum value 1 for a single product firm (complete specialization). On the other hand, it will achieve the maximum value k when the firm's activities are equally spread.

Berry (1971) defined an index of diversification for a firm as

$$d_B = 1 - \sum_i h_i^2, \qquad (1.19)$$

where h_i is the value of firm's output in industry i as a proportion of the total value of the firm's output. (The value of a firm's output in an industry is given by the volume of its output in the industry multiplied by the price of the product.) d_B becomes zero if the firm is completely specialized and it increases as the firm diversifies equally into an increasing number of industries.

Clarke and Davies (1983) looked at the relationship between market or industrial concentration and concentration at the level of the whole economy (aggregate concentration). Employing the Herfindahl-Hirschman index, they showed that the aggregate concentration is proportional to the weighted sum of concentration in constituent industries, where the factor of proportionality becomes amenable to an interpretation of a diversification index. In a later paper in 1984 they did the same exercise for the Hannah-Kay family.

To discuss the Clarke-Davies diversification formulae, let us consider an economy with n firms and k industries (or markets). Suppose that v_{ij} stands for the value of firm i's output in industry j, where v_{ij} may be zero for some j. The value of firm i's outputs is $v_i = \sum_{j=1}^{k} v_{ij}$, and the value of industry j's output is $v_{.j} = \sum_{i=1}^{n} v_{ij}$. We refer to $v = \sum_{i=1}^{n} v_i = \sum_{j=1}^{k} v_{.j} = \sum_{i=1}^{n} \sum_{j=1}^{k} v_{ij}$ as the size of the economy. Let $h_{ij} = v_{ij}/v_{.j}$ and $h_i = v_i/v$. The proportion h_{ij} is the value of firm i's output in industry j as a fraction of the value of industry j's output. On the other hand, h_i is the value of firm i's outputs as a proportion of the size of the economy.

Denote the reciprocals of $(\sum_{i=1}^{n} h_i^\alpha)^{1/(1-\alpha)}$ and $(\sum_{i=1}^{n} h_{ij}^\alpha)^{1/(1-\alpha)}$ by V_A and V_j respectively, where $\alpha > 0$ and $\alpha \neq 1$. V_A is the Hannah-Kay concentration index for the economy as a whole and V_j is its analogue at the level of industry j. Clarke and Davies (1984) shows that

$$V_A = [\sum_{j=1}^{k} V_j^{\alpha-1} . w_j^\alpha]^{1/(\alpha-1)} [\sum_{i=1}^{n}(1-T_i)^{\alpha-1} . v_i^\alpha / \sum_{i=1}^{n} v_i^\alpha]^{1/(1-\alpha)} \quad (1.20)$$

where $w_j = v_{.j}/v$ and

$$T_i = 1 - (\sum_{j=1}^{k} v_{ij}^\alpha)^{1/(\alpha-1)}/v_i^{\alpha/(\alpha-1)}. \quad (1.21)$$

The first term on the right hand side of (1.20) is a weighted sum of market concentrations with weights $w_i^{\alpha/(\alpha-1)}$. Note that T_i defined above is a generalization of the Berry diversification index at the firm level. T_i equals zero for complete firm specialization and becomes $(1 - k^{1/(1-\alpha)})$ when a firm operates equally in all k markets.

Let us define

$$T = 1 - [(\sum_{i=1}^{n}(1-T_i^{\alpha-1})v_i^\alpha / \sum_{i=1}^{n} v_i^\alpha]^{1/(\alpha-1)}. \quad (1.22)$$

Note that if $T_i = 0$ for all i, then $T = 0$. However, if some firms operate in more than one markets ($T_i > 0$ for some i), then $T > 0$. Thus, T can be interpreted as an index of diversification. T varies between zero (for complete specialization) and $(1 - k^{1/(1-\alpha)})$ for equal operation in all k markets by all n firms.

Using (1.22) we rewrite (1.20) as

$$V_A = [\sum_{j=1}^{k} V_j^{\alpha-1} w_j^{\alpha}]^{1/(\alpha-1)} (1-T)^{-1}. \tag{1.23}$$

Therefore, (1.23) shows that aggregate concentration depends positively on market concentrations and also, ceteris paribus, positively on an aggregate diversification index. The relationship depends crucially on the parameter α. The case $\alpha = 2$ in (1.23) was discussed by Clarke and Davies (1983). In this particular case concentration is measured by the Herfindahl-Hirschman index and T_i in (1.21) is the Berry diversification index at the firm level. Correspondingly, when $\alpha = 2$, the Clarke-Davies aggregate diversification index T in (1.22) can be referred to as the Berry aggregate index of diversification. Applying the case $\alpha = 2$, Clarke and Davies (1983) shows that roughly 10% of the increase in the UK manufacturing aggregate concentration was attributable to the increase in diversification between minimum list heading industries in 1963-68.

To develop a diversification index corresponding to the case $\alpha = 1$, it is convenient to work with the Shannon (1948) entropy formula. The aggregate (inverse) concentration and (inverse) concentration for an arbitrary industry j in this case are given respectively by

$$E = -\sum_{i=1}^{n} (v_i/v) log(v_i/v)$$

and

$$E_j = -\sum_{i=1}^{n} (v_{ij}/v_{.j}) \log(v_{ij}/v_{.j}).$$

It can be seen that

$$E = \sum_{j=1}^{k} E_j \frac{v_{.j}}{v} - \sum_{j=1}^{k} \frac{v_{.j}}{v} \log \frac{v_{.j}}{v} - F, \tag{1.24}$$

where

$$F = \sum_{j=1}^{k} F_j \frac{v_{.j}}{v} \tag{1.25}$$

is the aggregate diversification with

$$F_i = \sum_{j=1}^{k} \frac{v_{ij}}{v_i} \log \frac{v_{ij}}{v_i} \tag{1.26}$$

being the diversification of firm i. Equation (1.24) shows that the aggregate (inverse) concentration has been additively decomposed into a weighted average of industry (inverse) concentration indices, an entropy expression involving the sizes of different industries and an aggregate diversification index.

Jacquemin and Berry (1979) used the Shannon entropy formula to decompose the diversification by an arbitrary firm i in the whole economy F_i^T, into between and within industry diversification. That is,

$$F_i^T = F_i^B + \sum_{r=1}^{k} F_{ir}^W v_{ir}/v_i. \tag{1.27}$$

The first term on the right hand side (1.27) is firm i's diversification between industries and the second term is a weighted average of this firm's within industry diversifications, where the weights add up to one. An aggregate version of the above decomposition is

$$F^T = F^B + \sum_{r=1}^{k} F_r^W v_{.r}/v. \tag{1.28}$$

Hence the aggregate entropy diversification can be written as the sum of between industry diversification and a weighted average of within industry diversifications.

In the same paper, Jacquemin and Berry used the Shannon entropy and the Berry indices of firm diversification to carry out an empirical exercise based on data for 460 of the largest US manufacturing corporations in 1960 and 1965. Both the indices have been calculated at both the two and four digit level and both the measures demonstrated increasing diversification over time. The entropy measure also shows a greater degree of diversification within rather than between two digit industry groups in both the years. An attempt to decompose change in four digit diversification into within and between two digit diversification components has been made. It has been observed that diversification to new two digit categories as well as diversification to old two digit categories have been related to the growth rate of the relevant firms in positive manner.

Concentration: some theoretical implications

The purpose of this part is to see how concentration in a particular market may be able to influence the behavior of the firms in the market. (In presenting the materials here we will follow Stigler (1964), Hannah and Kay (1977) and Hay and Morris (1991).) We begin by analyzing a case involving the ability of each firm to keep watch on other firms' activities. Let us consider a very simple set up to illustrate this. A firm clearly will have some idea about its expected market share and any unlikely fluctuation will certainly alert it.

An example is the market for a homogeneous good where a price leader sets the price and other firms follow. (We discuss the price leadership model in detail in Chapter 2.) A firm may try to offer secret price discount to increase its sales. What are the chances of detecting such secret discounts? Stigler (1964) shows that the Herfindahl- Hirschman index is related to a reasonable measure of the ease of detecting cheating. To see this, suppose that there are n_s sellers of a homogeneous good and s_i is the output share of seller i. A few of the buyers are new, but over moderate period of time most are regarded as old. The number of new and old buyers are n_w and n_o respectively. A buyer will compare the increased probability of secret price discount that comes from shifting among suppliers with the economies of repeat purchase (which include smaller transaction cost and less product testing). We denote this probability of repeat purchase by p. In case of a potential price discount for old customers by firm j, firm i will lose $(1 - p)n_o s_i$ of old customers and firm j will gain $(1-p)n_o s_i s_j/(1-s_i)$ of them with a variance $(1-p)n_o s_i s_j (1-s_i-s_j)/(1-s_i)^2$. If we sum over all $i(\neq j)$, the variance of firm j's sales to old customers of rivals becomes (approximately) $(1-p)n_o s_j(1+I_H-2s_j)$, where I_H is the Herfindahl-Hirschman index. Thus, the variance of a firm's sales due to switching will be least when I_H will be least. So a firm that does well consistently will be more quickly suspected of cheating.

Hannah and Kay (1977) analyzed a case where the price discipline of a group of firms might break because of the retaliatory action by a subgroup of firms under the belief that random fluctuation in market shares is a consequence of secret price discount. Suppose there are n customers and each buys the same amount. Each customer has the probability s_i of buying from firm i. Thus, the expected market share of firm i is s_i, with the standard deviation $\sqrt{s_i(1-s_i)/n}$. Variability of market share is measured by the coefficient of variation $\sqrt{n^{-1}(s_i^{-1}-1)}$, the ratio between the standard deviation and the expected market share. This variability coefficient is greater for small firms. The market situation is assumed to be stable, unless firms with an aggregate share of s_a (say) believe that there is a secret price discount. Each firm will set its level of minimum expected sale such that the probability of selling less than this amount is p. If the firm sells less than this minimum amount it will join the group of disappointed firms. Therefore, its contribution to this frustrated group of firms is s_i with probability p and zero with probability $(1-p)$. This distribution possesses the mean ps_i and variance $p(1-p)s_i^2$. Summing over all firms, the fraction of output arising from the disappointed group of firms turns out to be p and the variance of that fraction is $p(1-p)\sum_i s_i^2$. Thus, the probability of the critical level s_a being exceeded depends on the variance, which is proportional to the Herfindahl-Hirschman index. That is, the probability of stability of the market situation depends directly on the Herfindahl-Hirschman measure.

The next implication is concerning the interdependence of firms in the market. Consider an n-firm industry producing a homogeneous good. The total consumer demand X of the good is a function of the good's price p and the demand function is denoted by

$$X = X(p). \tag{1.29}$$

This function is assumed to be downward sloping and differentiable. Because of monotone decreasingness of the function it is invertible. The inverse function is referred to as the inverse demand function and is denoted as follows:

$$p = f(X). \tag{1.30}$$

Note that p as a function X, that is, f is also monotonically decreasing. The revenue for firm i from the sale of its output is px_i. So marginal revenue, the change in revenue due to one unit change in output, is

$$MR_i = \frac{dpx_i}{dx_i} \tag{1.31}$$

$$= p + x_i \frac{df(X)}{dX} \tag{1.32}$$

$$= p(1 + \frac{x_i}{X} \frac{X}{f(X)} \frac{df(X)}{dX}). \tag{1.33}$$

Thus, the marginal revenue in (1.33) depends on the output share of firm i. We define the average marginal revenue AMR for the entire industry as the weighted average of individual firms' marginal revenues, where the weights are the output shares of the firms. That is,

$$AMR = [\frac{1}{X}\sum_{i=1}^{n} px_i + \sum_{i=1}^{n} x_i^2 \frac{dp}{dX}] \tag{1.34}$$

$$= p + p\sum_{i=1}^{n}(\frac{x_i}{X})^2 \frac{X}{p}\frac{dp}{dX} \tag{1.35}$$

$$= p[1 - I_H/\epsilon], \tag{1.36}$$

where $-\epsilon = (dX/dP)(p/X) < 0$ is the price elasticity of demand and I_H is the Herfindahl-Hirschman concentration index. Therefore, for a given ϵ, with $-1/\epsilon$ being small, a low concentration will mean that the divergence between p and AMR is not high. Loosely speaking, this implies that on an average, for all the firms, the marginal revenues will not differ significantly from the price. Consequently, the output share distribution of the firms is not very unequal. Hence no firm will be likely to be able to exercise any influence on market price. On the other hand, for a given ϵ, with $-1/\epsilon$ being small, a high value of I_H implies that AMR differs significantly from p which in turn means that there are some firms with high output shares. Hence they have some monopoly power.

Determinants of concentration

Although concentration is a way of expressing the oligopolistic nature of a market, it cannot be regarded as exogenous. It has been argued that various concentration indices are positively related to the Lerner (1934) type market power for the industry as a whole (see Chapter 2). Therefore, an equivalent way of asking the question why market power exists is that why concentration exists. The determinants of concentration try to explain the interindustry variations in concentration. Concentration has been traditionally considered to be determined by scale economies, capital intensity, barriers to entry, advertising intensity and size of the market. (See Chapter 5 for detailed discussion.) Some researchers take a different view, believing that probabilistic factors are important. (See Chapter 6.) Arguments have also been put forward to stress that technological innovation and invention are fundamental determinants of concentration. (See the next part of this chapter.) Hirsch and Addison (1986) hypothesize that large firms in concentrated markets may find the organization and structure of a union relatively more useful (or less detrimental) than would small firms in an unconcentrated market, suggesting that unionization may lead to a more concentrated market.

Some researchers point out the importance of studying determinants of concentration industry by industry basis because of the belief that the determinants differ in different segments of the economy. We take up this issue in Chapter 5.

Dynamic issues in concentration measurement

Dynamic analysis of concentration involves several issues including intertemporal change in concentration and changes in the levels of various determinants of concentration. An important constraint in the analysis of intertemporal concentration is that each industry considered for analysis must be comparable over time. That is, in terms of the product mix the broad character of the industry should remain unaltered. It may be the case that because of technological advancement the nature of the product has changed. An industry might have diversified its activities over time. Therefore, while making intertemporal comparison of industries we should take care of such constraints.

For analyzing changes in concentration over two periods, we can apply the concentration curve dominance criterion. However, such a study requires that the same firms be observed in the two periods being analyzed. Another condition which needs to be fulfilled here is that no change in the ranking of firms should occur between the periods. Several studies for the U.S.A. and the U.K. considered correlations over time between firms' shares or rank positions (see Curry and George (1983) and Schmalensee (1989)). The estimated correlations turned out to be very fairly high for some industries. This means that an analysis of concentration change over time using indices that are consistent with the concentration curve ranking rule will not be quite inappropriate. But if the rank correlation is not maximum, the concentration curve dominance criterion is not the proper technique. The criterion, however, can be used under some modifications. The modified system will enable us to study rank changes among firms and changes in the identity of the leaders simultaneously. The former gives us an idea about the mobility of the firms and the latter is concerned with concentration change.

The technique involves the construction of a pseudo concentration curve, which is defined as follows. Denote the output vector in an n-firm industry at time t by x(t), where t=1,2. (Thus, we assume that a firm observed in period 1 survives in period 2 also.) We get the pseudo concentration curve for x(2) by ordering firms by their ranks in period 1 but plotting cumulative shares of the total output X(2), the total output in period 2. (See Kakwani (1980) and Chakravarty (1990) for further details.) If there is no change in the rank orders of firms between two periods then the pseudo concentration curve for x(2) coincides with its concentration curve. The curve will lie below or above the concentration curve depending on the extent of rank changes. There is indeed no reason why the pseudo curve need be above no-concentration line, if the largest and the smallest firms are interchanged, we have a curve which will lie below the line. We refer to the reciprocal of twice the area above this curve as the pseudo concentration coefficient. We can now compare the concentration curve for x(1) with the pseudo concentration curve for x(2). The extent of divergence between the two curves are the resultant of mobility (rank changes between two periods) and concentration change.

We know that for any output distribution $x \in D^n$ its Gini index $G^n(x)$ and the Rosenbluth index $I_R^n(x)$ are related as $(I_R^n(x))^{-1} = n(1 - G^n(x))$, which is precisely twice the area above the concentration curve of x. Silber (1989) has shown that in terms of the nonincreasingly ordered output share vector s^o, $G^n(x)$ can be written as

$$G^n(x) = e'G_M s^o, \qquad (1.37)$$

where e' is the vector $(1/n, 1/n, \ldots, 1/n)$ and G_M is an $n \times n$ matrix whose diagonal elements are zero and off diagonal elements g_{ij} are 1 or -1 according as $i > j$ or $i < j$. Let $\hat{s}(2)$ be the ordered vector of output shares at time 2 where the ordering of firms is done according to their (nonincreasing) ranks in period 1. Using the nonincreasingly ordered output share vectors $s^o(1)$ and $s^o(2)$ in periods 1 and 2 respectively, we have

$$e'G_M(s^o(1) - s^o(2)) + e'G_M(s^o(2) - \hat{s}(2)) = e'G_M(s^o(1) - \hat{s}(2))$$

from which it follows that

$$-ne'G_M(s^o(1) - s^o(2)) - ne'G_M(s^o(2) - \hat{s}(2)) = -ne'G_M(s^o(1) - \hat{s}(2)). \qquad (1.38)$$

The first term on the left hand side of (1.38) is twice the area enclosed between the concentration curves for x(1) and x(2) and the second term is that enclosed between the concentration curve of x(2) and its pseudo concentration curve.

Therefore, the distributional change index given by the right hand side of (1.38) has been decomposed into two elements; the first term is a measure of the change in concentration and the second term reflects the intensity of the changes in the ranking of the firms (mobility). If there is no difference between the rank orders of firms in $x(1)$ and $x(2)$, there is no mobility ($s^o(2)$ coincides with $\hat{s}(2)$). In such a case distributional change is determined solely by concentration change. The relation (1.38) also shows that concentration may be stable over time but there may be significant variations in the ranking of the firms, which may generate distributional change between the periods. Therefore, attention should be given to both changes in concentration and changes in ranks.

Among important mechanisms by which concentration in an industry changes are entry into an industry, exit from the industry and a change in the firm sizes. In the small-firms property we have considered, if the firms entering/quitting the industry are of significant size, then there will be significant changes in the level of concentration. Now, entry into an industry will occur if the entrant finds it profitable. A firm's decision to enter an industry will be guided by several factors including the expected price of the product, costs of production, possible risks (e.g. variability in industry profits) it may have to face, expected retaliation from the existing firms etc. Further, the firm may face some entry barriers which also might make the entry quite tough. (See Chapter 5 for further analysis.)

Among the various factors that may force a firm to decide to take exit from an industry are low profits, less efficiency etc. Attempts have been made to treat exit as negative entry; factors which make entry less likely will make exit more likely. Some factors justify this interpretation:low or decreasing profit, slow growth etc. However, some entry barriers are not relevant to exit at all. An example is protection of patent rights. On the other hand, some entry barriers may make exit easier:in the case of existence of many diversified firms in the industry entry will be tough for a specialized firm but exit will be easy. Barriers to exit which may not make exit very easy may exist in an industry (see Caves and Porter (1976), Waterson (1984)). An example is a very high sunk cost, the portion of fixed cost that is not recoverable on exit. Another example is a very high capital cost where the capital does not have a profitable alternative use on exit. Clearly, with high entry barriers and low exit barriers profits are expected to be high. We have already noted that exit from an industry may take place through merger or takeover also.

It has been observed in many countries that aggregate concentration has risen during the post-war period (Geroski and Pomroy (1990)). Curry and George identified three possible sources for an increase in aggregate concentration:increase in concentration within individual industries, increase in diversification by large firms and increase in the control of manufacturing output by industries in which concentration is more than average.

Several general explanations have also been provided for increasing trend in concentration. We discuss the major ones very briefly. An efficient firm may increase its output share at the expense of one or more of its inefficient partners in the industry (Downie (1958)). This is similar in spirit to the output transfers principle we have analyzed before. Once a dominant group of firms in the industry emerges, it will enjoy all the benefits of size and consequently small firms may merge with the members of the dominant group giving rise to increased level of concentration. The role of management may also lead to increased concentration (Penrose (1959)). Control of financial and market power by big companies may allow them to increase their market shares (Meade (1968), Kay and King (1978), Prais (1981a)). Technological change which results in importance of the large scale production may cause centralization of capital which in turn will drive out smaller and higher cost competitors and thus creates dominance of the few (see, for example, Marx (1887), Engels (1887), Hilferding (1910), Sweezy (1942), Downie (1958), Galbraith (1967) and Scherer (1980)).

It will probably be interesting to formalize the idea that technical innovation may lead to increased concentration. For this we consider a model introduced by Dasgupta (1986) (see also Dasgupta and Stiglitz (1980)). The model is assumed to be timeless and devoid of any uncertainty. Assume also that firms cannot produce without engaging in Research and Development (R and D) activity. If a firm spends z on R and D, then it produces the commodity in question at unit cost $U(z)$, where U is decreasing and displays diminishing returns to scale, that is, U satisfies decreasingness and convexity along with $U(0) = \infty$. The model therefore makes the following assumptions:(i) there is a positive relation between R and D effort (that is, research inputs) and innovative output (Comanor (1965), Comanor and Scherer (1969) and Scherer (1980)). (ii) The cost related to the development of something increases more than proportionately with the contraction of the period of development (Mansfield et al. (1971)). (iii) The technological possibilities between R and D inputs and innovative outputs do not show any economy of scale with respect to the firm size (Kamien and Schwartz (1975)).

Let p(X) be the market demand function with X being the total industry output of the commodity. Assume that p(X) is of the type

$$p(X) = \alpha X^{-\epsilon}, \quad \alpha, \ \epsilon > 0 \qquad (1.39)$$

and

$$U(z) = \beta z^{-\theta}, \quad \beta, \ \theta > 0. \qquad (1.40)$$

Assume also that there are n firms. All these n firms are engaged in R and D and final production. Firm i's output is x_i and its R and D expenditure is t_i.

All firms choose their R and D expenditure and output levels simultaneously. Consequently, profit earned by firm i is

$$\pi_i = (p(\sum_{j \neq i} x_j + x_i) - U(t_i))x_i - t_i. \qquad (1.41)$$

Note that $U(t_i)$ being the unit cost of manufacturing the commodity at R and D expenditure t_i, $x_i U(t_i)$ gives us the manufacturing cost of x_i amount of output. Therefore, firm's total cost is $U(t_i)x_i + t_i$. We subtract this from the firm's revenue $p(X)x_i$ to get profit π_i.

Let us now suppose that the number of firms in the industry is not a datum. The decision of whether or not to enter and decisions on how much to spend on R and D and how much to produce are made simultaneously by all firms. It is clear from (1.41) that R and D expenditure is a form of fixed cost and it creates a barrier for a new firm wishing to enter the industry.

Definition: We say that $(n^*, (t_1^*, x_1^*), (t_2^*, x_2^*), \ldots, (t_n^*, x_n^*))$ is an equilibrium with free legal entry if for $i = 1, 2, \ldots, n^*$

$$(p(\sum_{j \neq i} x_j^* + x_i^*) - U(t_i^*))x_i^* - t_i^*$$

$$\geq (p(\sum_{j \neq i} x_j^* + x_i) - U(t_i))x_i - t_i \qquad (1.42)$$

for all $x_i, t_i \geq 0$, and

$$(p((\sum_{i=1}^{n^*} x_i^* + a) - U(z))a - z \leq 0 \qquad (1.43)$$

for all $a, z \geq 0$.

Condition (1.42) in the above definition means that given the number of firms n^* no firm can increase its profit by deviating from the equilibrium R and D expenditure and output vector, given that the other firms adopt the equilibrium R and D expenditures and output levels. Condition (1.43) shows that the number of firms n^* is such that if one more firm enters the industry, then it cannot earn a positive profit. The first condition is essentially the Nash (1951) equilibrium concept for a noncooperative game. (We discuss this concept more elaborately in Chapter 2.) This combined with the latter condition gives us Nash equilibrium with free legal entry (see Novshek (1980), Dasgupta and Stiglitz (1980) for further discussions).

Dasgupta (1986) shows that if p(X) and U(z) satisfy (1.39) and (1.40) respectively then there exists $\bar{\theta}$ as a function of α, β and ϵ such that if $\theta \leq \bar{\theta}$, there is a Nash equilibrium with free entry. Since all the firms face the same cost function, the resulting solution is symmetric — all firms produce the same amount of output. Note that θ in (1.40) is the elasticity of invention possibility curve. Innovational opportunities decrease with θ. Therefore, symmetric equilibrium under technological competition with free legal entry exists if innovational opportunities are not excessive. (Dasgupta imposes a restriction to ensure uniqueness of the equilibrium.)

It then turns out that in the equilibrium

$$n^* = \epsilon(1+\theta)/\theta. \tag{1.44}$$

Since the output shares of all the firms are equal in the equilibrium, a natural measure of concentration here is $1/n^*$. From (1.45) we deduce that $(\delta n^*/\delta\theta) < 0$. This means given other things, industries facing greater innovative opportunities are more concentrated, which is what we wanted to demonstrate.

However, the view that industries facing greater technological and innovative activities tend to be more concentrated has been challenged often. In a recent study Geroski and Pomroy (1990) applied a dynamic model of market concentration to 73 U.K. industries for the cross section panels 1970-74 and 1975-79. They proposed to examine the effect of innovations on market structure for the sample of industries using the model

$$\Delta I_{it} = f_i + \alpha_1 z_{it} + \alpha_2 k_{it} + \alpha_3 \Delta z_{it} + \alpha_4 \Delta k_{it}$$
$$+\alpha_5 \Delta \tau_{it} + \alpha_6 \Delta \tau_{it-1} + \alpha_7 I_{it-1} + \mu_{it}. \tag{1.45}$$

where the subscripts i and t refer respectively to an industry and to a time period. The concentration index I_{it} is the 5-firm concentration ratio and z_{it} is the log domestic industry production on average throughout the period. Thus, z_{it} can be regarded as a measure of market size. k_{it}, which is given by the ratio of capital stock to industry production on average, measures capital intensity, τ_{it} is an index of technical innovation and Δ is the first difference operator. $\Delta \tau_{it}$ is simply the number of innovations introduced into the industry i during the five year period and Δk_{it} and Δz_{it} are the first differences of the respective variables between the beginning and end year of each period. The concentration index I_{it-1} is the 5-firm concentration ratio for the year 1970 or 1975 depending on whether the analysis is made for the interval 1970-74 or 1975-79. The difference $\Delta \tau_{it-1}$ is the number of innovations during 1945-70 divided by 5 for the interval 1970-74 and it is the actual innovation difference between 1970-74 for the analysis of 1975-79 period. Predicted values of I_t were very close to actual values (the correlation was about .95). The results were found to be consistent with the Blair (1972) hypothesis that innovation is deconcentrating. That is, this study provides some evidence on the evolution of market structure which is consistent with the Blair hypothesis. (Mansfield (1984) found mixed evidence on the Blair hypothesis, observing a clear deconcentrating effect of innovation in drugs, but not in steel, petroleum or chemicals. Carlsson (1984), on the other hand, observed a market deconcentrating effect in a case study of metal working.)

Thus, the overall contribution of technical innovation towards the explanation of increase in aggregate concentration may sometimes be difficult to judge. However, there are less disagreements on the importance of financial and market power of big companies and increasing dominance of large firms (see Curry and George (1983)). In addition to these, stochastic factors are also considered to be responsible for the rise in concentration. (See Chapter 6.)

Concluding remarks

This chapter began with a discussion of the conceptual problems associated with the definitions of the size of a firm, an industry and a market. In the main body of the chapter we considered the problem of measuring concentration and some implications and applications of concentration indices. Factors that make an industry concentrated and intertemporal issues of concentration have also been examined.

We now briefly discuss some additional indices of concentration which we did not examine in the main body of the chapter. Hart (1971) suggested an index, which for any $x \in D^n$, $n \in N$, is defined as

$$b_1^n(x) = 1 + \frac{1}{n} - \frac{\sum_{i=1}^n is_i^o}{n}. \tag{1.46}$$

b_1 is related to the Rosenbluth index I_R as follows:

$$b_1^n(x) = 1 + \frac{1}{n} - \frac{((I_R^n(x))^{-1} + 1)}{2n}. \tag{1.47}$$

Therefore, for a given $x \in D^n$, an increase in I_R^n increases b_1^n and vice versa. As Hannah and Kay pointed out b_1^n fails to meet the merger principle and the small-firms property. It will also violate zero output independence.

Hause (1977) introduced an index which in terms of the Herfindahl-Hirschman index I_H^n is defined as

$$b_2^n(x) = \sum_{i=1}^n s_i^{2-[s_i(I_H^n(x)-s_i^2)]^\alpha}, \tag{1.48}$$

where $\alpha \geq 1.5$. The constraint $\alpha \geq 1.5$ ensures that b_2^n is a decreasing, convex function of the number of firms, which Hause believes is a desirable property of a concentration index. In view of the complicated formulation it is difficult to examine the effects of properties like the merger principle and the output transfers principle on b_2^n. Hause, however, provides a reasoning from economic theory in support of his index.

As noted earlier it is often argued that concentration can be partly or completely characterized as a random process. A related argument is that some continuous type distribution fits the size distribution of firms and some parameter or some function of it can be regarded as a reasonable index of concentration (Hart (1971, 1975)). The two main candidates for describing the size distribution of firms are the Pareto and the lognormal. To make the discussion along this line rigorous suppose that the output z of a firm is a random variable defined on the interval $[0, \infty]$. Let $F: [0, \infty] \to [0,1]$ be the cumulative distribution function. $F(z)$ is the proportion of firms producing output less than or equal to z. Often F is assumed to be continuously differentiable. The continuous function f, the derivative of F, is called the density function. Loosely speaking, f(t) is the proportion of firms producing output t.

If the variable z follows the Pareto distribution, then

$$F(z) = \begin{cases} 0 & \text{if } z < z_o \\ 1 - (\frac{z_o}{z})^\alpha, & \text{if } z \geq z_o > 0, \end{cases} \quad (1.49)$$

where $\alpha > 1$ is a parameter. The restriction $\alpha > 1$ ensures that the distribution has a finite mean. In this case the number of firms of size z or greater can be expressed as

$$N_z = Az^{-\alpha}, \quad (1.50)$$

where $A > 0$. Consequently, α becomes the slope of the line showing the cumulative frequency of firms with output above each stated level plotted on a double log scale against the size of firm. Sometimes arguments have been made in favor of use of α as a concentration index. But it is a violator of many desirable properties of a concentration index.

A continuous type variable z is said to have lognormal distribution with parameters μ and σ^2 if log z follows a normal distribution with mean μ and variance σ^2. Equivalently, $(log z - \mu)/\sigma$ is a normal variate with means 0 and variance 1. The density function of the lognormal variate z is given by

$$f(z) = [\frac{1}{z\sqrt{2\pi}\sigma}e^{-\frac{(log z - \mu)^2}{2\sigma^2}}]. \quad (1.51)$$

Given that the size distribution of firms is lognormal, σ^2, the variance of the distribution, meets the output transfers principle (Hart (1975, 1979)). Of two lognormal distributions, the one with greater σ has a uniformly higher concentration curve. As $\sigma \to \infty$, the curve tends to the complete concentration line[3]. But if the size distribution of firms cannot be approximated by a lognormal form, then the use of the variance of logarithm of output levels $(x_1, x_2, \ldots x_n)$ as an index of concentration is not appropriate. At very high levels of output the index actually decreases instead of increasing with a transfer from a relatively small firm to a large firm (Atkinson (1970)). Further, even in the lognormal case the index does not respond correctly to the merger principle (Curry and George (1983)).

Notes

1. S-convexity is a weaker requirement than convexity. A function $f^n : D^n \to R^1$ is convex if $f^n(\theta x + \overline{1-\theta}y) \leq \theta f^n(x) + (1-\theta)f^n(y)$ for all $x, y \in D^n$ and for all $\theta \in [0, 1]$. For a strictly convex function the defining inequality is $f^n(\theta x + \overline{1-\theta}y) < \theta f^n(x) + \overline{1-\theta}f^n(y)$ for all $x, y \in D^n, x \neq y$ and for all $\theta \epsilon (0, 1)$. Strict convexity along with symmetry implies strict S-convexity, but the converse is not true (Berge (1961)). If f^n is (strictly) convex, then $-f^n$ is (strictly) concave.

2. Miller (1967) introduced the concept of the marginal concentration ratio- the fraction of total output supplied by the fifth to eighth largest firms. He used this alongside the four-firm concentration ratio as an element of market structure. Since the two measures are of similar nature, little is gained by doing this (Collins and Preston (1969)).

3. These claims follow from the fact that the equation of the Lorenz curve for a lognormal variate, with distribution function F and parameters μ and σ^2 is given by $\Phi^{-1}(F(t)) - \sigma$, where Φ is the distribution function of a normal variate with mean 0 and variance 1, and $0 \leq t \leq \infty$ (see Chakravarty (1990)).

2 Market power in oligopolistic models

Much of industrial economics is concerned with market power, the ability of firms to influence the price (prices) of the product (products) they sell and its consequences. We have already mentioned in the preceding chapter that at the level of a single firm the Lerner (1934) index of monopoly power, the proportional excess of price over marginal cost, has been widely used in the literature as a measure of market power of the firm. However, determination of market power at the industry level will require additional consideration. The industry market power is a notion which depends both on the average extent of power exercised by all firms and on the distribution of power within the industry. Some value judgements have to be employed for aggregating the individual market powers into a single indicator (see Donsimoni, Geroski and Jacquemin (1984)). By defining the industry wide market power as the arithmetic average of individual Lerner indices weighted by respective output shares, various concentration indices have been shown to be related to this average. For example, Saving (1970), in a dominant firms model, established a relationship between the industrial Lerner function and the k-firm concentration ratio. Rader (1972) and Cowling and Waterson (1976) provided a similar interpretation for the Herfindahl-Hirschman concentration index in a Cournot - Nash framework. (See Clarke and Davies (1982), Clarke, Davies and Waterson (1984) and Encaoua, Jacquemin and Moreaux (1986) for further discussions.) However, Encaoua and Jacquemin (1980) have demonstrated that these results are extremely sensitive to the method employed to compute the Lerner index for the industry. For instance, instead of arithmetic averaging rule if we adopt the geometric averaging principle, then the aggregate market power becomes a function of the entropy concentration formula. (See also Hause (1977), Dickson (1979), Waterson (1984), Jacquemin (1987) and Chakravarty (1993)).

One major purpose of this chapter is to discuss the alternative aggregation procedures of individual Lerner indices. A brief analysis of the properties for an arbitrary market power function is also presented in the chapter. Clearly, calculation of Lerner indices for a typical firm under alternative assumptions about the behaviors of the firms will lead to a better understanding of the properties for a global market power function. In view of this we present standard market structures and monopoly powers for an arbitrary firm in such structures in this chapter.

Evidently, the models of market power discussed above are the consequences of some achieved oligopoly equilibria. However, it will also be interesting to look at the capacity of a firm to modify market conditions in its own favor. More precisely, our interest is to look at the potential ability of firms to monopolize the market from a competitive fringe to a noncompetitive regime through coalition formation. d'Aspremont and Jacquemin (1985), in the framework of 'simple games', suggested the use of a firm's Shapley (1953) value, the incremental contribution of the firm to coalitions averaged over all coalitions of which it is not a member, as its power to monopolize the market (see also d'Aspremont and Jacquemin and Mertens (1987)). They also suggested an aggregate power index for the industry as a whole. We analyze the d'Aspremont-Jacquemin approach elaborately in the present chapter. To prepare the background for this analysis we make a brief discussion on game theory also. This discussion enables us to interpret some oligopoly models in terms of game theory.

A multimarket analogue to the single market equilibrium relationship between aggregate Lerner indices of the degree of monopoly power and various concentration indices was considered by Encaoua, Jacquemin and Moreaux (1986). Their analysis demonstrates that cross elasticities of demand play an important role in determining the conditions leading to a positive link between diversification and global market power. Analyses of individual homogeneous markets are not capable of detecting the function of cross elasticities. We discuss this issue explicitly here. Another important concern of this chapter is the welfare consequences of market power. As a sequel, policy issues regarding improvement of welfare are considered. Finally, we close the chapter with some extensions and remarks.

Standard market structures and monopoly power

Consider an industry of n firms producing a homogeneous good. Let $x_i > 0$ be the output of firm i. The industry output vector $(x_1, x_2, \ldots, x_n)$ is denoted by x. The set of all output vectors in this industry is $D_+^n = \{x \in D^n \mid x_i > 0$ for all $i\}$, the strictly positive part of D^n. Thus, we assume that all the firms in this industry are active. This assumption will be maintained throughout the chapter.

Now, the total consumer demand X for the good is a function of the good's price p and the demand function is denoted by $X = H(p)$, where $X = \sum_{i=1}^{n} x_i$. We assume that the demand function is monotonically decreasing. Consequently, an inverse of the function H exists, we call this the inverse demand function and write it as

$$p = f(X). \tag{2.1}$$

Note that f is also monotonically decreasing. Assume that it is twice differentiable.

Suppose that $Q_i(w, x_i)$ stands for the (total) cost function of firm i. That is,

$$Q_i(w, x_i) = \min\{w.z \mid z \in A(x_i)\}, \tag{2.2}$$

where $w = (w_1, w_2, \ldots, w_m)$, $w_i > 0$ for all i, is the input price vector and $A(x_i)$ is the input requirement set faced by firm i. The set $A(x_i) \subseteq R_+^m$ is the collection of all input bundles that are capable of producing at least x_i. (See Chapter 3 for further discussions on input requirement set.) For the rest of this chapter we take the factor prices as constant so that the conditional cost function can be written only as a function of the level of output of the firm. That is, $Q_i(w, x_i)$ can be rewritten as $C_i(x_i)$ for some numerical function C_i whose domain is D^1. Assume that C_i is twice differentiable.

The profit of firm i, which is its revenue in excess of total cost, is then given by

$$\pi_i(x) = x_i f(X) - C_i(x_i), i = 1, 2, \ldots, n. \tag{2.3}$$

The first order conditions for maximization of profits by firm i are

$$p + x_i f'(X)\frac{dX}{dx_i} - C_i'(x_i) = 0, i = 1, 2, \ldots, n, \tag{2.4}$$

where ′ denotes derivative. C_i' is firm $i's$ marginal cost, the increase in the total cost of firm i when its output increases by 1 unit. Given (2.4) we have

$$\frac{p - C_i'(x_i)}{p} = -f'(X)\frac{x_i}{f(X)}\left(\frac{dX}{dx_i}\right). \tag{2.5}$$

Define the Lerner index of monopoly power L_i of firm i as the proportionate gap between price and the marginal cost of firm i, and denote the elasticity of demand (in absolute term) faced by the industry by ϵ. Then we rewrite (2.5) as

$$L_i = \frac{p - C_i'(x_i)}{p} = \frac{q_i s_i}{\epsilon}, \tag{2.6}$$

where $s_i = x_i/X$ is the output share of firm i and $q_i(= dX/dx_i)$ is firm i's conjectural industry output variation, the rate of change in industrial output in response to a change in its own output. The term q_i measures how the given firm i assumes that the industry output will change as its own output changes.

Note that we can rewrite $q_i s_i$ in (2.6) as $(dX/dx_i)(x_i/X)$, which can be regarded as the elasticity conjectured by firm i of the total (industry) output with respect to changes in its own output. Since in the homogeneous good case, the total output X depends on price only, this elasticity gives us an indication of the level of influence that firm i believes it can exert on the price level.

We can express q_i also as

$$q_i = 1 + \sum_{j \neq i} \frac{dx_j}{dx_i}. \tag{2.7}$$

The second term on the right hand side of (2.7) is the conjectural variation suggested by Bowley (1924) and Frisch (1951) and it measures firm $i's$ belief or perception about responses of other firms to its own output changes. It is the sum of the rate of change in all firms $j's$ outputs anticipated by firm i in response to its own changes $(j = 1, 2, \ldots, n, j \neq i)$. From (2.6) we observe that nonnegativity of L_i ensures that $q_i \geq 0$ (since both s_i and ϵ are positive).

Evidently L_i indicates how much is left to the ith firm on the margin, as a proportion of price level, when its output increases by 1 unit. Equation (2.6) relates firm $i's$ ability to hold price above marginal cost to three variables, which describe market structure and rivals' conduct:

1. Firm $i's$ conjectural industry output variation, which points out whether rivals will cooperate in restricting output or compete for customers.

2. The output share of firm i, which gives us an idea about the size of the market, that is, the number of customers.

3. The price elasticity of demand, which shows how fast the customers may leave the market because of price increase.

We will now calculate the value of the Lerner index for a typical firm in standard market models. The firm's conjectural variation may be helpful for such an exercise.

We begin by assuming that the industry is perfectly competitive. In this case each firm believes that it will not be able to influence the price. In standard textbooks a perfectly competitive industry is described as an industry in which there are a large number of firms producing a homogeneous good. It is inferred from this that no firm will be able to influence the price, that is, each firm acts as a price taker. As Basu (1993) pointed out, if we assume that each firm believes that it cannot influence the price, then 'the assumption about the large number of firms is no longer germaine to perfect competition. Nor is it important for firms to be identical in the sense of having identical cost functions' (op cit., p. 28). Thus, while making its supply decision each firm takes price as given.

A price p is a perfectly competitive equilibrium price if there exist $(x_1, x_2, \ldots, x_n)$ such that

$$p = C_i'(x_i), i = 1, 2, \ldots, n,$$
$$\sum_{i=1}^{n} x_i = X = H(p). \tag{2.8}$$

For deriving the first condition in (2.8) we make use of the fact that price is treated as given. (Since $p = f$ is given, differentiating π_i in (2.3) with respect to x_i and setting the derivative to zero, we have $p = C_i'(x_i)$ for all $i = 1, 2, \ldots, n$.) This condition means that the value that a consumer places on purchasing the good is exactly equal to the marginal cost of production. We can refer to this property as consumption efficiency. Another property that holds at the competitive equilibrium is that the product is produced at the minimum possible cost. This is production efficiency. The second condition in (2.8) means that demand equals supply[1].

Because of each firm's inability to influence the price level, both q_i (as given by (2.6)) and its elasticity are zero here. Consequently, for each firm in a perfectly competitive industry the Lerner index takes on the value zero.

At the opposite extreme of perfect competition we have the case of monopoly. In this case the industry consists of only one firm. This firm faces the entire demand for the product. The monopolist makes two decisions: how much to produce and at what price the produced quantity should be sold. If firm i is a monopolist, that is, if it constitutes the single-firm industry under consideration, then the first order condition for its profit maximization turns out to be

$$x_i f'(x_i) + f(x_i) - C_i'(x_i) = 0. \tag{2.9}$$

From the above equation we see that the Lerner index $(p - C_i')/p = (f(x_i) - C_i'(x_i))/f(x_i)$ becomes $1/\epsilon$. The elasticity of the conjectural industry output variation here is unity[2].

It may be interesting to note that a monopolist's output price will be an increasing function of his marginal cost. This seems intuitively reasonable. Since the monopolist controls the entire output market, an increase in his marginal cost will motivate him to increase the price for maintaining profit at maximal level. (For a proof of this result, see Tirole (1988) and Basu (1993).) We can demonstrate this graphically. Assume that the monopolist's marginal cost function is constant. The term $x_i f'(x_i) + f(x_i) = d(x_i f(x_i))/dx_i$ is his marginal revenue. We can rewrite this as $f(x_i)(1 + x_i f'(x_i)/f(x_i)) = p(1 - 1/\epsilon)$, since $p = f(x_i)$. Positivity of marginal revenue requires that the elasticity of demand is greater than unity in the absolute value. If this were not true, marginal revenue would be nonpositive and hence could not be equal to the positive marginal cost. It is clear from (2.9) that the profit maximizing output level is determined from this equality. Note also that the marginal revenue curve lies below the average revenue curve, that is, the demand curve. If the marginal cost is given by c_1, the profit maximizing output level is x_i^1 and the corresponding price is p_1. When marginal cost increases from c_1 to c_2, the profit maximizing output quantity reduces to x_i^2 and the price goes up to p_2. Thus, given $c_2 > c_1$, we have $p_2 > p_1$.

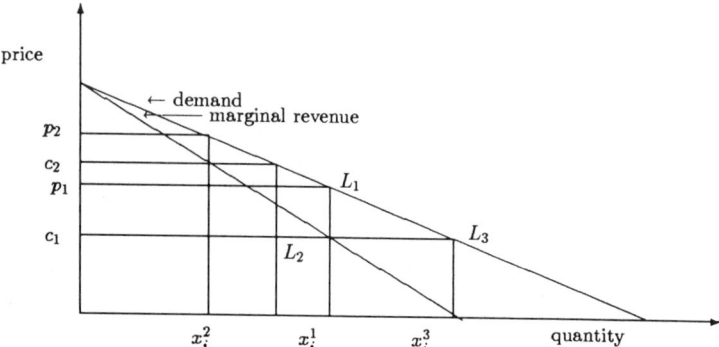

Figure 2.1 Determination of the monopoly price

We have noted that in the case of perfect competition the firms choose their actions so as to maximize their profits knowing all the consequences of the actions of the others. Each firm is a price taker here. On the other hand, for a monopolistic situation the single firm is the sole price setter. It will now be interesting to look at the market power of firms in oligopolistic industries:the type of industries that are neither competitive nor monopolized, but somewhere in between. In such a set up there are only a few competitors and a firm can have some effect on the price it will receive because it produces a substantial share of the total output. With only two firms such an industry is called a duopoly.

We first study the situation where the firms are Cournot maximizers (see Cournot (1897)). Here each firm i believes that the other firms will not change their output decisions, that is, firm $i's$ belief is that a change in its output by δ unit will change the industry output by δ unit only. A situation of this type can also arise when firm i 'has been convinced by its competitors that, no matter what it does, they will not change their output'. An example of this latter case 'is one in which sellers are bound to their buyers by long-term contracts for fixed quantities of supply' (Jacquemin (1987, p. 55)). In the case of Cournot maximization $q_i = 1$ and the conjectural elasticity becomes the firm's output share.

The first order condition for profit maximization of firm i (under the assumption that $q_i = 1$) becomes

$$f(X) + x_i f'(X) - C_i'(x_i) = 0. \tag{2.10}$$

We formally say that the firms in the industry are in Cournot equilibrium if (2.10) holds simultaneously for all $i = 1, 2, \ldots, n$. We refer to the function describing firm $i's$ optimal choice given other firms' outputs as its reaction function. A Cournot equilibrium is simply a point of intersection of the reaction functions. To illustrate this graphically, suppose that there are two firms. Then we rewrite (2.10) as

$$\frac{\delta \pi_i(x_1, x_2)}{\delta x_1} = f(x_1 + x_2) - x_1 f'(x_1 + x_2) - C_1'(x_1) = 0,$$

$$\frac{\delta \pi_2(x_1, x_2)}{\delta x_2} = f(x_1 + x_2) - x_2 f'(x_1 + x_2) - C_2'(x_2) = 0.$$

Firm $1's$ first order condition for profit maximization will determine its optimal choice of output as a function of its belief about firm $2's$ choice of output. This relationship is firm $1's$ reaction function. The reaction functionn represents firm $1's$ reactions given its alternative beliefs about the output choices of firm 2. Thus, if we write $r_1(x_2)$ as the reaction function of firm 1, then $r_1(x_2)$ is defined implicitly by firm $1's$ first order condition for profit maximization. More precisely, $(\delta \pi_1(r_1(x_2), x_2))/\delta x_1 = 0$. Similarly, we can define $r_2(x_1)$, firm $2's$ reaction function. Since a Cournot equilibrium satisfies the two first order conditions stated above, the intersection of the two reaction functions will simply give us Cournot equilibrium.

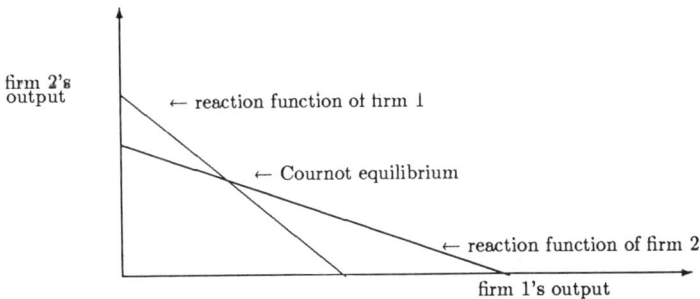

Figure 2.2   Cournot equilibrium

Clearly, for a Cournot firm i the Lerner index L_i is s_i/ϵ. (For further analysis of Cournot equilibrium, see Chapter 4. A discussion on this equilibrium with free entry has already been made in Chapter 1.)

We will next examine the case of an asymmetric oligopoly where a small number of large firms are dominant and there is a competitive fringe of small firms. Stackelberg's (1934) attempt is probably one of the first which have introduced asymmetry in oligopoly. In Stackelberg's duopoly model one firm acts as a leader and chooses its profit maximizing output level by taking account of the other firm's reaction function. Thus, while in the Cournot model one firm takes other firm's actions as given, in the Stackelberg model one firm will regard the responses or the reactions of the other as given. Suppose firm 1 is the leader and will choose its output by taking account of firm $2's$ reaction function. Thus, firm 1 chooses the value of x_1 that maximizes $\Pi_1(x_1, r_2(x_1))$. Denote this output level by $\hat{x}_1$. Then the output vector $(\hat{x}_1, \hat{x}_2)$ constitutes a Stackelberg equilibrium, where $\hat{x}_2 = r_2(\hat{x}_1)$. To see this graphically, consider the isoprofit curve of firm 1. This curve is the locus of all output levels of the two firms that generate a constant profit for firm 1. Firm 1 will operate at that point on firm $2's$ reaction curve where it has the highest possible profit. That is, the Stackelberg equilibrium is determined by the point of tangency between firm $1's$ isoprofit curve and firm $2's$ reaction function. This is shown in Figure 2.3.

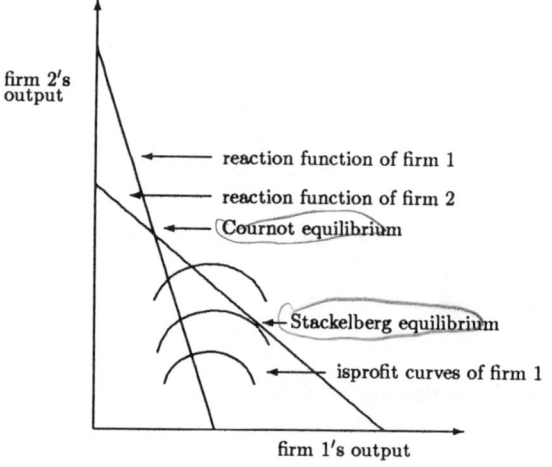

Figure 2.3 Stackelberg equilibrium

In the asymmetric oligopoly model we consider next, following Encaoua and Jacquemin (1980), the dominant group consisting of k firms of the industry will set up a selling price knowing the total quantity that the competitive firms will be able to produce at this price. The competitive firms will produce the output level at which their marginal cost will be equal to the price. Evidently, this is a price leadership oligopoly model. (Stigler (1950) considered a price leadership model that consists of one dominant firm and a fringe of competitive firms.) An example of a model of this type is the world petroleum market in which the major countries are leaders and the dependents are followers (see Dixit and Stern (1982)).

To examine the Encaoua-Jacquemin (1980) model in more detail, suppose that the first k firms of the industry form the dominant group and the remaining $(n-k)$ firms constitute the competitive fringe. The demand faced by the industry is $X = g(p)$ and the aggregate supply function of the fringe is $X_c = \phi(p)$. Then the (residual) output demand that the dominant cartel faces is

$$X_D = X - X_c = H(p) - \phi(p) = B(p). \qquad (2.11)$$

Basu (1993) provided a rational expectation argument supporting the existence of a price that defines (2.11). 'The fringe determines its supply on the basis of a conjectured price. If, given such a supply, the market-clearing price happens to be the conjectured price', that is, if (2.11) holds, 'then the price satisfies rational expectations' (op cit., p. 35).

Now, the profit function of an arbitrary firm i of the dominant group is

$$\pi_i(x_1, x_2, \ldots, x_k) = x_i h(X_D) - C_i(x_i), \qquad (2.12)$$

where $p = B^{-1}(X_D) = h(X_D)$ is the inverse residual demand function. The first order condition for profit maximization by firm i belonging to this group will then require that

$$h(X_D) + x_i \frac{dh(X_D)}{dX_D} \frac{dX_D}{dx_i} - C'_i(x_i) = 0, i = 1, 2, \ldots, k. \qquad (2.13)$$

To solve the system explicitly it is necessary to describe the behavior of the dominant firms. The price policy may be determined either through a process of competition among the dominant firms or by a cartel where the firms' objective is joint profit maximization. In the latter case, which is a situation of collusive price leadership, a monopolistic price solution will be obtained. An example of a successful cartel is the mercury cartel formed by Spain and Italy. These two countries control 80% of the world production of mercury (see Carlton and Perloff (1990)).

In the case of noncollusive price leadership, the price imposed on the competitive fringe will be a consequence of rivalry among the dominant firms. We assume that the k dominant firms adopt Cournot behavior among themselves : $dX_D/dx_i = 1$ for all $i = 1, 2, \ldots, k$. Hence

$$p - C'_i(x_i) = h(X_D) - C'_i(x_i) = \frac{x_i}{[-\frac{dX}{dp} + \frac{dX_C}{dp}]} \qquad (2.14)$$

from which we have

$$L_i = \frac{s_i}{\epsilon + \eta(1 - I_k^n(x))}, i = 1, 2, \ldots, k, \qquad (2.15)$$

where $\eta = (dX_C/dh(X_D))(h(X_D)/X_C)$ is the (positive) elasticity of supply of the competitive fringe and I_k^n is the k-firm concentration ratio.

We may note here the relationship between L_i in (2.15) and L_i in the case when all the n firms in the industry are Cournot maximizers. The additional term $\eta(1 - I_k^n(x))$ in the denominator appears simply because of partitioning of the industry into a dominant group and a competitive fringe. Evidently, for any firm in the fringe the Lerner index will be zero.

If, on the other hand, the first k firms follow a collusive behavior, then the market price and the dominant firms' aggregate supply will be a solution to the problem

$$\text{Maximize} \sum_{i=1}^{k} \pi_i(x_1,\ldots,x_k) = \sum_{i=1}^{k}[x_i h(X_D) - C_i(x_i)] \qquad (2.16)$$

with respect to $(x_1, x_2, \ldots, x_k)$. The monopoly powers of different firms in this case are

$$\begin{aligned} L_i &= \frac{I_k^n(x)}{\epsilon + \eta(1 - I_k^n(x))}, i = 1, 2, \ldots, k \\ &= 0, i = k+1, \ldots, n. \end{aligned} \qquad (2.17)$$

Thus, as expected, the monopoly powers of the members of the dominant group are equal. Other than the two industry characteristics ϵ and η, this common power depends on their joint output share. If all the n firms in the industry would have adopted a collusive behavior, then for each firm i, L_i would have been $1/\epsilon$, which is in fact the market power of a monopoly firm. (For a discussion of price leadership oligopoly in dynamic framework see Encaoua and Jacquemin (1980) and Jacqumin (1987).)

To illustrate the price leadership model graphically, let us suppose for simplicity that the deomiant group consists of only one firm. This firm has a constant marginal constant c. In Figure 2.4 we depict the aggregate demand curve and supply surve of the fringe. The residual demand curve, which is obtained by subtracting X_c from X at each price level is given by TT_1. The dominant firm treats this as its demand curve and selects the profit maximizing price. Given that c is its marginal cost, p is the price, OT_4 is the quantity supplied by the dominant firm and T_4T_2 is the supply of the fringe.

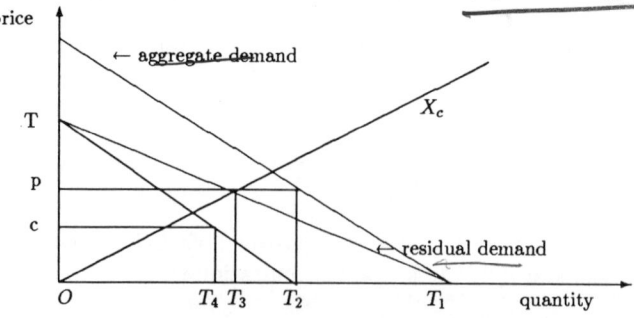

Figure 2.4 Price leadership oligopoly

Our calculations for Lerner indices in alternative market structures show that market power or monopoly power of a firm determines its ability to set price profitably above the competitive level (that is, above marginal cost).

Properties for an industrial market power function

We begin by assuming that the global or industrial market power is a real valued function $G(L_1, L_2, \ldots, L_n)$ of the individual firms' Lerner indices $L_1, L_2, \ldots, L_n$. In many branches of economics there is a convention of defining a global index as a function of local indices. For instance, in welfare economics, a social welfare function is defined as a real valued function of individual utility functions. Now, each L_i is a number belonging to the set $[0, 1]$. We can therefore write the industry level market power function as $G : [0, 1]^n \to R^1$, where $[0, 1]^n$ is the n-fold Cartesian product of $[0, 1]$.

We now propose some properties for an arbitrary industry market power function G. Of these normalization and the merger criterion were proposed by Encaoua and Jacquemin (1980).
Continuity (CN):G is a continuous function of its arguments.
Monotonicity (MO):G is increasing in individual arguments.
Normalization (NM):If all the $L'_i s$ assume a constant value b, then $G = b$.
Boundedness (BD):G is bounded between zero and one, where the lower bound is achieved if and only if all the $L'_i s$ take on the value zero.
Merger Criterion (MC):If two or more firms in the industry merge, then G should not decrease.

Continuity means that small changes in one or more arguments of G should have little impact on its functional value. Therefore, if G is continuous, then it will not be oversensitive to small errors in observations on price and marginal costs. According to monotonicity if market power of one firm increases, the rest remaining fixed, then the overall market power should increase. For example, suppose that the market power of firm i increases because of a reduction in its marginal cost, whereas the price level as well as the marginal costs of the other firms remain unaltered. Clearly, the overall market power in such a situation should increase.

Normalization is concerned with cardinality properties of G. This postulate requires that if the degree of market power is constant across firms, then irrespective of other characteristics of the firms (e.g. their market shares, which ned not be identical) the global market power will assume this constant value. Encaoua and Jacquemin (1980) pointed out that this situation 'can be realized through at least two important polar ways: (i) either the industry is perfectly competitive (all the producers are price takers), the quantity produced and sold being priced at the marginal cost of each producer; (ii) or the industry is perfectly cartelized between its different producers' (op cit., p. 93). The property also shows that if the industry is monopolized by a single firm, then the local and global powers are the same. Boundedness principle shows that G has natural bounds, where the necessary and sufficient condition for attainability of the lower bound is that the market is perfectly competitive. The merger criterion is concerned with the direction of change in G whenever there is a merger of some firms in the industry. If two or more firms in the industry merge, then the degree of competition in the industry is expected to reduce (see Chapter 4. See also Carlton and Perloff (1990).) It is therefore reasonable to expect that the global market power will not decrease under a merger.

A general form of industrial market power

To construct a general index of overall market power, let us consider a continuous, increasing function F of the market power vector $L = (L_1, L_2, \ldots, L_n)$ of the industry under consider consideration. Clearly, F satisfies CN and MO, but it need not meet the other postulates. However, such a function may be helpful in constructing a general average of $L'_i s$, which we refer to as the representative market power L_e. L_e is that level of market power which if shared by all firms would yield the same level of F as L. Formally,

$$F(L_e.1^n) = F(L), \qquad (2.18)$$

where 1^n is the n-coordinated vector of ones. L_e is a particular numerical representation of F. Now, assume for simplicity, that $F(L) = \sum_{i=1}^{n} s_i g(L_i)$, where $g : [0,1] \to R^1$ is continuous and increasing, and s_i is the output share of firm i. In this case L_e is given by

$$L_e = g^{-1}[\sum_{i=1}^{n} s_i g(L_i)], \qquad (2.19)$$

where g^{-1} is the inverse function of g. L_e in (2.19) is the quasilinear mean of individual firms' degrees of monopoly weighted by respective output shares. (Eichhorn (1978) and Chakravarty and Eichhorn (1991) provide further examples of quasilinear economic functions.) One can certainly come with up other aggregation procedures of $L'_i s$. But the novelty of L_e lies in the fact that it unifies the earlier literature.

We then have

Theorem 2.1:(i) The representative market power index L_e given by (2.19) satisfies CN, MO, NM and BD. (ii) If the elasticity of demand is a constant and all the firms have a constant conjectural industry output variation (that is, q_i in (2.6) is a constant for all i), then L_e satisfies MC.

Proof:(i) Recall that both $p = f(X)$ and C_i have been assumed to be twice differentiable at the outset. Since differentiability implies continuity[3], both p and C'_i are continuous from which continuity of $p - C'_i$ follows. This shows that $L_i (= (p - C'_i)/p)$ is a continuous function taking values in the closed set[4] $[0, 1]$. Continuity of $g : [0, 1] \to R^1$ shows that the composite mapping $g(L_i)$

is continuous. For any arbitrary $s = (s_1, \ldots, s_n)$ and L, $\sum_{i=1}^{n} s_i g(L_i)$ is a real number and hence belongs to the range of g. Now monotonicity of g shows that g^{-1} is well defined. Since g is continuous and increasing on the compact set[5] $[0,1]$, g^{-1} is continuous and increasing on the interval $[g(0), g(1)]$. This establishers continuity and monotonicity of L_e.

Next, let $L_i = b$ for all i. Since $\sum_{i=1}^{n} s_i = 1$, $L_e = g^{-1}(\sum_{i=1}^{n} s_i g(b)) = g^{-1}(g(b)) = b$. Hence L_e is normalized. Since for any arbitrary s and L, $\sum_{i=1}^{n} s_i g(L_i)$ is in the range of g, L_e is in the domain of g, that is, $0 \leq L_e \leq 1$. Normalization ensures that L_e will be zero whenever L_i is zero for all i. Conversely, let $L_e = 0$, from which we have $\sum_{i=1}^{n} s_i g(L_i) = g(0)$. Using the fact that $\sum_{i=1}^{n} s_i = 1$, this identity can be written as

$$\sum_{i=1}^{n} s_i [g(L_i) - g(0)] = 0. \qquad (2.20)$$

Now, given that the output domain is D_+^n, we have $s_i > 0$ for all i. Since the minimal value of L_i is zero, increasingness of g shows that $(g(L_i) - g(0))$ will be nonnegative for all i. Thus, the left hand side of (2.20) is the sum of n nonnegative terms. Since the right hand side of (2.20) is zero, we must have $s_i(g(L_i) - g(0)) = 0$, which gives $(g(L_i) - g(0)) = 0$ for all i. Increasingness of g shows that $L_i = 0$, which is the market power in a perfectly competitive framework. This therefore demonstrates that L_e satisfies boundedness. (ii) If q_i is a constant, say k, for all i, then L_i in (2.6) becomes ks_i/ϵ. Since by assumption ϵ is a constant, increasingness of g shows that it is increasing in s_i. Therefore, by theorem 1.8(b), $\sum_{i=1}^{n} s_i g(L_i)$ will increase under a merger. By increasingness of g^{-1}, L_e also will not decrease under a merger. This completes the proof of the theorem. □.

From theorem 2.1 we see that the merger criterion has a different status from the other axioms. The other properties can all be verified under quite general assumptions. For MC to hold we need to know something about the firms' behavior. Further, the Encaoua-Jacquemin (1980) result used for demonstrating that L_e verifies MC for constant conjectural variation assumption, of which Cournot behavior is a particular case, is only a sufficient condition. This sufficient condition for the merger criterion to hold depends crucially on the assumption about the conjectural variation. For instance, q_i may be a function of the vector s. In such a case we cannot express L_e in a form analogous to that adopted by Encaoua and Jacquemin (1980) or an ordinal transform of it. A necessary condition here will probably isolate the set of all $q_i's$ for which MC is satisfied.

We may now illustrate the general formula (2.19) under alternative assumptions about the firms' conduct and the function g. We note that if q_i in (2.6) is zero, we have perfectly competitive set up and hence $L_e = 0$. Again, if $q_i = 1/s_i$ we have perfect collusion, joint profits are maximized and the equilibrium solution is a monopoly: $L_e = 1/\epsilon$. While these two extreme cases can be obtained independently of the functional form of g, an intermediate case with nonidentical $L'_i s$ will require explicit specification of g. To illustrate this, let g be of the power function type, that is,

$$\begin{aligned} g(L_i) &= A + B\frac{L_i^{\alpha-1}}{\alpha - 1}, \alpha > 0, \alpha \neq 1 \\ &= A + B\log L_i, \alpha = 1, \end{aligned} \quad (2.21)$$

where $B > 0$ and A are constants. Continuity of g will require $\alpha \neq 1$ whenever $L_i = 0$.

When firms are Cournot maximizers, $L_i = s_i/\epsilon$ for all i. Then L_e associated with g in (2.21) becomes

$$\begin{aligned} L_e &= \frac{(\sum_{i=1}^n s_i^\alpha)^{\frac{1}{(\alpha-1)}}}{\epsilon}, \alpha > 0, \alpha \neq 1 \\ &= \frac{\pi_{i=1}^n s_i^{s_i}}{\epsilon}, \alpha = 1. \end{aligned} \quad (2.22)$$

The numerator of L_e in the above expression is the Hannah-Kay (1977) concentration index I_α^n (see Chapter 1). Under ceteris paribus assumptions, L_e is increasing in concentration I_α^n and decreasing in absolute elasticity ϵ. For $\alpha = 2$, I_α^n is the Herfindahl-Hirschman concentration index and the corresponding relation in (2.22) was established by Rader (1972) and Cowling and Waterson (1976). For $\alpha = 1$, I_α^n is the entropy concentration formula and its association with L_e is due to Encaoua and Jacquemin (1980) (see also Jacquemin (1987)). As $\alpha \to \infty$, $L_e \to \max_i s_i/\epsilon$, which is simply the 1-firm concentration ratio as a fraction of ϵ.

Encaoua and Jacquemin (1980) and Jacquemin (1987) added the $L'_i s$ of the dominant firms in (2.15) weighted by the output share of each firm in the dominant group to obtain the following overall power index

$$G_E = \frac{J_k^n(x) I_k^n(x)}{\epsilon + \eta(1 - I_k^n(x))}, \quad (2.23)$$

where $J_k^n(x) = \sum_{i=1}^k (s_i/I_k^n(x))^2$, the Herfindahl-Hirschman index for the dominant cartel. Now, let g be of form (2.21) (with $\alpha = 2$), where arguments of g are given by $L'_i s$ in (2.15) for $1 \leq i \leq k$ and $L_i = 0$ for $k+1 \leq i \leq n$ (since in a price leadership oligopoly model with a fringe of competitive firms the market power of the fringe firms will be zero). Then L_e in (2.19) becomes $I_k^n(x) G_E$. Thus, in this case L_e becomes a multiple of G_E. Since continuity of g in (2.21) requires $\alpha \neq 1$ whenever $L_i = 0$, the global market power index L_e for such a model cannot be expressed as a function of the truncated entropy concentration formula.

From the relation in (2.23) we see that given ϵ and η, an increase in aggregate monopoly power may result from an increase in the output share of the dominant group (I_k^n) or from an increase in the asymmetry of the size distribution within this group (J_k^n) or from both. Thus, in this case we have two aspects of asymmetry:asymmetry between the leaders and the followers and asymmetry among the leaders (J_k^n). It should also be noted that in (2.23) ϵ or η or both can reduce aggregate market power under ceteris paribus assumptions.

The Saving (1970) formula for global market power is obtained by the weighted average of $L_i's$ in (2.17), where the weights are the market shares of different firms. This formula turns out to be

$$G_S = \frac{(I_k^n(x))^2}{\epsilon + \eta(1 - I_k^n(x))}. \quad (2.24)$$

It is easy to see that L_e in (2.19) becomes G_S if g is of the form (2.21) (with $\alpha = 2$), where arguments of g are given by $L_i's$ in (2.17).

Thus, given an assumption about the conduct of the firms we get a corresponding industry wide market power function L_e for a continuous, increasing g. These functions will differ only in the manner how g is defined[6]. For choosing a particular form of g one may need to employ some value judgement. For instance, if we wish to attach proportionally higher weights to the firms with high market powers, then g should be convex.

An important point that needs to be mentioned at this stage is that in an industrial configuration both concentration and monopoly power are determined jointly from an equilibrium relation and there is a no causal relationship between the two in the sense that one is exogenous (which may be regarded as an independent variable) and the other is endogenous (which may be considered as the dependent variable). To understand this more explicitly, let us consider a formulation due to Jacquemin (1987). Suppose that the n firms in a homogenous good industry follow a behavior described by the following conjectural variation considered by Dixit and Stern (1982):

$$q_i = \frac{dX}{dx_i} = 1 + \theta \sum_{j \neq i} \frac{x_j}{x_i}. \quad (2.25)$$

Thus, an increase of 1% in the output of firm i is believed to provoke an increase of θ% in the output of each of the other firms. If $\theta = 0$, we have Cournot behavior. On the other hand, when $\theta = 1$ each firm believes that the other firms will maintain their output shares. The cases $\theta < 0$ may arise in a situation of the type where the firms agree to adjust their outputs for keeping price constant. It can then be said that the model allows collusive behavior which may be tacit.

The first order conditions for maximization of profits (equation system (2.4)) under the above assumption about q_i then become

$$p + x_i f'(X)[1 + \theta \sum_{j \neq i} \frac{x_j}{x_i}] - C_i'(x_i) = 0, i = 1, 2, \ldots, n, \quad (2.26)$$

which can be simplified to

$$p(1 - [\theta + (1-\theta)s_i]/\epsilon) = C'_i(x_i), i = 1, 2, \ldots, n. \qquad (2.27)$$

Suppose that each firm has a constant marginal cost, that is, for each i, $C'_i(x_i) = C'_i$, which is independent of x_i. Assume also that elasticity of demand is constant. Then from (2.27) we get

$$p = \frac{\bar{C}}{1 - \frac{\theta}{\epsilon} - \frac{1-\theta}{n\epsilon}}, \qquad (2.28)$$

where $\bar{C} = \sum_{i=1}^n C'_i/n$. Using the equilibrium price given by (2.28), we calculate the output share of firm i (by dividing (2.27) by (2.28)) as

$$s_i = \frac{\epsilon - \theta}{1 - \theta} - \frac{C'_i}{\bar{C}}(\frac{\epsilon - \theta}{1 - \theta} - \frac{1}{n}). \qquad (2.29)$$

Thus the market shares depend on technological variables ($\bar{C}$), demand conditions (ϵ) and the behavior of the firms (θ). Consequently, all concentration indices depend on these variables. Hence concentration indices approximate market power rather than acting as its predictors. Another issue is regarding elasticity of demand. The interindustry and intertemporal variations of demand elasticity may invalidate the relation (obtained by regressions) between the aggregate market power and concentration. We discuss this issue more elaborately in Chapter 5.

The analyses presented above have so far assumed that the firms produce the same product. We can now extend our exercise to the case of differentiated products which are close substitutes, if not perfect. We consider a group of n firms whose products are substitutes from demand point of view and each product is produced by only one firm. Such a marekt structure is called monopolistically competitive since it combines flavors of both monopoly (each product is produced by a single firm only) and competition (the goods are close substitutes - the firms compete for customers) (see Chamberlin (1956)). If the vector $(y_1, y_2, \ldots, y_n)$ represents the outputs of n products, then the inverse demand function of firm i, which gives the price of its product as a function of $(y_1, y_2, \ldots, y_n)$, is $p_i = f_i(y_1, y_2, \ldots, y_n)$. The profit function of firm i is

$$\pi_i(y_1, y_2, \ldots, y_n) = y_i f_i(y_1, y_2, \ldots, y_n) - C_i(y_i). \qquad (2.30)$$

Firm i will choose y_i so that its profit is maximized, that is, it will choose y_i that will satisfy

$$f_i(y_1, y_2, \ldots, y_n) - y_i \frac{\delta f_i(y_1, y_2, \ldots y_n)}{\delta y_i} - C'_i(y_i) = 0. \qquad (2.31)$$

An output vector $(y_1, y_2, \ldots, y_n)$ is a monopolistically competitive equilibrium if (2.31) is satisfied by this vector simultaneously for all $i = 1, 2, \ldots, n$.

Let ϵ_i denote the absolute value of the elasticity of demand of firm $i's$ product. Then from (2.31) we have

$$L_i = \frac{p_i - C_i'}{p_i} = \frac{1}{\epsilon_i}. \qquad (2.32)$$

In this differentiated product case we write the market shares in terms of turnover: $s_i = p_i y_i / \sum_{j=1}^n p_j y_j$. Encaoua and Jacquemin (1980) defined the aggregate monopoly power G_D in the industry as the share weighted geometric average of $L_i's$:

$$\begin{aligned} G_D &= \pi_{i=1}^n (L_i)^{s_i} \\ &= \pi_{i=1}^n s_i^{s_i} \pi_{i=1}^n (\frac{1}{s_i \epsilon_i})^{s_i} \qquad (2.33) \\ &= I_1^n \pi_{i=1}^n (\frac{1}{s_i \epsilon_i})^{s_i}, \end{aligned}$$

where I_1^n is the entropy concentration formula. If the n products are not differentiated, then $s_i \epsilon_i = \epsilon$, the absolute elasticity of demand. Consequently, as expected, in this case the relation (2.33) coincides with the relation (2.22) when $\alpha = 1$. To see how an increase in concentration may generate an increase in market power, consider a rank preserving transfer of market share from firm j to firm k, where $p_j y_j < p_k y_k$. It is easy to see that, given other things, if $\epsilon_j > \epsilon_k$, then such a transfer increases concentration and the aggregate market power[7].

Throughout our presentation we have assumed that a firm chooses its output in an attempt to maximize its profit. Bertrand (1883) argued that it is more reasonable to assume that firms act as price setters rather as quantity setters. We discuss Bertrand's suggestion in the concluding part of this chapter.

Industrial market power and diversification

In this part we look at the relationship between the degree of global market power defined at the level of the entire economy and several market characteristics. Let us consider an economy consisting of a set of n firms and a set of k industries characterized by Cournot behavior. Each firm $i (i = 1, \ldots, n)$ is a producer of all the k commodities. That is, each firm is a member of all the k industries.

The following notation will be adopted throughout this discussion.
y_j^i:Quantity of commodity j supplied by firm i, where $j = 1, 2, \ldots, k$ and $i = 1, 2, \ldots, n$;
$y_j = \sum_{i=1}^n y_j^i$:total quantity of commodity j;
$p_j = f_j(y_1, y_2, \ldots, y_k)$:the inverse demand function for commodity j that expresses the price of the commodity as a function of $(y_1, y_2, \ldots, y_k)$;

$C_i(y_1^i, y_2^i, \ldots, y_k^i)$:Cost function of firm i;
$\epsilon_{jl} = -\frac{\delta p_j}{\delta y_l} \frac{y_l}{p_j}$: absolute value of the elasticity of the price of commodity j with respect to the quantity of commodity l;
$v_j^i = p_j y_j^i$:the sale of commodity j by firm i;
$v^i = \sum_{j=1}^k v_j^i$:total sale by firm i;
$v_j = \sum_{i=1}^n p_j y_j^i$:total sale of industry j.
Evidently, $\sum_{i=1}^n v^i = \sum_{j=1}^k v_j = v$ (say).

Now, each firm i will choose y_j^i to maximize its profit π_i:

$$\pi_i = \sum_{j=1}^k f_j(y_1, y_2, \ldots, y_k) y_j^i - C_i(y_j^i, \ldots, y_k^i). \tag{2.34}$$

Since the firms have been assumed to be Cournot maximizers, the first order conditions for profit maximization for each firm i are:

$$\frac{\delta \pi_i}{\delta y_j^i} = p_j + \sum_{l=1}^k \frac{\delta p_l}{\delta y_j} \cdot y_l^i - \frac{\delta C_i}{\delta y_j^i} = 0, j = 1, \ldots k, \tag{2.35}$$

from which the degree of monopoly power for firm i in the industry for commodity j turns out to be

$$\begin{aligned} L_j^i &= \frac{p_j - \delta C_i / \delta y_j^i}{p_j} \\ &= \epsilon_{jj} \frac{y_j^i}{y_j} + \sum_{l \neq j} \epsilon_{lj} \frac{p_l y_l^i}{p_j y_j}, \quad j = 1, \ldots, k, \; i = 1, \ldots, n. \end{aligned} \tag{2.36}$$

The average degree of monopoly power of firm i is defined as

$$L^i = \frac{\sum_{j=1}^k p_j y_j^i L_j^i}{\sum_{j=1}^k v_j^i}. \tag{2.37}$$

Using (2.36) we can write L^i as

$$L^i = \sum_{j=1}^k \epsilon_{jj} \frac{v_j}{v^i} (\frac{v_j^i}{v_j})^2 + \frac{1}{2} \sum_{l,j \in \bar{J}} \frac{1}{v^i} (\frac{\epsilon_{lj}}{v_j} + \frac{\epsilon_{jl}}{v_l})(v_j^i + v_l^i)^2 d_{l,j}^i. \tag{2.38}$$

where $\bar{J}$ is the set of ordered pairs (l, j) such that (a) $(l, j) \in \bar{J}$ implies that $(j, l) \notin \bar{J}$, (b) for all $(l, j) \in J$ either $(l, j) \in \bar{J}$ or $(j, l) \in \bar{J}$ with J being the set of ordered couples (l, j), $l \neq j, l, j = 1, 2, \ldots, k$;

$$d_{(l,j)}^i = 1 - \frac{(p_j y_j^i)^2 + (p_l y_l^i)^2}{(p_j y_j^i + p_l y_l^i)^2} \tag{2.39}$$

is the Berry (1975) index of diversification of firm i operating on the pair of markets j and l. Note that $d^i_{(j,l)} = d^i_{(l,j)}$.

At the level of the whole economy the average degree of monopoly power is defined as

$$L = \frac{\sum_{i=1}^{n} v^i L^i}{\sum_{i=1}^{n} v^i} \qquad (2.40)$$

which in view of (2.38) becomes

$$L = \sum_{j=1}^{k} m_j \epsilon_{jj} I_{H_j} + \frac{1}{2v} \sum_{(l,j) \in J} [\sum_{i=1}^{n} (v^i_j + v^i_l)^2] (\frac{\epsilon_{lj}}{v_j} + \frac{\epsilon_{jl}}{v_l}) d_{(l,j)}, \qquad (2.41)$$

where $m_j = v_j/v$, the share of industry j in the whole economy and I_{H_j} is the Herfindahl-Hirschman index for industry j.

From (2.41) it appears that given other things, a high degree of concentration in each industry and a relatively large share of the concentrated industries in the economy are positively related to a high L. For every industry pair (j, l), if j is a substitute for l ($\epsilon_{lj} > 0$), then a diversification into j by firms selling in l will be positively related to l. This supports the popular view that 'if the same firms are acting in distinct industries producing substitute products, the intensity of competition will be less than in an economy where different firms act in different industries' (Encaoua, Jacquemin and Moreaux (1986, p. 529)). Similarly, when l and j are complements ($\epsilon_{lj} < 0$) diversification into j by firms selling in l will imply a constrained exercise of market power. In case of independence all cross elasticities are zero and there will be no relation with performance. Thus, the relationship between the monopoly power and diversification will differ depending upon the nature of link between the products into which the firms have diversified.

In the particular case when there are only two industries, the index of diversification that emerges from (2.41) is the Clarke-Davies (1983) diversification index. However, in the general case of k industries, optimizing behavior does not lead to such a decomposition formula.

It should be noted that both monopoly power and the degre of diversification are jointly determined from the equilibrium system (2.35). Therefore, it will not be correct to conclude that there is a causal relation between diversification and market power.

We will now consider an example to illustrate the methodology described above. Let us consider the following situation:

	Industry I	Industry II
Case 1	a, b	d, e
Case 2	a, b	a, b.

In case 1, there are four nondiversified firms: a,b in industry I and c,d in industry II, whereas in case 2 the two diversified firms a,b occupy the two industries simultaneously. Each firm possess a constant unit cost of production c, $0 < c < 1$. The firms follow Cournot behavior. The inverse demand functions faced by the two industries are given respectively by

$$p_1 = 1 - y_1 - \delta y_2,$$
$$p_2 = 1 - \delta y_1 - y_2, \qquad (2.42)$$

where $\delta \in (-1, 1)$.

For case 1, the profit maximizing solutions are symmetric Cournot equilibrium $(y_1^a = y_1^b, y_2^d = y_2^e)$. It turns out that the aggregate productions in the two industries are identical and is given by $2(1-c)/(3+2\delta)$. The common price level is $[1 + 2(1 + \delta)c]/(3 + 2\delta)$. Therefore the Lerner index becomes $(1-c)/[1 + 2(1+\delta)c]$.

In the second case both the firms are diversified into the two industries. Given the symmetric nature of the equilibria, $y_1^a = y_1^b$ and $y_2^a = y_2^b$. At the equilibrium production of each firm is $(1-c)/3(1+\delta)$ and production for any industry is $2(1-c)/3(1+\delta)$. The common price level is $(1+2c)/3$ and the common Lerner index is $(1-c)/(1+2c)$.

To compare the above case we consider three aspects.

1 If the products in the two industries are substitutes, $0 < \delta < 1$, then production is larger and price and monopoly power are lower in the nondiversified case. On the other hand, if products are complements, $-1 < \delta < 0$, then the diversified situation implies a larger output, lower price and lower monopoly power.

2 The equilibrium values of m_j and I_{Hj} appearing in (2.41) remain unaltered due to a shift from case 1 to case 2. For case 1 the equilibrium value of direct elasticity of demand $\epsilon_{jj}(1) = [2(1-c)(3+2\delta)]/3[1+2(1+\delta)c]$ and for case 2 this value is $\epsilon_{jj}(2) = 2(1-c)/[(1+\delta)(1+2c)]$. For $\delta = 0$, $\epsilon_{jj}(1) = \epsilon_{jj}(2)$ and for $\delta < 0$, $\epsilon_{jj}(1) > \epsilon_{jj}(2)$. Consequently, a policy of diversification will reduce the first term on the right hand side of (2.41). Since the Lerner index is higher for case 1, this reduction must get outweighed by the positive effect of the second term.

3 Finally, we modify the example to illustrate that diversification may permit economies of scope. (An economy of scope exists if it is cheaper to produce two or more products jointly than separately. While this notion corresponds to some sort of externality in the production of two or more products, it implicitly assumes the existence of some common properties of cost functions and certain indivisibilities (see Jacquemin 1987).) Let θ be the cost saving resulting from firms' decision for joint production, compared with a situation of separate production. Assume that $0 < \theta < c$. At equilibrium the Lerner functions for cases 1 and 2 are given respectively by $L(1) = (1-c)/[1+2(1+\delta)c]$ and $L(2) =$

$[1-(c-\theta)]/[1+2(c-\theta)]$. Clearly, $L(1)/L(2)$ is less than unity if $\delta > 0$ and it reduces further with $\theta > 0$. Thus, if products are substitutes, then existence of economies of scope (which increases output and decreases price) reduces the degree of monopoly induced by diversification.

Game theory: a brief discussion

The purpose of game theory is to model competition among a group of decision makers in the form of a game of strategies that describe the behavior of each decision maker. In our context, a decision maker is a firm and its output, price, etc. will be determined by the strategies it adopts. Game theory in this set up therefore describes how firms will frame their strategies and how these strategies will determine the values of the concerned variable.

A distinction is made between cooperative and noncooperative games depending on whether firms can make some binding agreements to cooperate or they act independently since they are not allowed to make binding agreements. We will start with a brief discussion of noncooperative games.

Two forms of models are used to characterize a noncooperative game: the strategic or normal form and the extensive form. Loosely speaking, these correspond respectively to presenting the game through strategies and through a move by move description. There are three elements of describing a normal form game:a set $S = \{1, 2, \ldots, n\}$ of players (firms); for each firm i, a nonempty set T_i whose elements are the strategies open to it and a payoff (profit) function $\pi_i : T \to R^1$, where T is the strategy space. The strategy space is the Cartesian product of individual strategy sets:$T = T_1 \times T_2 \times \ldots, \times T_n$. A normal form game is symbolized simply by (S, T, π), where π stands for the vector $(\pi_1.\pi_2, \ldots, \pi_n)$.

The concept of Nash (1951) equilibrium is central to a game in which firms cannot make binding agreements. A strategy combination $t^* \in T$ is a Nash equilibrium if for all $i = 1, 2, \ldots, n$, $\pi_i(t^*) \geq \pi_i(t_1^*, t_2^*, \ldots, t_{i-1}^*, t_i, t_{i+1}^*, \ldots, t_n^*)$ for all $t_i \in T_i$. In other words, a set of strategies is a Nash equilibrium if, holding the strategies of all other firms constant, no firm can increase its profit by adopting a different strategy.

To state a result that shows the existence of a Nash equilibrium we need some technicalities like compactness, convexity, quasiconcavity and continuity. A set $B \subseteq R^m$ is called convex for all $z_1, z_2 \in B$ and for all $0 \leq \theta \leq 1$, $\theta z_1 + (1-\theta)z_2 \in B$. A function $F : B \to R^1$ is called quasiconcave if for all $z_1, z_2 \in B$ and for all $0 \leq \theta \leq 1$, $F(\theta z_1 + 1-\theta)z_2) \geq \min(F(z_1), F(z_2))$. For a strictly quasiconcave function, the defining inequality is $F(\theta z_1 + (1-\theta)z_2) > \min(F(z_1), F(z_2))$ for all $0 < \theta < 1$ and for all $z_1, z_2 \in B$, where $z_1 \neq z_2$. Continuity and compactness have been discussed earlier.

A game $G(S, T, \pi)$ has at least one Nash equilibrium under the following conditions:(i) the number of firms n is finite, (ii) T_i is a compact and convex subset of R^m, $i = 1, 2, \ldots, n$, (iii) $\pi_i(t)$ is continuous, $i = 1, 2, \ldots, n$ and (iv) $\pi(t)$ is quasiconcave with respect to $t_i, i = 1, 2, \ldots, n$. (See Friedman (1986) and Tirole (1988).)

Evidently, the Cournot market model can be interpreted in game theory terms. Given continuity of the demand and cost functions, the profit function π_i of firm i is continuous. We can choose an arbitrary large number k such that every firm's output level will be in the set $[0, k]$, which is compact and convex. Assuming quasiconcavity of π_i (which is fulfilled under quite general assumptions about demand and cost functions), we see that a Cournot equilibrium is a Nash equilibrium. This is why the Cournot model is also referred as the Cournot-Nash model. The reasoning behind this equivalence is that under Cournot assumption each firm believes that a change in its output has no effect on the quantity its competitors wish to produce, which is essentially the Nash assumption. By presenting the Stackelberg model as a game in which firms move sequentially we can interpret the Stackelberg equilibrium as a Nash equilibrium. The game is played in two stages. Firm 1 (say) chooses its output first without observing firm 2's output. At the second stage, firm 2 observes firm 1's output and then chooses its own output. Think of the game from firm 1's view point. It knows that its profit depends not only its own output, but also the output of its rival. Unllike the Cournot model, however, firm 1 knows that firm 2 observes firm 1's output before choosing its own profit maximizing output. This shows that the Stackelberg model can be justified in a game theoretic framework according to a formulation which is different from the one required in the case of the static Cournot model.

An interesting example of a normal form game is prisoner's dilemma attributed to A.W. Tucker in Luce and Raiffa (1957). We shall reframe it to fit our oligopolistic structure. Suppose that two firms can choose one of two output levels: a high output, O^H and a low output, O^L. The profits of the firms are given in Table 2.1.

Table 2.1

		Firm 1	
		O^L	O^H
Firm 2	O^L	8,8	-4,12
	O^H	12, -4	0,0

If one produces the low output and the other produces the high output, the low output firm makes a loss of 4 units and the high output firm earns a profit of 12 units. If both adopt high (low) output strategy, then each one makes a profit of 8(0) units. From firm 1's view point O^H is a dominant strategy; that is, it is the better choice for each possible choice of its rival. By a similar argument O^H is firm 2's dominant strategy. The strategy combination (O^H, O^H) is the unique (pure strategy) Nash equilibrium of this game[8]. This can be contrasted with the case where the firms collude and agree to produce the low output. Since each firm has an incentive to deviate from the committed output level such an agreement will not be sustainable. We will return to the nonsustainability issue after sometime.

It is important to note that the result we have stated above regarding the existence of Nash equilibrium is inapplicable to the games in which the players have finite strategies. Thus, the prisoner's dilemma is an example in which we cannot apply the result. We can get rid of this problem if we allow the players to use mixed strategies. A mixed strategy for firm i is a probability distribution over T_i. The strategy space of firm i is given by the set of all probability distributions over T_i. The profits (payoffs) for mixed strategies will be the expected values of the corresponding pure strategy profits. For a game $G(S, T, \pi)$ with finite strategy sets its mixed strategy counterpart possesses at least one Nash equilibrium.

The Nash equilibrium has come under attack from different perspectives. One criticism is that a game may possess too many Nash equilibria. Argument has therefore been put forward in favor of refinement so that for every game only a subset of the Nash equilibria will be the set of outcomes. 'It can also be argued that the Nash equilibrium concept is too 'narrow' to be able to predict outcomes accurately and what we need is not a refinement but a coarsening' (Basu, (1993, p.12)). (Further discussion along this line is beyond the scope of this book and the reader is referred to Tirole (1988), Kreps (1990) and Basu (1993).)

In extensive form representation a game is characterized by:the order of play, the payoffs of players and (may be) a probability distribution for moves. (See Tirole (1988) and Kreps (1990).) Such a game may be finite or infinite depending on the length of the sequence of moves. It may have a repeated or a nonrepeated strcuture. Repeated games are also called supergames because a player can adopt a strategy over many one period games. A supergame is a stationary world where firms repeatedly interact in the same environment. The same basic game (e.g. the game whose payoffs are given in Table 2.1) is repeated from one period to the next. The only link between the periods is the memory that players have of actions chosen by them and their rivals in previous iterations.

The main advantage of a multiperiod game over a single period game is that the former allows for more realistic interactions between firms. For instance, in the single period prisoners' dilemma model, each firm takes its rival's strategy as given and assumes that it cannot influence this strategy. The essential problem is that firms may have an incentive to deviate from collusive agreements and such deviations remain unpunished in a game that involves no future interactions. Clearly, this point has relevance to Cournot and Stackelberg models. Any collusive agreement (other than the outcome predicated by the model) cannot be sustained in these models. But if the game is played repeatedly, each firm can influence its rival's strategy by sending signal or threatning to punish. Given that the firms, if they wish, may be able to take punitive actions to retaliate against defections, it is likely that firms will cooperate in a repeated version of the game. (However, any repeated game may not result in collusion. If the game is repeated a finite number of times and both firms know the termination date with certainty and all the information of the repeated game is known to all firms, then cooperation may not be sustained in any period. We can talk about two ways in which game theorists have tried to sidestep this problem. One is to assume that players interact for a finite number of periods but the terminal period is not known with certainty. The other way retains finite repetition, certain terminal period assumptions but introduces some uncertainty in the firms' knowledge about the way their opponents may react.)

In the repeated game based on the basic game of Table 2.1, a strategy profile (an array of strategies with one strategy for each firm) where firm $i's$ ($i = 1, 2$) strategy is to choose O^H in each iteration of the game is a Nash equilibrium profile. These strategies satisfy a stronger requirement: they are subgame perfect. Subgame perfection (Selten (1975)) requires that the threats implicit in a player's Nash equilibrium strategy be credible, that is, if the firm is called upon to implement its proposed threat at any stage in the game, it should have no incentive to back off. A subgame perfect Nash equilibrium is a set of strategies for each firm such that it is not only an overall equilibrium but in any subgame of the original game the restriction of the strategies constitute a Nash equilibrium for the subgame concerned. (Any subgame of the original game is a game in its own right.) That is, in this case the original strategies will still be a Nash equilibrium for any game that start in any period t irrespective of whatever might have happened in the game upto period $(t-1)$. For a finite period game under certain conditions, collusion is a subgame perfect Nash equilibrium. The folk theorem describes a set of subgame perfect Nash equilibrium for infinitely long games in which there is little or no time discounting. According to the folk theorem any combination of output levels could be repeated infinitely as long as each firm's profit at these levels will be at least as large as the minimum that each firm can earn in a one period game. Before we wind up this discussion we may mention that much of recent research in multiperiod games is concerned with subgame perfection. (For more discussions, see the references cited above.)

We now turn to the theory of cooperative games where the main point of interest is the way in which the players bargain together over the division of the payoffs, rather than the way of achieving the payoffs through strategic behavior. The value and the core are the two kinds of equilibria. The value approach determines the vector of payoffs by taking account of threat capabilities of the players ((Nash (1953), Shapley (1953)). The core, on the other hand, is the set of all payoff vectors which, in some sense, will be acceptable by all players.

An arbitrary n person game is defined by a set of players $S = \{1, 2, \ldots, n\}$ and a characteristic function $v : \mathcal{P}(S) \rightarrow \mathrm{R}^1$ such that (a) $v(\phi) = 0$, and (b)

$v(S_1 \cup S_2) \geq v(S_1) + v(S_2)$ for all sets $S_1, S_2 \subseteq S$ such that $S_1 \cap S_2 = \phi$, where $\mathcal{P}(S)$ is the collection of all subsets of S and ϕ is the empty set. Any subset S_1 of S is a coalition and $v(S_1)$ is the worth of the coalition S_1, that is, the payoff which S_1 can assure for itself. The condition $v(\phi) = 0$ means that the empty coalition does not get anything. Condition (b) is called superadditivity. According to superadditivity when two disjoint coalitions combine they can get at least as much as the two coalitions could get seperately.

The game we require for our analysis in the next part is a simple game. Such a game is helpful for formulating shareholders' voting criteria. In a simple game the coalitions are classified into 'winning' and 'losing'. The characteristic function is dichotomous:$v(S_1) = 1$ if S_1 is winning and $v(S_1) = 0$ if it is losing. A coalition S_1 is called a minimal winning coalition if it does not have a proper subcoalition S_2 which is winning, that is, there is no $S_2 \subset S_1$ such that $v(S_2) = 1$. A simple game is monotonic if for all $S_1, S_2 \subset S$, $S_1 \subset S_2$, $v(S_1) \leq v(S_2)$. Voting games where the players possess different number of votes and winning is defined as a majority vote are an important class known as weighted majority games. An n-person weighted majority game with weights $(a_1, a_2, \ldots, a_n)$ and quota k is defined as

$$v(S_1) = 1 \; if \sum_{i \in S_1} a_i \geq k$$
$$= 0 \; if \sum_{i \in S_1} a_i < k. \qquad (2.43)$$

Distribution of power in voting games can be analyzed using power indices defined in terms of a model of coalition formation. A well known measure of voting power is the Shapley-Shubik index (Shapley and Shubik (1954)), which is a specialization of the Shapley value (Shapley (1953)) for a general game to simple games. The Shapley value for a general game is a vector $\psi = (\psi_1, \psi_2, \ldots, \psi_n)$ containing, for each player, the expected value for participating in the game. In the following presentation we show how this value, with reference to simple games, can be used for developing monopoly power indices.

Power to monopolize the market: a game theoretic approach

We have demonstrated earlier that the relationship between market power and concentration indices is sensitive to the procedure employed to aggregate the Lerner indices of different firms. It has also been noted that both concentration and price cost margins are jointly determined in the equilibrium relation which means that it will not be correct to assume a causal relationship between the two.

As an alternative it might be interesting to have indicators of probability of market monopolization. An attempt along this line has been made by d'Aspremont and Jacquemin (1985), which constitutes the basis of this analysis. Two types of questions will illustrate the need for such a measure, the first is the link between the output share of a firm and its capacity to contribute towards monopolization and the other is concerned with the size and number of coalitions allowing monopolization. We have already noted that a concentration index does not get affected much by the existence/addition/deletion of very small firms. In contrast, the role of a small firm can be very significant to form a coalition sufficient for controlling a market. This is understood easily in a context where a structural change like a merger may induce a switch into a particular oligopolistic regime when a small firm joins the set of merging firms. The second issue is related to the size of coalitions required to induce a change of regime. Given the problem of enforcing a coalition between a large number of firms and the role of corresponding costs, monopolization is easier in markets where the number of colluding firms required to induce a shift in the regime is small. That is, the smaller the number of firms which will collude to elevate price above marginal cost, the higher is the chance of noncompetitive behavior. A switch to a more noncompetitive regime may result from several alternative coalitions of different firms. The larger the number of such coalitions, the higher is the probability that there will be a switch.

Many antitrust authorities have adopted thresholds of concentration of output shares above which it is assumed that a monopoly, a dominant position or a harmful cartel will be created. For instance, in the German law a firm is presumed to be market dominating if its market share is one third. A policy maker will regard a coalition/merger leading to a configuration that reaches or exceeds the critical threshold as unacceptable, because above this threshold it is presumed that the new equilibrium will reduce social welfare significantly. (See the next part of this chapter for definition of social welfare. We will take up this issue more explicitly in Chapter 4.) Our analysis here assumes the existence of such a threshold.

From our discussion on weighted majority games it should be clear that they can be used to find an index of power to monopolize the industry. The determination of potential winning coalitions can be based on output shares of the firms. To see this, let us suppose that for an n-firm industry the following data are available:

(a) distribution of output shares $(s_1, s_2, \ldots, s_n)$;

(b) a given value $\bar{k}$ of critical threshold corresponding to a (weighted or unweighted) sum of output shares.

Now, for any coalition S_1 of firms, that is, $S_1 \subseteq \{1, 2, \ldots, n\} = S$, define a simple game as follows:

$$v(S_1) = 1 \quad if \sum_{i \in S_1} s_i > \bar{k} \qquad (2.44)$$
$$= 0 \quad otherwise.$$

This game is determined by a family of subsets (of n firms) capable of inducing a shift of the regime.

Since coalition formation can be random, we should look at the expected power of a firm rather than its power in a specific coalition. This is accomplished by the Shapley value. That is, this value can be regarded as a measure of power of a firm to monopolize the industry. The Shapley value ψ_i for a firm i is the incremental contribution of that firm to coalitions averaged over all coalitions of which it is not a member. For a simple game ψ_i turns out to be

$$\psi_i = \sum_{S_1 \subset S,\, i \notin S_1} \frac{t!(n-t-1)!}{n!} [v(S_1 U\{i\}) - v(S_1)], \qquad (2.45)$$

where t is the number of firms in S_1. The third bracketed term is the increment to the characteristic function with the addition of firm i to coalition S_1. The coefficient of this term is the ratio of the number of orderings of the firms given the coalition S_1, to the orderings of total number of firms. Therefore, it can be interpreted as the probability of formation of coalition S_1. Thus, the Shapley value is a mathematical expectation, given a model of random coalition formation.

Now, for the special form of characteristic function given by (2.45), the bracketed term will be zero except for any coalition S_1 which is losing but $S_1 U\{i\}$ is winning. Thus, this specific Shapley value ψ_i reflects the ability of firm i to change a coalition form losing to winning by joining it and can be interpreted as the expectation of happening this, given that random coalition formation is allowed. (Strictly speaking, we have to consider only minimal winning coalitions, since any simple game is characterized by the set of its minimal winning coalitions.) Clearly a firm with small market share may have great market power if it is necessary to make a losing coalition winning.

To discuss some additional properties of ψ_i in (2.45), let G^S be the collection of all simple games with the set of firms $S = \{1, 2, \ldots, n\}$. The vector $\psi = (\psi_1, \psi_2, \ldots, \psi_n)$ have been shown to be the only formula satisfying some properties which have interesting interpretations in industrial economics. The first axiom defines a class of games which are anonymous in the sense that the individual power indices should be independent of names of the firms. Thus, the power indices remain the same if two firms trade their places. Formally we have,

Anonymity: For any permutation ρ of S and for any $(S, v) \in G^S$ if $(S, \bar{v})$ is such that for all $S_1 \subset S$, $\bar{v}(\rho(S)) = v(S)$ then $\psi_i(S, v) = \psi_{\rho(i)}(S, \bar{v})$, $i \in S$.

The second axiom is concerning the firms which do not increase the power of any coalition by joining it. Such firms are null firms. Formally, $i \in S$ is a null firm in a game (S, v) if for all $S_1 \subset S$, $v(S_1 U\{i\}) = v(S_1)$.

Null Player Condition: If i is a null firm in a game $v \in G^S$, then $\psi_i(v) = 0$.

The next postulate is an additivity condition which describes a way of calculating the sum of values of two n-firm simple games.

Additivity: If for $v, \bar{v} \in G^S$ and for any $i \in S$,

$$\psi_i(v) + \psi_i(\bar{v}) = \psi_i(v \vee \bar{v}) + \psi_i(v \wedge \bar{v}), \qquad (2.46)$$

where for any arbitrary $S_1 \subset S$ the union $v \vee \bar{v}$ and the intersection $v \wedge \bar{v}$ are defined respectively by

$$\begin{aligned}(v \vee \bar{v})(S_1) &= \max\{v(S_1), \bar{v}(S_1)\},\\ (v \wedge \bar{v})(S_1) &= \min\{v(S_1), \bar{v}(S_1)\}.\end{aligned} \qquad (2.47)$$

Condition (2.46) can be interpreted in the following way. If firms have market power in two different markets, then the total power of a firm will be the sum of its power in a single market and its power when its control is exercised on both markets at a time. This can be illustrated by a situation of two imperfect substitutes: there is some power resulting from control of one of the two products because of product differentiation and their is some power that results from the degree of substitution between the products. The power resulting from product differentiation is the first term on the right hand side of (2.46) and the second term gives power generated from substitutability.

The last axiom is

Normalization: For any $v \in G^S$, $\sum_{i=1}^n \psi_i(v) = 1$.

This condition means that sum of the values over all firms must be equal to the amount which the grand coalition $\{1, 2, \ldots, n\}$ can guarantee itself.

Let us now illustrate the individual power indices by an example. Conser a 3-firm industry with output shares $(.10, .40, .50)$ and $\bar{k} = .65$. We have $v(\{1\}) = v(\{2\}) = v(\{3\}) = 0$, $v(\{1,2\}) = v(\{1,3\}) = 0$ and $v(\{2,3\}) = v(\{1,2,3\}) = 1$. The only minimal winning coalition here is $\{2,3\}$. The Shapley value for this example is $(0, 1/2, 1/2)$. Therefore, firm 1 is a null player though it has a positive output share. Firms 2 and 3 have equal power inspite of different shares. That is, the contributions of firms 2 and 3 to reach the critical threshold are the same despite their unequal output shares.

We will now develop an index for measuring overall power to monopolize an industry. That is, we determine the danger of monopolization in a given industry on the basis of a given family of winning coalitions. We assume that the required index determining the extent of power of monopolization in an n-firm industry is a real valued function F defined on G^S. The following axioms are considered for F:

(a) Anonymity: For any permutation ρ of $\{1, 2, \ldots, n\}$ and for any $v \in G^S$, if $\bar{v}$ is such that for all $S_1 \subset S$, $\bar{v}(\rho(S_1)) = v(S_1)$, then $F(v) = F(\bar{v})$.

(b) Null Player Condition: If n' is a null player and $S' = S \cup \{n'\}$, then for any $v' \in G^{S'}$, $v'(S_1) = v(S_1)$, where $S_1 \subset S$ is arbitrary.

(c) Additivity: For any $v, \bar{v} \in G^S$, $F(v) + F(\bar{v}) = F(v \wedge \bar{v}) + F(v \vee \bar{v})$.

(d) Boundedness: For any $v \in G^S$, $0 \leq F(v) \leq 1$.

(e) Minimal Winning Coalition: Let $v, \bar{v} \in G^S$ be such that except for one firm j, they have the same family of r disjoint minimal winning coalitions

$\{M_1, M_2, \ldots, M_r\}$ and $\{M_1 \setminus j, M_2, \ldots, M_r\}$ respectively, where $M_1 \neq M_1 \setminus \{j\} \neq \phi$, then $F(v) < F(\bar{v})$.

Properties (a) - (c) are similar to the corresponding postulates we have studied for the individual power indices. Property (d) shows that the overall power index is bounded between zero and one. Property (e) asserts that under ceteris paribus assumption, once the minimal winning coalition M_1 is reduced, the overall power index increases. The other minimal winning coalitions are assumed to be disjoint from each other and from M_1 to reflect pure size effect of minimal winning coalitions.

d'Aspremont and Jacquemin showed that F defined on G^S satisfies postulates (a) - (e) if and only if for some positive Borel measure μ on $(0, 1]$ which is bounded by but not concentrated on 1, the following integral formula is fulfilled: for any $(S, v) \in G^S$ with minimal winning coalitions $\{M_1, M_2, \ldots, M_r\}$, $r \geq 1$,

$$\begin{aligned} F(S,v) = \int_0^1 [\sum_{i=1}^{r} \alpha^{|M_i|} - \sum_{i=1}^{r-1} \sum_{j=i+1}^{r} \alpha^{|M_i \cup M_j|} \\ + \sum_{i=1}^{r-2} \sum_{j=i+1}^{r-1} \sum_{k=j+2}^{r} \alpha^{|M_i \cup M_j \cup M_k|} \\ - \ldots \\ + (-1)^{r-1} \alpha^{|M_1 \cup M_2 \cup \ldots \cup M_r|}] d\mu(\alpha), \end{aligned} \qquad (2.48)$$

where for any set S_1, $|S_1|$ denotes the number elements in it.

A Borel measure μ referred to in (2.48) is a set function satisfying certain conditions and it takes values in $[0, 1]$. A representative element of the class in (2.48) can be found by specifying certain value of α in $(0,1)$ and then applying the formula for μ concentrated on α. Any other function in the class will be a linear combination of representative elements. Since F is based on minimal winning coalitions, it can be regarded as a weighted average of individual power indices.

The formula is obtained by showing that if there exists an F satisfying postulate (a) and (b), then there will be a function defined on S such that for any game v_M, $M \subset S$,

$$F(v_M) = f(m), \qquad (2.49)$$

where m is the number of firms in M. The function f can now be specified using other axioms.

To illustrate the formula, let us consider a 3-firm industry and use $f(m) = \alpha^m$ with $\alpha = 1/2$. Assume that the minimal winning coalitions are $M_1 =$

$\{1,2\}$, $M_2 = \{2,3\}$ and $M_3 = \{1,3\}$. Then F becomes

$$\begin{aligned} F &= \sum_{i=1}^{3} f(|M_i|) - \sum_{\substack{i,j \\ i \neq j}} f(|M_i \cup M_j|) + f(|M_1 \cup M_2 \cup M_3|) \\ &= 3(\frac{1}{2})^2 - 3(\frac{1}{2})^3 + (\frac{1}{2})^3 \\ &= .50. \end{aligned}$$

(2.50)

Using numerical example d'Aspremont and Jacquemin (1985) shows that in the particular case of a single minimal winning coalition, the index obtains the maximum value when there is only one firm in the coalition and it decreases as the number of firms in the coalition increases. This property seems intuitively reasonable. On the other hand, the value of F increases as the number of disjoint minimal winning coalition increases. This happens because of the fact that with the increase in the number of disjoint minimal winning coalitions the probability of a shift of the regime gets augmented.

Welfare consequences of market power

A major focus of industrial economics is on the analysis of the markets which are imperfect. In such set ups prices differ from the marginal costs of production which in turn imply positivity of market power. These situations, as opposed to competition, are inefficient ways of organizing production.

It is necessary to see what gains or losses in welfare, defined as the sum of consumers' surplus and producers' surplus, are involved in moving from one set up to another. The basic devices from which we can determine changes in welfare are none other than simple demand and supply curves. Consumers' surplus is given by the area under the consumers' demand curve above the price level. It is a measure of the amount that consumers would be willing to pay for any given quantity of the good purchased minus the amount the market requires them to pay. It should be noted that since aggregate demand curve is the sum of demand curves of all consumers, the consumers' surplus is the sum of monetary surplus obtained by each consumer. No distinction is made among consumers. A dollar's worth of surplus to one consumer is treated as having the same weight as a dollar's worth to another, regardless of their income levels. Thus, distributive implications are disregarded entirely.

Producers' surplus is the difference between the total amount producers receive for any given quantity of the product and the minimum amount which they would be willing to accept for that quantity. It is measured diagrammatically by the area above the supply curve but below the price at which that quantity is sold. (The supply curve can be interpreted as the aggregate supply curve for the good by a competitive industry.)

For assessing whether a particular move is worthwhile or not, we look at the change in welfare resulting from the move. If the change is positive, then it is regarded as desirable. That is, policy prescriptions are based on the notion that a policy change will improve welfare. If, as in almost all cases, all the producers' surplus may be regarded as economic profits, then a move is worthwhile whenever:

$$\Delta W = \Delta \pi + \Delta CS > 0, \qquad (2.51)$$

where W, π and CS stand respectively for welfare, profit and consumers' surplus, and Δ indicates change.

An interesting case that can be analyzed in the above framework is the situation where a perfectly competitive industry becomes monopolized. Suppose that the competitive industry has constant marginal cost of production which is the marginal cost for the monopolist as well. The competitive industry's supply curve coincides with its marginal cost curve. The monopoly charges higher price and produces less than the competitive set up does. Refer to Figure 2.1. When marginal cost is c_1, competitive output is x_i^3 and the monopoly output is x_i^1. Monopoly price in this case is p_1 which is greater than the competitive price c_1. The producers' surplus which is zero in the competitive case becomes positive under monopoly. However, consumers' surplus decreases under monopolization. We can easily see that the net change in welfare is negative. It is called the deadweight loss resulting from monopolization (market power). In the context of Figure 2.1, this deadweight loss is given by the area of the triangle $L_1 L_2 L_3$. This loss is a measure of the loss of welfare resulting from monopolistic output restriction.

From public policy point of view we should be concerned about the divergence between price and marginal cost. Such problems of inefficiencies that arise out of the existence of excessive market power call for government intervention via legislation or regulation to enforce competition. But sometimes interventions are costly. The desirability of a government action towards an industry should therefore rely on the comparison between the benefits and the costs of intervention.

The theory of intervention has been investigated in the context of oligopolistic framework by Dansby and Willig (1978). They developed tools capable of assessing the gain in welfare $W(y) - W(y^o)$ resulting from intervention, where y^o and y are the vectors of outputs of the firms in the industry before and after the intervention. Note that the formulation is quite general in the sense that firms may produce differentiated products. Now the first order approximation of $W(y) - W(y^o)$ is

$$\begin{aligned} W(y) - W(y^o) &= \sum_i W_i(y^o)(y_i - y_i^o) \\ &= \nabla W \Delta y, \end{aligned} \qquad (2.52)$$

where W_i is the partial derivative of W with respect to the output of firm i.

Clearly, a necessary condition for intervention activity to be socially desirable is that $\nabla W \triangle y$ exceeds the cost of intervention.

Observe that $\nabla W \triangle y$ will depend on the particular direction of industry output changes. While this may be appropriate for evaluation of a particular policy, a practical evaluation of industry performance requires specification of an index which should be independent of policy detail. Dansby and Willig (1979) therefore developed an index 'that measures the sensitivity of social welfare to the locally best changes in the outputs of the firms in an industry' (op cit., p.250).

To discuss their measure explicitly, consider the initial price vector weighted distance function

$$d(\Delta y, p^o) = [\sum_i (p_i^o \Delta y_i)^2]^{1/2}, \qquad (2.53)$$

where p_i^o and Δy_i stand for the ith coordinate of the vectors p^o and Δy respectively. Note that p_i^o is the (current) price of the product of firm i. Dansby and Willig solved for the vector $y^*(\theta)$ which maximizes W subject to $d(\Delta y, p^o) \leq \theta$. That is, $W(y^*) - W(y^o)$ is the maximum increase in welfare obtained by output adjustments whithin the distance θ from y^o. The 'best direction' of changes in outputs then becomes proportional to $(y^*(\theta) - y^o)$ and the average rate of change in welfare, given that the outputs are adjusted in the best direction is $(W(y^*(\theta)) - W(y^o))/\theta$.

The industry performance gradient index ϕ is then defined as the 'best instantaneous rate of change of welfare', at the present position of the industry:

$$\phi = \lim_{\theta \to 0}(W(y^*(\theta)) - W(y^o))/\theta. \qquad (2.54)$$

The index ϕ is a measure of the sensitivity of social welfare to output adjustments of different firms in the industry.

Theorem 2.2 (Dansby and Willig, 1979): Assume that W is continuously differentiable. Then for the distance function defined in (2.53) the industry performance gradient index ϕ at y^o is

$$\phi = [\sum_i ((p_i^o - C_i'(y_i^o))/p_i^o)^2]^{1/2}, \qquad (2.55)$$

where C_i' is the marginal cost of firm i. Further, the associated best direction of adjustment in the firms' base price weighted outputs is

$$d(p_i^o y_i^*(\theta))/d\theta \mid_{\theta=0} = \frac{p_i^o - C_i'(y_i^o)}{\phi p_i^o}. \qquad (2.56)$$

Proof: The Lagrangian for the maximization of $W(y)$ subject to $d(\Delta y, p^o) \leq \theta$ can be written as

$$V = W(y) + \mu[\theta^2 - \sum_i (\Delta y_i p_i^o)^2].$$

where μ is the Lagrange multiplier. The first order conditions, necessarily satisfied at the solution $(y^*(\theta), \mu)$, are: (a) $W_i(y^*(\theta)) = 2\mu(p_i^o)^2(y_i^*(\theta) - y_i^o)$ and (b) $\mu[\theta^2 - \sum_i (\Delta y_i p_i^o)^2] = 0$, $\mu \geq 0$ and $d(\Delta y, p^o) \leq \theta$. By the envelope theorem[9], $dW(y^*(\theta))/d\theta = \delta V/\delta \theta = 2\mu\theta$. Squaring (a) and dividing through by $(p_i^o)^2$ for each i, summing over i, and using (b) yields $2\mu\theta = [\sum_i W_i(y^*(\theta))^2/(p_i^o)^2]^{1/2}$. As $\theta \to 0$, $y^*(\theta) \to y^o$ and by continuity $W_i(y^*(\theta)) \to W_i(y^o)$. Then $\phi = \lim_{\theta \to 0} dW(y^*(\theta))/d\theta = \lim_{\theta \to 0} 2\mu\theta$.

In view of the fact that $W_i(y) = \delta W(y)/\delta y_i = p_i(y) - C_i'(y_i)$, ϕ now becomes the expression given by (2.55). Equation (2.56) follows from using (a) to solve for the limit, as $\theta \to 0$, of $[y_i^*(\theta) - y_i^o]/\theta$. □

The index ϕ in (2.55) is a symmetric function of the Lerner indices of different firms in the industry. It becomes exactly the Lerner index in a single-firm case. The index ϕ shows that the sensitivity of welfare to optimal quantity adjustments is directly related to the proportionate gap between prices and marginal costs. If for any firm i, price exceeds its marginal cost then the optimal adjustment suggests output increase. In case $p_i^o = C_i'(y_i^o)$ for all i, then y^o is a local maximum of W and optimal adjustments would be 'no change at all'. If W is strictly concave, then an y at which $\phi = 0$ is the unique global welfare optimum. For any other y, W is lower and ϕ is higher. (See Dansby and Willig (1979) for a proof of this.) Therefore ϕ is an inverse indicator of welfare performance.

If W is concave, then

$$W(y) - W(y^o) \leq \sum_i (W_i(y^o)/p_i^o)(p_i^o(y_i - y_i^o)).$$

By Cauchy-Schwartz inequality[10] we have

$$\sum_i (W_i(y^o)/p_i^o)(p_i^o(y_i - y_i^o))$$
$$\leq (\sum_i (W_i(y^o)/p_i^o)^2)^{1/2} (\sum_i (p_i^o(y_i - y_i^o))^2)^{1/2}$$
$$= \phi(y^o) d(\Delta y, p^o).$$

This shows that the welfare difference $W(y) - W(y^o)$ is bounded above by $\phi(y^o) d(\Delta y, p^o)$. Hence for intervention to be beneficial, this bound should exceed the cost.

For an n-firm homogeneous good industry using (2.6) we can write ϕ in (2.55) as

$$\phi = \frac{1}{\epsilon} (\sum_{i=1}^n (s_i q_i)^2)^{1/2}. \tag{2.57}$$

The notation adopted in (2.57) have been explained earlier. If $q_i's$ are the same for all firms, then ϕ increases under a transfer of output from a small frim to a large firm. This gives ϕ in (2.57) a flavor of concentration. In fact, under standard Cournot hypothesis ϕ becomes $\sqrt{I_H^m}/\epsilon$, where I_H^m is the Herfindahl-Hirschman index of concentration. Though this gives a precise welfare theoretic interpretation of the Herfindahl-Hirschman index, it should be noted that the welfare gradient index in (2.55) depends crucially on the behavioral hypothesis. Another set of assumptions on firm behavior (for instance, a price leadership model) will give us an alternative form of ϕ. Therefore the rate of potential welfare improvement depends not only on industry structure but also on conduct of firms. However, given such limitations we can make some unambiguous statements which may be helpful for the specific objective we have in mind.

While in (2.55) the price cost margins have generated an industry performance gradient index, we can also use them to express the link between consumers' surplus and concentration. If we put $\alpha = 2$ in (2.22), we have

$$L_e = \frac{I_H^m}{\epsilon}, \tag{2.58}$$

the Rader (1972) and Cowling-Waterson (1976) relation between price cost margins and concentration. Using notation adopted there, we rewrite (2.58) as

$$\frac{pX - \sum_{i=1}^n x_i C_i'}{pX} = \frac{I_H^m}{\epsilon} \tag{2.59}$$

which gives us

$$p = \frac{\sum_{i=1}^n x_i C_i'}{X(1 - I_H^m/\epsilon)}. \tag{2.60}$$

Since consumers' surplus is a decreasing function of price, we have

$$CS = h_1(p) = h_1(\frac{\sum_{i=1}^n x_i C_i'}{X(1 - I_H^m/\epsilon)}). \tag{2.61}$$

where h_1 is decreasing in its argument. For a given share weighted average of marginals ($\sum_{i=1}^n x_i C_i'/X = \sum_{i=1}^n s_i C_i'$), an increase in I_H^m will decrease the consumers' surplus. An increase in the consumers' surplus may result from a decrease in average of marginals, keeping concentration constant. Thus, this latter situation of increase in consumers' surplus does not result from a reduction in concentration. Hence (2.61) presents different components of consumers' surplus which might be of interest to a policy maker. We again stress that this conclusion, as in many cases, is model specific.

Blackorby, Donaldson and Weymark (1982) argued that indices of concentration by themselves are not sufficient to evaluate industry performance. They presumed the existence of preferences (by a policy maker, say) over all possible configurations of output vectors for a particular industry. By imposing certain structures on evaluator's preferences they showed that the industry performance E can be measured by a Cobb-Douglas function of the total output X and a numbers equivalent $n_e(x)$:

$$E(x) = (X)^\nu (n_e(x))^{1-\nu}, \qquad (2.62)$$

where x is the vector of outputs in an n-firm homogeneous good industry and the parameter ν, $0 < \nu < 1$, characterizes the trade off in the Cobb-Douglas representation. A higher value of E indicates a better performance. But for comparison of alternative vectors to be meaningful we need a reference framework.

Next, we analyze a case of mixed oligopoly. The analysis is based on De Fraja and Delbono (1989) and Basu (1993). An industry is said to possess a mixed character if both private and nationalized firms coexist. A private firm will maximize its profit and a nationalized firm will maximize social welfare. We can characterize the Cournot equilibrium of such an industry. Comparative static exercises relating to some relevant issues can be carried out here. For instance, we can investigate how welfare will change when the entire industry is nationalized. We can also look at the consequences of privatization of nationalized or public firms in terms of output and welfare.

Suppose that there are n private firms, $1, 2, \ldots, n$ and m public firms, $n+1, \ldots, m+n$. We assume that the inverse demand function is linear:

$$p = a - X, \qquad (2.63)$$

where $X = \sum_{i=1}^{n+m} x_i$, with x_i being the output of firm i and a is a constant. Each firm's conditional cost function is given by

$$C_i(x_i) = b + \frac{k}{2} x_i^2, \qquad (2.64)$$

where b and $k > 0$ are constants. For any private firm i, that is, for any $i \in \{1, 2, \ldots, n\}$, the profit function is

$$\pi_i(x) = x_i p - C_i(x_i), \qquad (2.65)$$

where $x = (x_1, x_2, \ldots, x_{n+m})$ and for any public firm j, $j \in \{n+1, \ldots, n+m\}$, the optimizing function is

$$W^j = \int^X p(t)dt - \sum_{i=1}^{n+m} C_i(x_i). \qquad (2.66)$$

Let us now assume that $m = 1$, that is, there is only one public firm. The symmetric Cournot equilibrium shows that the common output level for each private firm is

$$x_i = \frac{ak}{(1+k)^2 + nk}, i = 1, 2, \ldots, n, \qquad (2.67)$$

71

and the output level of the public firm is

$$x_{n+1} = \frac{a(k+1)}{(1+k)^2 + nk}. \qquad (2.68)$$

Aggregate welfare in equilibrium turns out to be

$$W = \frac{a^2(1+k)^3 + nk(nk + 2 + 4k + k^2)a^2}{2((1+k)^2 + nk)^2} - n(1+b). \qquad (2.69)$$

We can now look at the consequence of privatization of the single public firm. In such a case there are $(n+1)$ private firms which are Cournot maximizers. The equilibrium output of firm i becomes

$$\hat{x}_i = \frac{a}{2+k+n}, i = 1, \ldots, n+1. \qquad (2.70)$$

and aggregate welfare in equilibrium is

$$\hat{W} = \frac{a^2(3+k) + a^2(4+k)n + a^2n^2}{2(2+k+n)^2} - (n+1)b. \qquad (2.71)$$

To analyze the consequence of privatization we need to compare W and $\hat{W}$. It turns out that W exceeds $\hat{W}$ as n reduces. Thus, nationalization of one firm is worthwhile if the industry is highly concentrated. This seems intuitively reasonable: given equal output distribution, one plausible way of making the industry more competitive (hence increasing welfare) is to increase the number of firms.

The idea of making an industry more competitive by altering the number of the firms was also considered by Perry (1984) under the assumption of economies of scale which, loosely speaking, requires decreasingness of average cost (see Chapter 5). Economies of scale gives rise to a trade off in the evaluation of structure of an industry. (See Chapter 4 for a discussion.) Scale economies are more exploited with a small number of firms, but then imperfect competition may emerge. On the other hand, if we allow the number of firms to increase then economies of scale are sacrificed (Williamson (1968)). A structural policy, as considered by Perry (1984), would regulate the number of firms not their behavior. Thus, a structural policy exercises direct control over the structural environment of an industry. This contrasts with a behavioral policy which exercises control over the objective of firms. For instance, a monopoly regulation to enforce marginal cost pricing is a behavioral policy.

Assuming a constant conjectural variation, Perry (1984) considers the equilibrium industry output for any given number of firms. The number of firms is then allowed to increase until each firm's profit is just nonnegative. Clearly, with imperfect competition market equilibrium under free entry assumption will result in unexploited scale economies. The structural optimum is then defined as the number of firms which maximizes aggregate welfare subject to the industry output equilibrium for any given number of firms. Perry's analysis can therefore be regarded as a formalization of the trade offs discussed by Williamson.

Concluding remarks

In this chapter we have concentrated on the notion of market power exercised by firms in an industry. Two alternative concepts of market power have been examined:one is conjectural variation-based and the other is game theory-based. We considered the problem of aggregating the market powers of different firms into an overall indicator. Some other aspects like market power for diversified firms and welfare consequences of market power have also been studied.

We have noted that prices instead of outputs can as well be treated as instruments controlled by firms. As stated, this idea originated from an article of Bertrand publishied in 1883. To illustrate the Bertrand model, let us consider a 2-firm homogeneous good industry where each firm produces the good at a constant average cost a. Given that consumers are perfectly informed of offered prices, they all will buy from firm i if its price p_i is smaller of the two prices, where $i = 1, 2$. But if p_i is higher than firm i's rival's price, then firm i sells nothing and all consumers buy from the rival. Consumers are indifferent between the two firms if the prices are identical. In this case we can assume without loss of generality that firm i gets half of the consumers. Let $H(p)$ be the total demand function. Then we can write firm i's output demand function as

$$\begin{aligned} x_i &= H(p_i), \text{ if } p_i < p_j \\ &= \frac{1}{2} H(p_i), \text{ if } p_i = p_j \\ &= 0, \text{ if } p_i > p_j. \end{aligned} \quad (2.72)$$

The profit function of firm i is given by

$$\begin{aligned} \pi_i(p_i, p_j) &= H(p_i)(p_i - a), \text{ if } p_i < p_j \\ &= \frac{1}{2} H(p_i)(p_i - a), \text{ if } p_i = p_j \\ &= 0, \text{ if } p_i > p_j. \end{aligned} \quad (2.73)$$

We say that the firms use the Bertrand conjecture if each firm sets its price in an attempt to maximize its profit assuming that other firms will not change their prices. It is easy to check that the unique Bertrand equilibrium for the duopoly under consideration is $(p_1, p_2) = (a, a)$. There is no profitable deviation from (a, a). So in this equilibrium both firms charge a price equal to marginal cost, earn zero profits and hence this equilibrium is same as the social optimum (competitive equilibrium). The Lerner indices for both the firms in this case become zero. Clearly, the Bertrand model can be interpreted as a game in which the firms' strategies are their prices. The Bertrand equilibrium is a Nash equilibrium in prices.

Edgeworth (1897) presented a variant of the Bertrand model. He showed that if the firms have limited capacity then there is no Bertrand equilibrium. To illustrate this, suppose that if $p_i = p_j = a$, then the total output of the firms can just fulfill the market demand. If firm i charges a higher price while firm j maintains its price at marginal cost, then all consumers will try to buy from firm j. However, because of its limited capacity this firm cannot satisfy the demands of all consumers. Hence the frustrated consumers will come to firm i which can now choose a price to maximize its profit by acting like a monopolist with respect to the residual demand curve. This will generate positive profit for firm i. Therefore, $(p_i = a, p_j = a)$ cannot be a Bertrand equilibrium. One can also see that $p_j \neq p_i$ cannot be a Bertrand equilibrium. (See, however, Dasgupta and Maskin (1986) for existence of a more complex type of equilibrium. For further discussions along this line the reader is referred to Tirole (1988) and Carlton and Perloff (1990).)

With linear demand curve and constant marginal cost, Bertrand competitive equilibrium is a consistent conjectural equilibrium. A firm's conjecture is consistent if a rival's behavior coincides with the behavior predicted at the equilibrium and near the equilibrium. That is, consistency requires that a firm's conjecture should be correct at the equilibrium and also outside the equilibrium when firms are adjusting their behaviors to reach equilibrium (Kamien and Schwartz (1983)). To illustrate consistency consider a Cournot duopoly model. Consistency will then require that the actual profit maximizing rate of change of firm 1's output when firm 2's output changes, that is, the slope of firm 1's reaction function with respect to the output of firm 2 should equal the rate conjectured by firm 2.

In the conjectural variations models we have considered, each firm's conjectures are correct at the equilibrium. However, outside equilibrium their conjectures may be false.

To see this, we consider a Cournot duopoly with the same constant marginal cost a for both the firms. Let $r_1(x_2)(r_2(x_1))$ be the reaction function of firm 1(2). It turns out that $dr_1(x_2)/dx_2$ is not necessarily equal to zero, showing the inconsistency of the Cournot conjecture. In addition to inconsistency, specification of conjectures are arbitrary. Furthermore, multiperiod versions of conjectural variation models are implausible. However, game theoretic explanations of many such models make them attractive from a different perspective. More importantly, they are easy to explain and their empirical implementability is also easy.

Notes

1. With free entry competitive equilibrium wi yield normal profit for each identical firm in the long run. That is, they will receive just enough to pay for their production and no more. Free entry implies that if existing firms in the industry earn positive profits, then new firms will be attracted. As a consequence price goes down until profit becomes zero. If additional identical firms are unable to produce, then there could be positive profits, but firms still produce where price = marginal cost.

2. In the long run if a 'monopolist is to remain a monopolist, there must be some sort of barrier to entry' (Varian (1984, p.91)). See Chapter 5 for a discussion on entry barriers.

3. Results on continuous functions used in this proof can be found in Apostol (1974, Chapter 4).

4. A set $B \subseteq R^m$ is called closed if it includes its boundaries.

5. A set is called compact if it is closed and bounded.

6. For example, by choosing $g(L_i) = \exp(\theta L_i)$, $\theta > 0$, we get an alternative specification of aggregate monopoly power.

7. If firm i is earning a positive profit we would expect new firms to enter the industry and produce close substitutes of the product of firm i. Therefore, in the long run, firms would enter the industry until all firms earn zero economic profit, as in a competitive industry. With a downward sloping demand curve, a firm has some market power:its price is greater than its marginal cost.

8. A strategy is called pure if it does not have stochastic elements. Such a choice is made with certainty.

9. The envelope theorem concerns calculating how the optimal value of a function changes when a parameter of that function changes. For a rigorous statement, see Varian (1984, pp. 327-329).

10. See Apostol (1974, p.20).

3 Measuring efficiency

Modelling of production technology is generally done by means of a production function, which in the single output case will give the maximum output obtainable from an input vector. In the econometric literature this function is referred to as a frontier function since it describes the optimizing behavior of a producer and hence places limits on the possible output values. The extent to which the actual output of a production unit approaches its maximum is called the technical efficiency of production. This is output-based approach to technical efficiency. This approach takes inputs as given and determines the amount of output lost due to inefficiency.

The problem of measuring technical efficiency of a firm is important from both a theoretical and a policy point of view. From a theoretical perspective we will be mainly interested in developing an appropriate measure of efficiency and studying its properties. On the other hand, a policy maker's interest may lie in knowing how far a given firm can increase its efficiency without absorbing further resources. That is, a planner's motive is to see how much more output could be obtained from the same inputs.

The most well known measure of technical efficiency is the Debreu (1951) - Farrell (1957) measure. This measure is essentially the inverse of the Malmquist (1953) - Shephard (1970) distance function, which measures the maximum amount by which an input vector can be shrunk along a ray while holding the output level constant. Note that here output is taken as given and we look at the scaled down levels of inputs which are still capable of producing this given output. Therefore, this is an input-based index of efficiency, an index that takes output as given and determines the potential input waste due to inefficiency. It may be interesting to note that for any output level, the Debreu - Farrell index is bounded below by the ratio of the minimal to actual input costs for producing the output. Evidently, this ratio is a natural measure of economic efficiency. It determines a firm's success in choosing an optimal set of inputs for producing a given (but arbitrary) level of output.

Alternatives and variations of the Debreu - Farrell index were suggested by
Färe and Lovell (1978), Färe and Grosskopf (1983), Zieschang (1984), Färe,
Grosskopf and Lovell (1985, 1993) and Russell (1985, 1988). We discuss the
Debreu-Farrell measure along with these alternatives and variations in this
chapter. The chapter also presents the properties for an arbitrary measure of
technical efficiency and studies their implications. We conclude the chapter
with some remarks.

Properties for an index of efficiency

Measures of technical efficiency were introduced by Debreu (1951) and Farrell
(1957). Their pioneering contributions have inspired several studies during the
past years. (See the extended bibliography for references to this literature.)
Our purpose here is to study briefly the properties for an arbitrary measure
of technical efficiency and their implications. Discussion along this line have
been made by Färe and Lovell (1978), Kopp and Diewert (1982), Zieschang
(1983, 1984), Russell (1985, 1988), Bol (1986), Färe, Grosskopf and Lovell
(1993) and many others.

Usually technical efficiency measures depend on the combination (u, b) of
an output vector $u \in R^n_+$ and an input vector $b \in R^m_+$ that can produce u, and
the technology that underlies the production. We characterize the production
technology of a firm by the input correspondence $A : R^n_+ \to \mathcal{P}(R^m_+)$, where
$\mathcal{P}(R^m_+)$ is the power set of R^m_+. (The power set of R^m_+ is the collection of all
subsets of R^m_+, including R^m_+ itself.) The input requirement set A assigns to
any output $u \in R^n_+$, the set $A(u)$ of input vectors that can produce at least
the output vector u. It is also called the upper level set mapping. Assume
that A satisfies the following conditions :

(A1) : $A(01^n) = R^m_+$.
(A2) : If $u \geq 01^n$, then $01^m \notin A(u)$[1].
(A3) : For all $u \in R^n_+$ and for all $\theta \geq 1$, $b \in A(u)$ implies that $\theta b \in A(u)$.
(A4) : For all $u \in R^n_+$ and for all $\theta \geq 1$, $A(\theta u) \subseteq A(u)$.
(A5) : For all $u \in R^n_+$, $A(u)$ is a closed set.

According to (A1) any amount of input could be employed (wasted) for
producing nothing (that is, the zero output vector). Consequently, the input requirement set for the zero output vector is the entire input domain.
Condition (A2) asserts that for producing positive amounts of one or more
outputs, we require positive quantity of at least one input. That is, something
out of nothing is ruled out. The third assumption means that if an output
vector could be produced by some quantities of the required inputs, then it
could also be produced by all scaled up quantities of these inputs. Shephard
(1970) referred to this condition as the weak disposability of inputs. Clearly,
a stronger version of (A3) is the free disposability property

(A3') : If $b \in A(u)$ and $b' \geq b$, then $b' \in A(u)$, where $u \in R_+^n$ is arbitrary.

Postulate (A4) demands that the input requirement set for any output vector u is always larger than the corresponding set for any scaled up version of u. A stronger version of (A4) is

(A4') : For any $u \in R_+^n$, if $b \in A(u)$ and $u' \leq u$, then $b \in A(u')$.

Evidently, both (A3) and (A4) ((A3') and (A4')) can be regarded as monotonicity properties. While (A3) reflects a kind of monotonic behavior of the input requirement set for a given output vector, (A4) considers output variations in a particular way and demands some type of monotonicity of the input requirement set. Finally, (A5) means that for any output vector u, the input requirement set contains its own boundaries. We write $\mathcal{A}$ for the collection of all upper level set mappings that satisfy (A1) - (A5). It may be noted that we can also model the technology by the output correspondence $O(b) = \{u \in R_+^n : b \text{ can produce } u\}$.

To define a technical efficiency measure rigorously, we consider the following :

$$U = \{u \in R_+^n \mid u \geq 01^n \text{ and } A(u) \text{ is nonempty}\}. \tag{3.1}$$

$$B = \{(u,b) \mid u \in U \text{ and } b \in A(u)\}. \tag{3.2}$$

$$d(u,b,A) = max\{\theta > 0 \mid \frac{b}{\theta} \in A(u)\}, \tag{3.3}$$

where $u \in U$ and $b \in A(u)$.

$$\begin{aligned} IsoA(u) &= \{b \in R_+^m \mid b \in A(u) \text{ and } \theta b \notin A(u), \text{ where } 0 \leq \theta < 1\} \quad (3.4) \\ &= \{b \in R_+^m \mid d(u,b) = 1\}, \text{ where } u \in U. \tag{3.5} \end{aligned}$$

$$\begin{aligned} EffA(u) &= \{b \in R_+^m \mid b \in A(u) \text{ and } \bar{b} \leq b \text{ implies } \bar{b} \notin A(u)\} \\ &= \{b \in R_+^m \mid d(u,b) = 1, d(u,\bar{b}) < 1 \text{ for all } \bar{b} \leq b\}, \text{ where} \\ & u \in U. \tag{3.6} \end{aligned}$$

The sets U and B are self explanatory. The function $d : UXD^mX\mathcal{A} \to D^1$ is the Malmquist (1951) - Shephard (1970) distance function which gives the maximum amount by which the input vector b can be scaled down such that it is still in the input requirement set $A(u)$. Given (A1) - (A5), $d(u,b,A(u))$ is well defined, continuous and positive. It is decreasing in u for every b, increasing in b for every u and concave in b for every u. Further, it satisfies a homogeneity property :

$$d(u, tb, A(u)) = td(u, b, A(u)) \tag{3.7}$$

for all $t \geq (d(u, b, A(u))^{-1}$. Clearly,

$$\theta_o = d(u, b, A(u)) \geq = 1 \Leftrightarrow \frac{b}{\theta_o} \in A(u). \tag{3.8}$$

Using $d(u, b, A(u))$ we can rewrite $A(u)$ as

$$A(u) = \{b \in R_+^m \mid d(u, b, A(u)) \geq 1\}. \tag{3.9}$$

The set $IsoA(u)$ defined in (3.4) is the input isoquant corresponding to the output vector u. That is, it is the set of all inputs vectors that can produce exactly u. $EffA(u)$ is the set of efficient input vectors (in the sense of Koopmans (1951)) that can produce the output vector u. $EffA(u)$ shows that an input vector is efficient for output vector u if there is no way to produce u with less inputs. Clearly, for any $u \in R_+^n$, $EffA(u) \subseteq IsoA(u)$. But the converse is not true. While any element of $EffA(u)$ is an efficient input vector for u, we will say that an input vector b is weakly efficient for u, if $b \in A(u)$ and $b > \bar{b}$ implies that $\bar{b} \notin A(u)$.

Sometimes for defining an efficiency index we will require the free disposal property (A3'). We therefore need to modify the input requirement set. The modified set is defined by

$$\overline{A}(u) = A(u) + R_+^m \tag{3.10}$$

where $u \in U$. $\overline{A}(u)$ is the free disposal hull of $A(u)$. For any $u \in U, \overline{A}(u)$ is simply the input requirement set $A(u)$ translated by the set R_+^m. If $A(u)$ satisfies (A1) - (A5), then $\overline{A}(u)$ also satisfies them. Furthermore, if $b \in \overline{A}(u)$ and $b' \geq b$, then $b' \in \overline{A}(u)$, which is the free disposability requirement (A3'). Now, define the extended Malmquist-Shephard distance as

$$d(u, b, \overline{A}) = max\{\theta > 0 \mid \frac{b}{\theta} \in \overline{A}(u)\}, \tag{3.11}$$

where $u \in U$. Given (A1) - (A5), the extended distance is well defined and satisfies the following monotonicity property :

$$d(u, b, \overline{A}) \geq d(u, b', \overline{A}), \tag{3.12}$$

where $u \in U$, b, $b' \in \overline{A}(u)$ and $b \geq b'$.

We can also define here the input isoquant and efficient subset for any output vector $u \in U$:

$$Iso\overline{A}(u) = \{b \in R_+^m \mid b \in \overline{A}(u) \text{ and } \theta b \notin \overline{A}(u) \text{ where } 0 \leq \theta < 1\}. \tag{3.13}$$

$$Eff\overline{A}(u) = \{b \in R^m_+ \mid b \in \overline{A}(u) \text{ and } \overline{b} \leq b \text{ implies that } \overline{b} \notin \overline{A}(u)\}. \quad (3.14)$$

Note that although $IsoA(u) \neq␣Iso\overline{A}(u)$, $EffA(u) = Eff\overline{A}(u)$.

Measuring technical efficiency of an input vector b producing output quantities u means answering the question : to what extent b is efficient for u? Therefore, a technical efficiency index E is a real valued function defined on the Cartesian product of the output domain, input domain and the technology set such that different output input combinations can be meaningfully compared using values of E. Rigorously, we have $E : U X D^m X \mathcal{A} \to (0,1] \cup \infty$ with the property that $E(u,b,A) \in (0,1]$ if and only if $b \in A(u)$.

Färe and Lovell (1978) suggested the following properties for an arbitrary technical efficiency index E :
Maximum Efficiency Principle (ME) : For all $u \in U$,

$$E(u,b,A) = 1 \quad (3.15)$$

if and only if $b \in Eff(u)$.
Homogeneity (HM) : For all $(u,b) \in B$ and for all $t \in [(d(u,b,A))^{-1}, \infty)$,

$$E(u,tb,A) = t^{-1}E(u,b,A). \quad (3.16)$$

Monotonicity (MO) : For all $u \in U$, $b \in A(u)$, if $b' \geq b$ and $b' \in A(u)$, then

$$E(u,b',A) < E(u,b,A). \quad (3.17)$$

The first property is concerned with efficient input vectors. It says that the efficiency measure achieves its maximum attainable value (assuming that for producing any arbitrary output vector we use inputs from the corresponding requirement set) if and only if the input vector is technically efficient in the sense of Koopmans. Property (3.16) is a homogeneity property and demands that a feasible scaling of an input vector should lead to an inverse scaling of the efficiency of that input vector. Finally, MO is a monotonicity condition. It means that increasing at least one input, while holding all others constant, will lower the value of the efficiency index. Thus, it requires efficiency to vary inversely with input usage. It should be evident that for any $u \in U$, a higher value of $E(u,b,A)$ will indicate a higher degree of efficiency.

We now study an implication of the properties ME, HM and MO. The following theorem shows that any technology satisfying (A1) - (A5) is incompatible with an efficiency measure E that meets these properties.

Theorem 3.1 (Bol, 1986) : For any technology satisfying (A1) - (A5) there does not exist an efficiency index that fulfills ME, HM and MO.

Proof : The proof consists of an example. Let $A(1) \subset R^3_+$ be defined by

$$A(1) = \{b \in R^3_+ \mid b_1 \geq 1, b_2 \geq 1, b_3 \geq e^{-(b_1-1)(b_2-1)}\}. \quad (3.18)$$

Note that A(1) is closed, convex and $01^3 \notin A(1)$. Further, $b \in A(1)$ and $b' \geq b$ implies that $b' \in A(1)$. Observe also that Eff A(1) is not closed.

The input correspondence $A : R_+^1 \to \mathcal{P}(R_+^3)$ defined by $A(u) = uA(1)$ for $u > 0$ and $A(0) = R_+^3$ fulfills (A1) - (A5). It also meets the free disposability principle $(A3')$.

For any $k > 0$, b^k defined by $(2, 1+k, e^{-k})$ is an element of Eff (1), but $b^0 = (2, 1, 1)$ is not contained in Eff (1). Observe that $b^0 \leq e^k \cdot b^k = (2e^k, (1+k)e^k, 1) \in A(1)$. For any efficiency measure E, by the condition HM, we have $E(1, e^k \cdot b^k, A(1)) = e^{-k} E(1, b^k, A(1))$. Now, since $b^k \in Eff(1)$, by ME $E(1, b^k, A(1)) = 1$. Hence $E(1, e^k b^k, A(1)) = e^{-k}$, which converges to 1 as $k \to 0$. On the other hand, $E(1, b^0, A(1)) < 1$ and, therefore, $E(1, b^0, A(1)) < E(1, e^k \cdot b^k, A(1))$ for sufficiently small k, in contradiction to monotonicity. This proves the theorem. □

In view of Bol's result it will be interesting to investigate whether by relaxing one or more properties of a technical efficiency measure we can make it well defined for all technologies. Russell (1985) suggested the following :
Weak Monotonicity (WM) : For all $u \in U, E(u, b', A(u)) \leq E(u, b, A(u))$ if $b' \geq b$, b, $b' \in A(u)$.
WM means that increasing at least one input while holding all other inputs constant, cannot increase efficiency measure.

Using Bol's argument (see also Russell (1988)) one can demonstrate
Theorem 3.2 : For any technology satisfying (A1) - (A5) there does not exist an efficiency measure that meets ME, HM and WM.

Theorem 3.2 shows that in order to retain properties HM and WM we must modify ME. Following Russell (1988) we therefore consider :
Weak Maximum Efficiency Principle (WE) : For all $u \in U$. $E(u, b, A(u)) = 1$ if and only if b is weakly efficient.

However, WE turns out to be incompatible with HM :
Theorem 3.3 (Russell, 1988) : For all technologies satisfying (A1) - (A5), there does not exist an efficiency index that will meet WE and HM.
Proof : Consider any level set A(u) with $b \in A(u)$ where $b > 01^m$. For any $\theta > 1$, $\theta b \in A(u)$ (property (A(3))). Since $A(u) \subseteq R_+^m$, b and θb are weakly efficient. Therefore, WE implies that $E(u, b, A(u)) = E(u, \theta b, A(u)) = 1$. But this violates HM.□

Russell (1988) pointed out that we can retain WM and HM if we further weaken the maximum efficiency principle to weak maximum efficiency principle on restricted domain:
(WE') : For all $b > 01^m$, $E(u, b, A(u)) = 1$ if and only if b is weakly efficient, where $u \in U$.

Another important property for efficiency measures is the commensurability principle (CM) considered by Russell (1988).
(CM) : If $\hat{u} = G_1 u$ and $\hat{b} = G_2 b$, where G_1 and G_2 are positive diagonal matrices of dimensions n and m respectively, then $E(\hat{u}, \hat{b}, \hat{A}) = E(u, b, A)$,

with $\hat{A}(\hat{u})$ being the requirement set $\{\hat{b} \in R_+^m \mid b \in A(u)\}$.

According to CM if units of measurement of different inputs are changed, which also generate changes in the output units, then the value of the efficiency index should not alter. In other words, the efficiency index is independent of the choice of units of measurement of inputs and outputs.

In the next part of this chapter it will be shown that HM, WM, WE' and CM are consistent in the sense that there exists an efficiency index that satisfies these assumptions for all technologies.

Indices of efficiency

We are now ready to discuss alternative indices of technical efficiency. We begin with the Debreu-Farrell index, which is defined by

$$E_{DF}(u,b,A) = (d(u,b,A))^{-1}, \; if\, b \in A(u) \qquad (3.19)$$
$$= \infty, \; if\, b \notin A(u), \qquad (3.20)$$

where $u \in U$ is arbitrary. E_{DF} gives the maximum amount by which an input vector b producing output u can be proportionately decreased such that u can still be produced. Let $t^0 = min\{t > 0 \mid tb \in A(u)\}$. Using t^0, we can express $E_{DF}(u,b,A)$ as

$$E_{DF}(u,b,A) = \frac{\| t^0 b \|}{\| b \|}, \qquad (3.21)$$

where $\| \;\; \|$ denotes the Euclidean distance. Thus, E_{DF} is the ratio of two distances computed along the same ray. Evidently, $\{b \mid d(u,b,A) = 1\} = EffA(u)$ if and only if $IsoA(u) = EffA(u)$, so that (u,b) is judged efficient by E_{DF} if and only if $b \in IsoA(u)$. In terms of t^0 defined above, we have $t^0 = 1$ if and only $E_{DF} = 1$. The input vector b is not efficient if $t^0 < 1$ and in this case E_{DF} falls below unity.

The Debreu-Farrell output-based measure is

$$E'_{DF}(u,b,A) = \frac{\| u \|}{\| u/t_0 \|}, \qquad (3.22)$$

where $t_0 = min\{t > 0 \mid b \in A(u/t)\}$. Therefore, the output-based measure E'_{DF} is the ratio between two distance measures computed along the same ray.

The two measures E_{DF} and E'_{DF} will coincide if and only if the technology is subject to constant returns to scale (see Färe and Lovell (1978)). In the literature discussion and applications of input-based measures are more common. In view of this we will concentrate only on input-based measures. Analogous discussions can be made for output-based measures also.

We may note that E_{DF} has many useful features which make it highly suitable for various empirical applications. For instance, it is non-parametric since it does not require the specification of a functional form of an explicit frontier production function. It develops an efficiency ranking of firms (or plants) solely from the observed data of inputs and outputs where no input and output price data exist. This is particularly useful for enterprises in the public sector, such as public schools and hospitals, where the concept of profit cannot be easily defined. It also allows the direct measurement of inefficiency (Hanoch and Rothschild (1972), Diewert and Parkan (1983), Färe , Grosskopf and Lovell (1985, 1993)) in terms of the gap between the two subsets of a given observed set of firms, one efficient and one inefficient.

It will also be interesting to note that E_{DF} has many attractive properties which provide support for resurrecting it form economic perspective. (We may add that both Debreu (1951) and Farrell (1957) emphasized the relationship between technical efficiency and economic efficiency.) The following discussion, which is based on Russell (1985), shows that even if market prices are not known, economic efficiency is not irrelevant to the analysis of technical efficiency.

A natural measure of economic efficiency F of a firm is the ratio of the minimal to actual input costs for a producing a given (but arbitrary) output vector u. That is,

$$F(u, w) = \frac{Q(u, w)}{(w.b)} \qquad (3.23)$$

where $w \in D_+^m$, the strictly positive part of D^m, is the input price vector and Q is the cost function defined by

$$Q(u, w) = \min_b \{w.b \mid b \in A(u)\}. \qquad (3.24)$$

The following duality relationship is well known (Shephard (1970)) :

$$Q(u, w) = \min_b \{w.b \mid d(u, b, A) \geq 1\}. \qquad (3.25)$$

$$d(u, b, A) = \min_w \{w.b \mid Q(u, w) \geq 1\}. \qquad (3.26)$$

The two functions are related by

$$Q(u, w)d(u, b, A) \leq w.b \qquad (3.27)$$

for all (u, b, w). We rewrite (3.27) as

$$\frac{Q(u, w)}{w.b} \leq \frac{1}{d(u, b, A)}. \qquad (3.28)$$

That is, for all (u, b, w)

$$F(u, w) \leq E_{DF}(u, b, A). \qquad (3.29)$$

Thus, the Debreu-Farrell measure of technical efficiency is an upper bound on the measure of economic efficiency.

The inequality (3.29) is related to the decomposition of economic efficiency into allocative and technical efficiencies (Kopp and Diewert (1982) and Zieschang (1983)) :

$$\frac{Q(u,w)}{w.b} = (\frac{Q(u,w)}{w.b}.d(u,b,A))\frac{1}{d(u,b,A)} \qquad (3.30)$$
$$= a(u,b,A).E_{DF}(u,b,A), \qquad (3.31)$$

where $a(u,b,A)$ is the allocative efficiency. Decomposition formula in (3.31) shows that in minimizing cost the production organizations must employ their inputs in most efficient manner (technical efficiency) and choose a combination of inputs that fulfill the cost minimizing conditions (allocative efficiency). Allocative inefficiencies arise whenever cost minimizing conditions do not hold. Thus, if a firm is allocatively inefficient, it does not operate on its least cost expansion path.

We will now provide a graphical illustration of the decomposition formula in (3.31). In Figure 3.1, the point v represents the inputs of the two factors that the firm mploys for producing the output level u^o. The isoquant kk' represents the various combinations of the two factors that a perfectly efficient firm might use to produce u^o. Now the point v^1 represents an efficient firm using the factors in the same ratio as v. It produces the same output level u^o as v using only a fraction Ov^1/Ov as much of each factor. Thus, the Debreu-Farrell measure of the firm corresponding to v is given by Ov^1/Ov.

Let us now look at the extent to which a firm uses the various factors of production in appropriate proportions, from the view point of their prices. The line ll' is the isocost line, the locus of all combinations of two factors that a firm can purchase for a given cost outlay, given the prices of the factors. It slope is equal to the ratio of the factor prices. Consequently, v^2 not v^1, is the cost minimizing point of production, since although both points represent 100 per cent technical efficiency, the cost of production at v^2 is only a fraction Ov^3/Ov^1 of that at v^1. This ratio is the allocative efficiency of the firm represented by v.

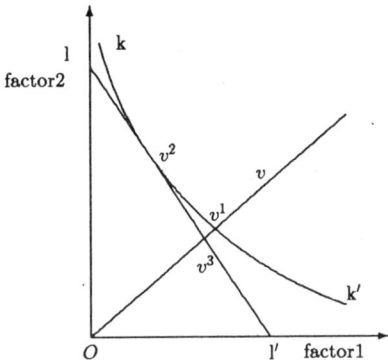

Figure 3.1 Allocative and technical efficiencies

We thus see that the difference between v and v^1 can be viewed as due to technical inefficiency while that between v^1 and v^2 is due to allocative inefficiency. The product of these two gives us global (in) efficiency. Note that if the firm is perfectly allocatively efficient, then the points v^1, v^2 and v^3 will coincide and global efficiency is determined by the Debreu-Farrell measure only.

The index E_{DF} can be provided an evocative economic interpretation even when market prices do not exist. The distance function $d(u, b, A)$ can alternatively be defined (derived) as the minimum ascribed value of a given input vector, subject to the constraint that the chosen shadow price vector will belong to the lower indirect level set $A^1(u)$, the set of prices at which affordable input prices can produce no more than the output vector u :

$$d(u, b, A) = \min_{w}\{w.b \mid w \in A^1(u)\} \qquad (3.32)$$
$$= k(u, b).b, \qquad (3.33)$$

where $k(u, b)$ is the shadow price vector. The shadow price vector used to evaluate the input vector b is given by the normal of the hyperplane that supports $A(u)$ at $b/d(u, b.A)$. That is,

$$\sum_{i=1}^{m} k_i(b_i - b_i/d(u, b, A)) = 0, \qquad (3.34)$$

where k_i is the ith component of $k(u, b)$. We therefore, have

$$E_{DF}(u, b, A) = (d(u, b, A))^{-1} \qquad (3.35)$$
$$= \frac{k(u, b).b/d(u, b, A)}{k(u, b).b} \qquad (3.36)$$
$$= \frac{Q(u, k(u, b))}{k(u, b).b}. \qquad (3.37)$$

From (3.37) we see that the Debreu-Farrell index can be written as the ratio of minimal to actual expenditures of inputs at shadow price vector $k(u,b)$.

The Debreu-Farrell measure does not meet WE' though it is weakly monotone and homogeneous. However, in view of our next theorem the extended Debreu-Farrell index $\bar{E}_{DF}$, considered by Färe and Grosskopf (1983), Färe, Lovell and Grosskopf (1985, 1993) and Russell (1988), is a more satisfactory measure, where

$$\bar{E}_{DF}(u,b,A) = (d(u,b,\bar{A}))^{-1} \; if \; b \in A(u) \qquad (3.38)$$
$$= \infty \; if \; b \notin A(u). \qquad (3.39)$$

Theorem 3.4 (Russell, 1988) : The extended Debreu-Farrell technical efficiency measure $\bar{E}_{DF}$ satisfies WE', HM, WM, and CM for all technologies that fulfill (A1) - (A5).

Proof : To show that $\bar{E}_{DF}$ satisfies WE' suppose that $b^1 > 01^m$ is weakly efficient but $E_{DF}(u,b^1,A) < 1$. Then $b^1 \in A(u)$ and $\theta b^1 \in \bar{A}(u)$ for some $\theta < 1$. Thus, there exists an input vector $b^2 \in A(u)$ such that $b^2 \leq \theta b^1 < b^1$ contradicting the supposition that b^1 is weakly efficient. Hence $E_{DF}(u,b^1,A) = 1$.

Next, suppose that b^1 is not weakly efficient. Then there exists an input vector $b^2 \in A(u)$ such that $b^2 < b^1$. Let $\epsilon = \min\{b_i^1 - b_i^2 \mid i = 1,2,...m\}$ and $\theta = (\parallel b^1 \parallel -\epsilon)/\parallel b^1 \parallel$. Then $\theta b^1 \geq b^2$. Hence $\theta b^1 \in \bar{A}(u)$. However, as $\theta < 1$, $\bar{E}_{DF}(u,b^1,A) = (d(u,b^1,\bar{A}))^{-1} < 1$. Hence $\bar{E}_{DF}$ satisfies WE'.

Homogeneity property of $\bar{E}_{DF}$ follows from (3.7). It is easy to verify that it follows WM.

Now, to show that $\bar{E}_{DF}$ satisfies CM, we need to show that

$$d(G_1 u, G_2 b, \hat{\bar{A}}) = d(u, b, \bar{A}). \qquad (3.40)$$

To see that this is so, note that

$$b \in \bar{A}(u) \;\Leftrightarrow\; \exists \hat{b} \in R_+^m \mid b - \hat{b} \in A(u)$$
$$\Leftrightarrow\; \exists \hat{b} \in R_+^m \mid G_2 b - G_2 \hat{b} \in \hat{A}(G_1 u)$$
$$\Leftrightarrow\; G_2 b \in \hat{A}(G_1 u) + R_+^m = \hat{\bar{A}}(G_1 u),$$

where the last equivalence makes use of positiveness of G_2. Consequently,

$$d(G_1 u, G_2 b, \hat{\bar{A}}) = \max\{\alpha > 0 \mid (G_2 b/\alpha) \in \hat{\bar{A}}(G_1 u)\}$$
$$= \max\{\alpha > 0 \mid b/\alpha \in \bar{A}(u)\}$$
$$= d(u,b,\bar{A}),$$

which is what we wanted to show. □

Färe and Lovell (1978) pointed out that there are some difficulties with the measure E_{DF}. First, which we have already noted, it is open to two interpretations. Consequently, it can interpret technical efficiency in two different for merger is also presented in the chapter. Finally, we make some concluding remarks.

Merger activity: reasons and some historical evidences

Mergers generate revacillation of property interests among the existing firms. A merger may offer various advantages to the merged entity. Before we analyze the reasons for mergers, let us briefly discuss some historical evidences.

The available data from various sources on the number of mergers for the U.S.A. reveal that four great merger waves have shaped the landscape of American industry (see Martin (1988) and Carlton and Perloff (1990)). The first two of them involved mainly horizontal mergers. The first wave started in 1883 and ended in 1904. A typical consequence of merger during this period was the emergence of a dominant firm in the industry. Creation of U.S. Steel by combining 180 independent firms is an example. (The end of this phase of merger came after the supreme court found that some horizontal mergers violated the antitrust law of the Sherman Act. The second merger wave began after the first world war and ended in 1929. By this time the antitrust laws changed. Mergers were not combinations of a large number of firms, now fewer firms combined and often formed the second/third largest firm in the industry. Precisely because of these natures of the two merger waves discussed above, Stigler (1950) called them merger to monopoly movement and merger to oligopoly movement respectively. The third wave took place during the later 1960s and early 1970s and it consisted mainly of conglomerate mergers. Finally, mid 1980s have witnessed the fourth wave of mergers for which there is no common name. Though the merger activity during 1980s has been great, its levels are not unprecedented. In the case of the U.K., 1960s witnessed the most substantial wave of merger activity since 1920s (see Hannah and Kay (1977, 1981) and Curry and George (1983)).

Mergers and acquisitions were not very uncommon in India as elsewhere in the world. In line with the changes in policy of the Union Government several mergers and acquisitions had taken place. But it was in a low key, mainly because of several restrictions like Monopolies and Restrictive Trade Practices (MRTP) Act 1969. In fact, merger used to be regarded mainly as an instrument of revival of sick units and obtaining tax benefits rather than as a vehicle for achieving corporate growth and expansion. However, with the current liberalization process of the Indian economy the scenario is changing quite fast. Since the announcement of the budget for 1993-94 on 28 February 1993, at least 34 mergers and 21 acquisitions have been announced, of which, by 15 July 1993, 8 mergers and 7 acquisitions have been completed (The Economic Times, Calcutta, 15 July 1993). The urge for vertical and horizontal expansion and technology upgradation with an eye on global market to meet competition at international levels are some of the main purposes of the recent merger proposals. The most important merger in the country's cor-

4 Merger, efficiency and concentration

The concept of merger has been internationally prevalent since the turn of the 20th Century. Merger or amalgamation results into a combination of two or more firms into one wherein the merging entities lose their identities by being absorbed in the merged entity. Ways that are similar to merger for creating new firms include the acquisition of one firm by another or the sale of a part of a firm. Mergers and acquisitions have played a dominant role in the growth of many leading corporations in the world.

Baumol, Panzar and Willig (1982) applied the notion of 'economies of scope' to investigate whether combining two or more multiproduct firms in an industry can lead to an increase in efficiency. Färe (1986) considered a Debreu (1951) - Farrell (1957) type measure to calculate the efficiency gain (loss) realized from a merger of two or more multiproduct firms. He also provided a cost interpretation of this gain function. It has been observed that in a homogeneous good case the Färe gain function, when interpreted in terms of costs, can be regarded as a concentration index (Chakravarty (1992)).

We discuss the Färe measure of efficiency of merger of multiproduct firms in this chapter. An interpretation of this measure as a concentration index is explored here. A dominance relation that implies and is implied by the Färe gain function is also developed. Next, a specific functional form of the gain index is derived under the assumption that the factor markets are perfectly competitive. In a limiting case it coincides with the entropy-based concentration formula.

Farrell and Shapiro (1990) provided an explicit analysis of how a merger between firms in the same industry will affect equilibrium output and welfare. They found general conditions under which mergers raise price and developed a procedure for analyzing the effect of merger on rivals and consumers and thus provided sufficient conditions for profitable mergers to raise welfare. It is shown that cost saving resulting from merger plays a large role in (merger) policy calculations without demanding much information. We consider these issues in this chapter. A brief discussion on historical evidence and reasons porate history is the recent merger of Reliance Petrochemicals with Reliance Industry, one of the largest producers of synthetic fibre textiles in India. This merger was aimed to increase the shareholders' values by realizing significant 'synergies' of both the companies. Another important merger was that of Renusagar Power Supply and Hindustan Aluminum Company. The merged entity expects to participate more vigorously in competitive market, consolidate the position of the company and diversify into capital intensive projects. Similarly Tata Tea acquired a leading position in plantation sector after it has taken over the Consolidated Coffee which has got the largest coffee growing activity in Asia. In addition to coffee and tea, these companies produce other agro products including spices, mushrooms, cardamom etc. With the economy moving towards globalization, mergers and acquisitions are expected to take place on a much larger scale than in the past.

Firms may expand horizontally, vertically or into unrelated markets. There are several reasons why it may be beneficial economically for two or more firms to consolidate into one. We briefly discuss some of them.

1 The merged entity derives benefits of combined services, manufacturing assets, man power and cash flow. The combined technology and managerial reserves of the merged firm may enhance the capability of the firm to implement more sophisticated projects to ensure rapid growth and enable it to compete globally. There will be reduction in advertising and other promotional expenditures because of merger. Mergers may provide a stronger distribution network.

2 There may be cost saving efficiency due to merger. It may be cheaper to produce different output levels together rather than producing them separately. A firm that controls many firms may be able to close the less efficient ones.

3 Merger may give rise to synergies. For instance, if two firms own complementary patents then they may combine and be able to produce more efficiently than either could alone.

4 The search for market power may motivate mergers. If a sufficient number of firms in a homogeneous good industry merge, then the merged firm would face less competition and possess additional market power. This additional market power might lead to smaller output (higher prices for consumers). Analogously, a supplier of an input may create market power in the following way. It may buy or vertically merge with the manufacturing firms which use the input and monopolize the final output market.

5 Merger can be used for achieving diversification of activities in order to avoid risks. If firms in industries which are subject to oscillatory

variations diversify into unrelated markets, they may be able to even out their instability in the income stream.

6. Mergers may also pave the way for better and more efficient running of the firm through its ability to attract superior managerial talents. Some managers wish to control large firms since they can enjoy more power.

7. The ability of the merged firm to absorb new technology and spend on Research and Development may increase.

8. The transaction cost of buying from or selling to other firms may be avoided through vertical integration.

9. Steady supply of an essential input may motivate vertical integration. This will eliminate uncertainty regarding delivery of the input.

10. Firms may vertically integrate to increase rivals' input costs. A vertically integrated firm possessing market power on an essential input may exercise the power over rivals which are nonintegrated and in turn can place them at a cost disadvantage.

11. Merger may offer incidental benefits like reduction in tax liabilities. This will certainty be the case when the sum of taxes on individual profits will be greater than the tax on merged entity's profit.

12. Apart from growing big, the fear of increasing competition from the rivals may force firms to seek merger. For instance, recently in India the tie ups between Godrej Soaps and Procter and Gamble, another important detergent producing corporation, forced Tata Oil Mill Company to merge with Hindustan Lever, whose giantness as a detergent producer is well known in the country. This will enable Hindustan Lever to make products in bigger plants and to use the retail outlets of Tata Oil Mill as a readymade resource[1].

Measuring efficiency of merger

Our purpose here is to discuss the Debreu-Farrell measure considered by Färe (1986) to gauge efficiency gains from the merger of two or more multiproduct firms.

Let $u = (u_1, u_2, ..., u_m) \epsilon D^m$ be a typical vector of outputs of a multiproduct firm. We write $w \epsilon D_+^k$ for the vector of input prices faced by the firm. Thus, the firm produces m different goods and uses k different inputs, where both m and k are arbitrary. The cost function of the firm is denoted by $Q(w, u)$. Suppose $u^1, u^2, ..., u^n$ are n multiproduct output vectors. Then the cost function Q is strictly subadditive if for all u^i

$$Q(w, \sum_{i=1}^{n} u^i) < \sum_{i=1}^{n} Q(w, u^i). \qquad (4.1)$$

Subadditivity means that it is cheaper to produce the various outputs together than to produce them separately.

Inequality (4.1) gives one formulation of economies of scope. For example, let u_1, u_2 stand for quantities of goods 1 and 2 respectively. Then for a strictly subadditive cost function

$$Q(w, u_1, 0) + Q(w, 0, u_2) > Q(w, u_1, u_2), \qquad (4.2)$$

which demonstrates the existence of economies of scope. These production economies achieved through making different products are distinct from economies of scale[2], though may can interact with them. For instance, if a multiproduct firm produces substitutes, an exploitation of scale economies in one product may decrease the demand for other goods and reduce the potential saving generated from economies of scope (see Waterson (1983)). In the multiproduct case the simultaneous presence of economies of scale and economies of scope is not sufficient for subadditivity (see Baumol et al. (1982), Jacquemin (1987)).

In a single good situation, 'everywhere decreasing marginal costs imply everywhere decreasing average costs and everywhere decreasing average costs imply subadditivity' (Tirole (1988, p. 19)). In this particular situation, subadditivity also follows from economies of scale, a weaker requirement than declining marginal cost (Jacquemin (1987, p. 20)). Sharkey (1982) pointed out that the existence of economies of scale is a sufficient but not a necessary condition for subadditivity.

If there is a commonly available technology Q(w,u) that produces u at factor prices w, then according to Baumol et al. (1982) an industry is a natural monopoly if over the relevant range of output Q is strictly subadditive. That is, a natural monopoly exists if there is no incentive to have more than one firm for producing the output when the aggregate output could be produced at less cost by a single firm.

From duality theory, strict subadditivity of a cost function for all factor prices w is equivalent to superadditivity of the corresponding input requirement set A(.) (Diewert (1982)). The set A(.) is superadditive if for all $u^1, u^2, ..., u^n$,

$$\sum_{i=1}^{n} A(u^i) \subset A(\sum_{i=1}^{n} u^i). \qquad (4.3)$$

Therefore estimation of efficiency gains from combining two or more multi-product firms with the common cost function Q can be done by comparing the frontiers of the sets $\sum_{i=1}^{n} A(u^i)$ and $A(\sum_{i=1}^{n} u^i)$.

For expositional ease, following Färe (1986), we consider a diagrammatic presentation in which the input quantities are denoted by b_i, i=1,2. Now, by superadditivity $\sum_{i=1}^{n} A(u^i)$ will be in the interior of $A(\sum_{i=1}^{n} u^i)$.

Let b^o be an input vector belong to the sum $\sum_{i=1}^{n} A(u^i)$. Evidently, $b^o \epsilon A(\sum_{i=1}^{n} u^i)$. The radial contraction of b^o along the ray through itself and the origin intersects the boundaries of $A(\sum_{i=1}^{n} u^i)$ and $\sum_{i=1}^{n} A(u^i)$ at t^1 and t^2 respectively. The ratio Ot^1/Oa is the Debreu-Farrell measure of efficiency of b^o relative to the reference technology $A(\sum_{i=1}^{n} u^i)$. Similarly, Ot^2/Oa determines the efficiency of b^o relative to the reference technology $\sum_{i=1}^{n} A(u^i)$. The quotient between these two measures which is given by Ot^1/Ot^2 yields the efficiency gain from combining the producers of $u^1, u^2, ..., u^n$.

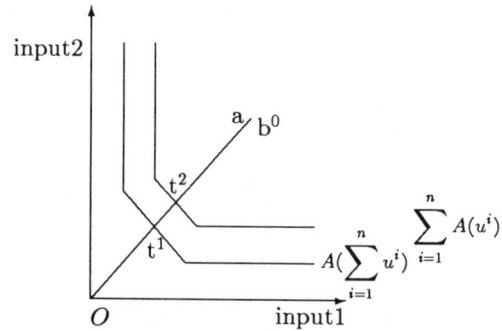

Figure 4.1 **Efficiency of merger**

Using arguments similar to that employed in the context of the decomposition formula in (3.31) we can demonstrate that if the input prices corresponding the input vectors at t^1 and t^2 are cost minimizing, then the above efficiency gain function considered by Färe turns out to be

$$G(u^1, u^2, ..., u^n, w) = \frac{Q(w, \sum_{i=1}^{n} u^i)}{\sum_{i=1}^{n} Q(w, u^i)}. \tag{4.4}$$

Therefore, under the stated conditions, strict subadditivity of the cost function will occur when the value of the measure of efficiency of merger in (4.4) is less than unity.

Efficiency of merger and concentration

In this part we relate the Färe (1986) measure of efficiency of merger G given by (4.4) to concentration.

It is assumed that all the n firms in the industry produce only one good. We denote the output level of firm i by $x_i \geq 0$. The $G(x, w) = Q(w, \sum_{i=1}^{n}$

$x_i)/\sum_{i=1}^{n} Q(w,x_i)$, where $x = (x_1, x_2, ..., x_n)$. Now, the change in G due to a transfer of output from a small firm to a large firm will depend on the difference between the marginal costs of the firms concerned. Consequently, the denominator of G will decrease if Q is strictly concave in output levels. The numerator of G remains unaltered under the transfer considered. Thus, given strict concavity of $Q(w, x_i)$ in x_i, efficiency of merger will increase as a result of the aforementioned transfer. But we know that with a transfer of output from a small firm to a large firm output concentration increases. Hence the measure G and concentration move in the same direction under output transfers. An analogous argument will establish that G reduces under replications.

Next, if the industry output is produced by a single producer the efficiency will be of a maximum and the gain function G achieves its upper bound 1. But this is also the case of complete concentration and a concentration measure takes on its highest value in this extreme situation. This establishes a coherence between the upper bounds of the two indices. A similar coherence occurs for the lower bound also. Clearly, G will be continuous if Q is continuous. We note that addition (deletion) of a firm with zero output to (from) the industry does not alter G if $Q(w, 0) = 0$. Finally, G remains invariant under any permutation of output levels. The above discussion enables us to state the following:

Theorem 4.1: Suppose that the singleoutput cost function Q is continuous, strictly concave in output levels and $Q(w, 0) = 0$. Then (in the single output case) the Färe measure of efficiency of merger G given by (4.4) can be regarded as a concentration index in the sense that it agrees with continuity, zero output independence, symmetry and the output transfers principle properties of a concentration formula.

To develop a ranking relation consistent with the ordering generated by the gain index G, let us consider any two output distributions x and y of a fixed total over two industries with n_1 and n_2 firms respectively, where n_1 and n_2 are arbitrary. In view of corollary 1.4, we know that the concentration curve of x dominates that of y if and only if x is regarded as more concentrated than y by all concentration indices that satisfy zero output independence, symmetry and the output transfers principle. Combining this result with theorem 4.1 we have

Theorem 4.2: For any arbitrary positive integers n_1 and n_2, let $x \epsilon\ D^{n_1}$ and $y\epsilon\ D^{n_2}$, where $\sum_{i=1}^{n_1} x_i = \sum_{i=1}^{n_2} y_i$, be also arbitrary. Then the following statements are equivalent:

(a) Concentration curve of x dominates that of y.
(b) $G(x, w) > G(y, w)$ for all cost functions Q that are strictly concave in output levels and Q(w,0) = 0.

Theorem 4.2 says that with a given total output an unambiguous ranking of any two output distributions by the Färe measure of efficiency of merger can be obtained through the pairwise comparison of the concentration curves of the distributions. The number of firms in the industries concerned need not be the same for this result to hold.

Next, we will derive a specific functional form of the concentration index. For this suppose that factor markets are perfectly competitive. The factor prices can now be taken as given. We therefore rewrite the gain function $G(x,w)$ as $G_1(x)$. Let us then consider $H(x_1, x_2, ..., x_n) = (G_1(x_1, x_2, ..., x_n))^\theta$, a normalized form of G_1, as a concentration index. The coefficient of normalization θ is assumed to be positive.

If we assume that $Q(w, x_i) = Kx_i^r$, where $0 < r < 1$ and $K > 0$ are constants, then all the conditions stated in theorem 4.1 about the cost function are satisfied. The constant K can be regarded as a function of input prices. Under this specification of Q, H turns out to be

$$H(x_1, x_2, ..., x_n) = (\sum_{i=1}^n s_i^r)^{\frac{1}{(r-1)}}, \ 0 < r < 1, \tag{4.5}$$

where s_i is the output share of firm i. The index in (4.5) is a subclass of the Hannah-Kay family of concentration indices. As $r \to 1$, $H \to \pi_{i=1}^n s_i^{s_i}$, which is one variant of the entropy concentration formula.

Note that theorem 4.1 also holds for a cost function of type $Q(w, x_i) = K_1(1 - e^{-x_i})$, where $K_1 > 0$ is a function of input prices. However, with this specification of Q, the form of H derived does not satisfy zero degree homogeneity in output levels. Strictly speaking, the function $Q(w, x_i) = Kx_i^r$ is the only cost function for which the index H satisfies the zero degree homogeneity condition (Chakravarty (1992)).

Price effects of horizontal mergers

In this part, following Farrell and Shapiro (1990), we examine the effect of a merger between firms in the same industry on aggregate output (and hence on price). This becomes the central question of merger analysis if we are concerned with consumer welfare only. It will be shown in the next section that this constitutes an important component of an analysis of aggregate welfare also.

We consider a homogeneous good industry consisting of n firms which are assumed to be Cournot maximizers. This assumption will be maintained throughout this part and the next part of the chapter. The number of firms n is given exogenously reflecting some important barriers to entry. (See Chapter 5 for a discussion on entry barriers.) The ith firm's output is x_i. Let $y_i = (X - x_i)$ stand for the aggregate output of all firms other than firm i, i=1,2, 3, ..., n. It will be assumed for the rest of the chapter that $x_i's$ are positive for all i, that is, all the firms are assumed to be active.

The cost function of firm i is $Q_i(w, x_i)$, where $w \in D_+^k$ is the vector of input prices which are assumed to be constant. We therefore rewrite $Q_i(w, x_i)$ as

$C_i(x_i)$. The inverse demand function showing market price p as a function of total output X is p = f(X). We may recall that firm i's first order condition for profit maximization is

$$f(X) + x_i f'(X) - C_i'(x_i) = 0, i = 1, ..., n. \quad (4.6)$$

As stated earlier, a Cournot equilibrium is a vector $(x_1, x_2, ..., x_n)$ such that (4.6) holds for all n firms. From Cournot equilibrium condition (4.6) we deduce that larger firms have lower marginal costs. That is, $x_i > x_j$ implies that $C_i'(x_i) < C_j'(x_j)$. Furthermore, the converse is also true.

We will now make two weak assumptions about the Cournot equilibrium. These assumptions will be required for the results to be presented in the remainder of the chapter. First, each firm's reaction curve is assumed to be downward sloping. Equivalently, for each firm i, an increase in rivals' aggregate output y_i decreases its revenue:

$$f'(X) + x_i f''(X) < 0, i = 1, 2, ..., n. \quad (4.7)$$

Inequality (4.7) is quite weak and is standard in Cournot analysis (see Dixit (1986) and Shapiro (1989)). This condition is satisfied if $f'(X) + X f''(X) < 0$. Novshek (1985) has shown that the condition $X f''(X) + f'(X) < 0$ is sufficient to gurantee the existence of a Cournot equilibrium. It is in fact somewhat weaker than $2f'(X) + x_i f''(X) - C_i''(x_i) < 0$, the usual second order conditions for Cournot maximization.

Next, for each firm i its residual demand curve is assumed to intersect its marginal cost curve from above. Equivalently,

$$C_i''(x_i) > f'(X), i = 1, ..., n. \quad (4.8)$$

Inequality (4.8) is satisfied if $C_i''(x_i) \geq 0$. This requirement is one of the weak stability conditions for Cournot maximization (Dixit (1986)). (Stability requires that a movement from the equilibirum position by any subgroup will not increase its profits.)

Let us now consider some comparative statics properties of Cournot equilibrium that will be important for our analysis. From (4.6) we note that the effect of a change in y_i on x_i is

$$\frac{dx_i}{dy_i} = r_i = -\frac{f'(X) + x_i f''(X)}{2f'(X) + x_i f''(X) - C_i''(x_i)}. \quad (4.9)$$

This is the slope of firm i's reaction function. In view of inequality (4.7) and the second order condition for firm i's profit maximization, $r_i \leq 0$. Condition (4.8) ensures that $-1 < r_i < 0$. This means that if the rivals of firm i increase their production, then it will contract, but by less than the expansion of the rivals. Since $dx_i = r_i dy_i$, we have $dx_i(1 + r_i) = r_i(dx_i + dy_i) = r_i dX$, which gives

$$dx_i = -\theta_i dX, \quad (4.10)$$

where $\theta_i = -r_i/(1+r_i)$

Using (4.7) and (4.8) we demonstrate that $\theta_i > 0$. It will in fact be easier to work with θ_i instead of r_i. Letting $\alpha(=-Xf''(X)/f'(X))$ be the negative of the elasticity of the inverse demand curve's slope, and $\mu_i(=x_i C_i''(x_i)/C_i'(x_i))$ be the elasticity of firm i's marginal cost curve with respect to its own output x_i, we have

$$\theta_i = \frac{s_i - s_i^2 \alpha}{s_i + \mu_i(\epsilon - s_i)}, \quad (4.11)$$

where $s_i = x_i/X$ is firm i's output share and $\epsilon(=-f(X)/Xf'(X))$ is the absolute value of the elasticity of demand. If ϵ is a constant, α equals $(1+1/\epsilon)$, so that θ_i becomes a function of s_i, ϵ and μ_i only. In case $C_i'(x_i)$ is a constant and the demand function is linear, $\alpha = \mu_i = 0$, which in turn implies that $\theta_i = 1$.

Now consider an exogenous change dx_1 in firm 1's output. For any firm $i \neq 1$, $dx_i = -\theta_i dX$ which implies that $dy_1 = -\sum_{i \neq 1} \theta_i dX$. Therefore, $dX = -\sum_{i \neq 1} \theta_i dX + dx_1$ from which we have $dX(1 + \sum_{i \neq 1} \theta_i) = dx_1$. With conditions (4.7) and (4.8), $\theta_i > 0$ for all i. Hence dX has the same sign as dx_1, but is smaller numerically. This establishes

Lemma 4.3 (Farrell and Shapiro, 1990):Consider an exogenous change in firm 1's output, and let the other firms' outputs adjust to reestablish a Cournot equilibrium among themselves. If firms' reaction curves slope downward (condition (4.7)), and if the stability condition (4.8) holds, then aggregate output moves in the same direction as firm's 1 output, but by less.

Note that for lemma 4.3 to hold we do not require that firm 1 should follow Cournot behavior.

Now, due to merger there will be a combination of the assets and of the control of the merging firms, whom we refer to as insiders. We denote the set of insiders by IN. Once the merger has taken place, a new Cournot equilibrium will be established between the merged entity M and the nonparticipant firms, whom we call outsiders. Merger may differ substantially depending on the extent to which productive assets can be combined and the extent to which output decisions can be coordinated usefully or anticompetitively. We have already noted that merger may increase productive efficiency and may create synergies. Consider a polar case in which all firms have constant and identical marginal costs and the merged entity has the same costs. In such a situation merger will be purely anticompetitive. A theory of merger will be helpful for policy purpose if it can incorporate all these possibilities which can be captured under alternative assumptions about the relationship between the merged entity's cost function C_M and those of the insiders.

The following theorem gives us a necessary and sufficient condition for equilibrium output to decrease under merger.

Theorem 4.4 (Farrell and Shapiro, 1990):A merger of a group of firms in Cournot oligopoly raises price if and only if the merging firms' price cost margin would be less than the sum of the pre-merger price cost margins of the constituent firms, where the merged entity produces as much as its constituent firms did together before the merger.

Proof: In view of lemma 4.3 we need to look only at the sign of the effect on the insiders' total output. For doing that it is necessary to determine whether the new firm M would increase or decrease its output if the outsiders do not change their outputs from pre-merger levels.

We write $\hat{x} = (\hat{x}_1, \hat{x}_2, ..., \hat{x}_n)$ for pre-merger output vector of the industry. Denote the sum $\sum_{i=1}^{n} \hat{x}_i$ by $\hat{X}$ and the insiders' aggregate pre-merger output by $\hat{X}_M$. At pre-merger output levels, M's marginal revenue is $f(\hat{X}) + \hat{X}_M f'(\hat{X})$. Thus, M will reduce its output if and only if $C'_M(\hat{X}_M) > f(\hat{X}) + \hat{X}_M f'(\hat{X})$, or $f(\hat{X}) - C'_M(\hat{X}_M) < -\hat{X}_M f'(\hat{X})$. The proof will be complete if we show that $-\hat{X}_M f'(\hat{X})$ equals the sum of merging firms' pre-merger price cost margins. Now, for any insider i, $C'_i(\hat{x}_i) = f(\hat{X}) + \hat{x}_i f'(\hat{X})$, which implies that $f(\hat{X}) - C'_i(\hat{x}_i) = -\hat{x}_i f'(\hat{X})$. If we sum this up over $i \in IN$, then

$$\sum_{i \in IN} [f(\hat{x}) - C'_i(\hat{X}_i)] = -\hat{X}_M f'(\hat{X}), \qquad (4.12)$$

as required. □

In the particular case when only two firms, say 1 and 2, are insiders, price will fall if and only if $(p - C'_M) > (p - C'_1 + p - C'_2)$, where p is the pre-merger price, C'_1, C'_2 are measured at pre-merger output levels $\hat{x}_1$ and $\hat{x}_2$, respectively and C'_M is measured at output $\hat{M} = \hat{x}_1 + \hat{x}_2$. That is, price will fall if and only if

$$C'_2 - C'_M > p - C'_1. \qquad (4.13)$$

Inequality (4.13) shows that for price to decrease M must have lower marginal cost than its constituent firms.

Using equation (4.6) we can rewrite (4.13) in terms of some pre-merger variables which may be easy to observe:

$$C'_M < p(1 - \frac{s_1 + s_2}{\epsilon}). \qquad (4.14)$$

From inequality (4.14) we see how much less than the current price the marginal cost of the merging entity must be for price to decrease.

Some illustrative calculations will now be presented to draw out some implications of (4.14) and theorem 4.4. In some cases the assets of the merging firms cannot be combined for improving their joint production capabilities. In such a case the merged entity M can probably allocate output across facilities, but its production possibilities will not be different from those of the constituent firms as a whole before the merger. In this case merger generates no synergies. Formally,

$$C'_M(\theta) = \min\{\sum_{i \in IN} C'_i(x_i) \mid \sum_{i \in IN} x_i = \theta\}. \qquad (4.15)$$

(Salant, Switzer and Reynolds (1983) show that this holds in a model considered by them with constant average cost. See also Perry and Porter (1985).)

The following theorem, which is stated without proof, shows that any merger not creating synergies will increase price

Theorem 4.5 (Farrell and Shapiro, 1990):If a merger generates no synergies, then it causes price to rise.

To illustrate the no synergy condition considered in (4.15), suppose that $C_i(x_i) = a_i\phi(x_i, k_i)$, where ϕ is a short run variable cost function, k_i gives the amount of capital good employed by firm i and a_i is an inverse measure of 'knowledge' at firm i. With this specification of the cost function, three types of cost savings can be distinguished under a merger:(a) Rationalizing output across facilities, that is, changing $x_i's$ but not $k_i's$ and $a_i's$, (b) changing the distribution of $k_i's$ without affecting total capital stock, (c) learning from each other, that is, changing $a_i's$. Farrell and Shapiro (1990) formally establishes the following intuitively reasonable result. 'A merger can raise output and make consumers better off only if it permits the merging firms to exploit economies of scale or if the participants learn from it' (op cit., p. 113).

Since the factors that determine a merger's effect on price have been identified, we can make use of inequality (4.14) to explain the influence of some key variables on these factors. For instance, we note that the larger are the output shares of the merging firms or the smaller is the elasticity of demand, the greater should be learning effect or scale economies for price reduction to materialize.

If we adopt the view that the objective of an antitrust policy should be maximization of consumers' surplus, then a merger should be blocked if and only if it raises price. The above discussion becomes helpful in making such an assessment. But conventionally, the proper goal of an antitrust policy is to maximize aggregate efficiency or welfare. This requires further analysis which, following Farrell and Shapiro (1990), we present below.

Welfare effects of horizontal mergers

Before we present the effects of a merger on aggregate welfare, we make a brief discussion on concentration-based traditional merger analysis.

We begin by mentioning that in the U.S. it is the policy of the antitrust laws, as embodied in Section 7 of the Clayton Act 1914, to prohibit mergers that decrease competition substantially. Mergers that do not increase concentration substantially or leave it low after the merger are permitted. (Mention may also be made of the Sherman Act 1890. Section 2 of the Sherman Act condemns monopoly that does not result from normal industrial development; it does not condemn monopoly that is achieved from competition on the merits. For the U.K., Japan and India the corresponding legislations are the Monopolies and Restrictive Practices (Inquiry and Control) Act 1948, the Antimonopoly Law 1947 and MRTP Act 1969 respectively. MRTP Act was introduced to check the concentration of economic power, control of growth of monopolies and prevent restrictive and unfair trade practices. Restrictions were imposed on expansion of enterprises, amalgamations and takeover of business enterprises including acquision of shares falling within the purview of this Act. However, over the last few years many changes have taken place in government policy, particularly in area relating to the MRTP Act.)

The prohibition of a concentration increasing merger by antitrust laws results from the belief that an increase in concentration is anticompetitive. That is, an inverse relationship between performance and concentration is assumed implicitly. In particular, it is presumed that a structural change, such as a merger that increases concentration will reduce welfare W, defined as the sum of producers' and consumers' surpluses. However, such an assumption need not be true always.

To see the danger of identifying changes in concentration with change in W, let us consider an n-firm homogeneous good industry. The concentration index we use here is the Herfindahl-Hirschman index I_H. (This index is used for evaluation of merger in the U.S.) The firms are Cournot maximizers. Following the notation adopted in the preceding part, we note that for any arbitrary change $\{dx_i\}$ in firms' outputs

$$dW = \sum_{i=1}^{n}[f(X) - C'_i(x_i)]dx_i. \qquad (4.16)$$

Given that the firms are practising Cournot behavior, $f(X) - C'_i(x_i) = -f'(X)x_i$. Hence

$$\begin{aligned}
dW &= -f'(X)\sum_{i=1}^{n}x_i dx_i & (4.17) \\
&= -f'(X)d(\sum_{i=1}^{n}x_i^2)/2 & (4.18) \\
&= -f'(X)(d(X^2 I_H))/2 & (4.19) \\
&= -f'(X)[2XI_H dX + X^2 dI_H]/2 & (4.20) \\
&= -f'(X)X^2 I_H(\frac{dX}{X} + \frac{1}{2}\frac{dI_H}{I_H}). & (4.21)
\end{aligned}$$

Now, $f'(X) < 0$. Therefore, dW has the same sign as $(dX/X + dI_H/2I_H)$. Since $p > C'_i(x_i)$ in equilibrium, increase in output $(dX > 0)$ tend to increase welfare (equation (4.16)). Now, if a firm with large market share increases its output, then I_H, X and W all will increase. Furthermore, it is also possible to have $dX < 0$, $dI_H > 0$ but yet $dW > 0$. It may be noted that if all the n firms produce the same output, then $I_H = 1/n$, which means that there is an inverse relationship between I_H and W, as n varies. But this is a very special circumstance.

It has been argued that large firms are large because of their efficiency. (See Demsetz (1973a, 1974)). This issue is taken up in more detail in Chapter 5.) If so, welfare may increase if these efficient firms acquire more of industry's productive capital and hence increase their output shares. This means that if X is fixed, then a transfer of output from a small (less efficient) firm to a large firm which has lower marginal cost in Cournot equilibrium will increase welfare. But the output transfer increases concentration also.

It, therefore, turns out that there is a complex relationship between concentration, output and welfare. Hence a careful analysis of the welfare effects of merger is needed. This is what we do in the remainder of this chapter.

We assume again the framework considered in the preceding analysis. Note that we can regard the change in equilibrium output by the insiders, ΔX_{IN}, as the integral of the infinitesimal changes dX_{IN} that make up ΔX_{IN}. Now,

$$dW = p dX_{IN} - dC_{IN} + \sum_{i \in O} [p - C'_i(x_i)] dx_i, \qquad (4.22)$$

where C_{IN} is insiders' total cost and O is the set of outsider firms.

From (4.10), for outsider firms $dx_i = -\theta_i dX$ and their price cost margins are $p - C'_i(x_i) = -x_i f'(X)$ (see equation (4.6)). Hence

$$dW = p dX_{IN} - dC_{IN} + \sum_{i \in O} f'(X) x_i \theta_i dX, \qquad (4.23)$$

which we can rewrite as

$$dW = (p dX_{IN} + X_{IN} dp - dC_{IN}) - X_{IN} f'(X) dX + \sum_{i \in O} f'(X) x_i \theta_i dx_i. \qquad (4.24)$$

In (4.24) the first three terms on the right hand side constitute the change in insiders' joint profits, $d\pi_{IN}$. Now, $d\pi_{IN}$ involves the change in cost dC_{IN} which is hard to observe. Consequently, determination of the sign of (4.24) will be difficult. However, this term drops out if we consider the external welfare effect $dW - d\pi_{IN}$. From (4.24)

$$dW - d\pi_{IN} = -X_{IN} f'(X) dX + \sum_{i \in O} f'(X) x_i \theta_i dX \qquad (4.25)$$

$$= [\sum_{i \in O} \theta_i x_i - X_{IN}] f'(X) dX. \qquad (4.26)$$

From (4.26) we note that the net externality from an infinitesimal merger that changes overall output by dX is $h(X) f'(X) dX$, where $h(X) = \sum_{i \in O} \theta_i x_i - X_{IN}$. Now, $h(X) f'(X) dX$ has the same sign as $h(X)$ if $dX < 0$. Converting $h(X)$ into output shares we have

Theorem 4.6 (Farrell and Shapiro, 1990):Consider any change in behavior by a subset of firms, 'insiders', in an oligopolistic industry. The net external effect of this change on other firms, 'outsiders', who are Cournot oligopolists, and on consumers depends only on the equilibrium change in the insiders' output, X_{IN}. A small reduction in X_{IN} has a net positive welfare effect on outsiders and consumers if and only if $\sum_{i \epsilon 0} \theta_i s_i > s_{IN}$, where s_{IN} is the initial (joint) market shares of the insiders.

Now, if a merger causes insiders' equilibrium output to change from X_{IN} initial (X_{IN}^i, for short) to X_{IN}^{final} (X_{IN}^f, for short), then the change in total welfare (ΔW) in excess for change in insiders' joint profits ($\Delta \pi_{IN}$) is given by

$$\Delta W - \Delta \pi_{IN} = \int_{X_{IN}^i}^{X_{IN}^f} (\frac{dW}{dX_{IN}} - \frac{d\pi_{IN}}{dX_{IN}}) dX_{IN}. \tag{4.27}$$

In (4.27) for each given X_{IN} the integrand is evaluated assuming a Cournot equilibrium among outsiders.

For simplicity, and as suggested by the discussion presented earlier, we consider only output reducing mergers, for which $\Delta X_{IN} < 0$. When X_{IN} reduces, we can rewrite (4.27) as

$$\Delta W - \Delta \pi_{IN} = \int_{X_{IN}^f}^{X_{IN}^i} -(\frac{dW}{dX_{IN}} - \frac{d\pi_{IN}}{dX_{IN}}) dX_{IN}, \tag{4.28}$$

which in view of (4.26) becomes

$$\Delta W - \Delta \pi_{IN} = \int_{X_{IN}^f}^{X_{IN}^i} h(X)(-(f'(X)) \frac{dX}{dX_{IN}} dX_{IN}. \tag{4.29}$$

where $h(X) = \sum_{i \epsilon 0} \theta_i x_i - X_{IN}$. Therefore, if $h(X) \geq 0$ before a merger, and if the merger causes a reduction in insiders' output, then the total externality $\Delta W - \Delta \pi_{IN}$ turns out to be positive.

A privately profitable merger ($\Delta \pi_{IN} > 0$) that makes total externality positive can be regarded as socially desirable. The following theorem, which is stated without proof, gives sufficient conditions for privately profitable merger to raise welfare.

Theorem 4.7 (Farrell and Shapiro, 1990):Consider a proposed merger among firms $i \epsilon IN$ and suppose that their initial (joint) market share s_{IN} does not exceed $\sum_{i \epsilon 0} \theta_i s_i$. Suppose further that f'', f''', and $C_i''(x_i)$ are all nonnegative and $C_i'''(x_i)$ is nonpositive in the relevant ranges and for all nonparticipant firms i. Then if the merger is profitable and would raise the market price, it would also raise welfare[3].

We consider an example to explain theorem 4.7. Suppose demand is given by $p = B - X$ and for all firms i the marginal cost function is of the form $\frac{1}{2}x_i^2/k_i$ (see Perry and Porter (1983)). Every merger in this set up will raise price.

Theorem 4.7 will apply. It can be seen that $\theta_i = x_i/p = s_i/\epsilon$. Consequently, a merger will possess positive externality if

$$s_{IN} < \frac{1}{\epsilon} \sum_{i \in O} s_i^2, \qquad (4.30)$$

where the output shares considered are pre-merger ones. Inequality (4.30) shows that a merger is likely to help insiders ($\Delta \pi_{IN} > 0$) and consumers ($\Delta W - \Delta \pi_{IN} > 0$) jointly if s_{IN} is small, that is, if the portion of the industry constituted by outsiders is more concentrated.

The intuitive reasoning behind this conclusion is that in this model for large firms θ_is are large ($\theta_i = x_i/p$). In economic words, when there are large outsiders, a reduction in X_{IN} 'will induce an especially large output response by them - which is just where increases in output are socially most valuable' (Farrell and Shapiro (1990, p.119). Thus, high concentration among outsiders will make output response socially desirable. Another important feature of (4.30) is that if demand is more inelastic, then merger is more likely to have a positive external effect. The reason is that with inelastic demand the price cost margins of outsiders are large and hence higher welfare benefit can be expected from their increased output. (Evidently, by varying assumptions about cost and demand functions, we can develop analogous conditions for positive externality.)

Following Williamson (1968) it has been a common practice to evaluate the effects of horizontal mergers in terms of a trade off between welfare loss caused by output reduction (price increase) and cost savings resulting from greater efficiency. 'Subsequent theoretical developments have shown the limitations of the naive trade off model, but the basic idea of an efficiency defence remains' (George and Jacquemin (1992, p. 153). However, cost savings are often difficult to observe. In the words of White (1987, p.18) 'Efficiencies are easy to promise, yet may be difficult to deliver'.

In contrast, Farrell and Shapiro (1990) focussed on the external effect of a merger rather than trying directly to determine the sign of its aggregate welfare effect. Availability of information required is a clear advantage of this approach. It is consistent with market oriented policy analysis. The antitrust authorities can look at the external effect 'to make use of the fact that only privately profitable mergers are proposed, and it would permit them to give cost savings a larger role in merger policy (as Williamson's (1968) calculations suggest they deserve) without demanding either information or credulity about alleged synergies' (Farrell and Shapiro (1990, p. 122)).

An important point that needs to be mentioned at this stage is that the Cournot assumption has been made to measure the mark ups $p - C_i'(x_i)$ by $-x_i f'(X)$ and to compute outsiders' response by θ_is. However, this assumption can be relaxed. Note that there are two effects of a change in X_{IN}. The first effect is $X_{IN} df(X)$ which causes a loss to consumers. Second, the *ith* outsider firm changes its output by some amount, say $\psi_i dX_{IN}$, and the overall change by outsiders is then $\sum_{i\in O}[p - C'_i(x_i)]\psi_i dX_{IN}$. Thus, the externality effect is positive if and only if

$$\sum_{i\in O}[p - C'_i(x_i)]\psi_i dX_{IN} - X_{IN} df(X) > 0. \qquad (4.31)$$

Equation (4.24) is a special case of equation (4.31) under an a priori assumption about ψ_i. Clearly, under alternative assumptions about ψ_i we can derive necessary and sufficient conditions for positive externality from the basic equation (4.31).

Concluding remarks

Baumol, Panzar and Willig (1982) initiated the idea that there may be a gain in efficiency from combining two or more multiproduct firms. Färe (1986) suggested an index to measure this type of efficiency gain. We show that in the single good case a cost variant of this function can be related to a concentration formula. Furthermore, the ordering generated by the Färe gain function is shown to be consistent with the concentration curve ranking criterion. Finally, a normalized form of the gain function satisfying a 'homogeneity' rule is shown to coincide with a subclass of the Hannah-Kay family of indices. This relationship is important because it shows the application of a concentration index as an index of efficiency of merger. With given factor prices, we only need output levels of different firms to calculate this index.

Following Farrell and Shapiro (1990) we have also examined the output and welfare effects of mergers in Cournot oligopoly. It was found that mergers typically raise price. For a merger to reduce price considerable economies of scale or learning is required. On policy issues, it was argued that privately profitable mergers that make 'externality effect' positive can be proposed.

Notes

1. For more extensive discussions on reasons for merger, see Carlton and Perloff (1990) and Farrell and Shapiro (1990).

2. A single good cost function $Q(w, z)$ has global economies of scale at production level $z > 0$ if for all $\theta > 1$, $\theta Q(w, z) > Q(w, \theta z)$. That is, the average cost will be decreasing in the neighbourhood of z.

3. The requirement $f'' \geq 0$ is satisfied by many demand functions, e.g. linear and constant elasticity type. Nondecreasingness of marginal costs ($C''_i(x_i) \geq 0$) is also fulfilled widely. For mergers involving moderate change in X_{IN}, the second order terms may be sufficient. Therefore, theorem 4.7 may hold even if $f''' < 0$ or $C'''_i(x_i) > 0$. For a large merger, third derivative conditions are necessary.

5 On structure performance relationships

The subject of this chapter is the relationship between industry structure and measures of industry performance. The major elements of market structure describe the ways in which the market departs from the conditions of perfect competition. In standard market models, such as 'models of monopoly and competition, market structure determines market conduct, the behavioral rules followed by buyers, sellers and potential entrants to choose the variables under their control. Market performance is assessed by comparing the results of market conduct to first best ideals such as perfect competition or feasible alternatives' (Schmalensee (1989, p. 954)). Thus, we see that an industry's structure (for example, concentration) determines the behavior of the firms which in turn determines industry performance (for example, profit). We begin this chapter with a brief discussion of three standard measures of market performance, viz., the rate of return, the price cost margin and Tobin's (1969, 1980) q.

Next, we use alternative measures of performance to investigate whether high concentration indicates high profitability. We consider the methodological issues as well as empirical implementation problems. The literature developed along this line is quite voluminous and this chapter is inevitably incomplete despite its length. Therefore, the studies quoted in the chapter can be regarded as illustrative examples of the main areas of research. Furthermore, the output of new studies is so extensive that any review will be out of date quite quickly. However, the reference list at the end is attempted to make biased towards recent works as far as possible.

A large part of this discussion is devoted to the examination of Bain's (1956) hypothesis, which states that firms in an industry can earn excess profits if they are protected by entry barriers. Then we consider some additional issues including contestability. In a contestable market entry and exit are easy, conditions of perfect competition are satisfied: price equals marginal cost and strategic behavior has no relevance (see Baumol, Panzar and Willig (1982)). The remainder of the main body of this chapter presents the Chicago

School's hypothesis which stresses that high profits are in fact a consequence of greater efficiency. As in the former case our discussion in these latter cases maintains a balance between theoretical arguments and empirical findings. Finally, we close the chapter with some important remarks.

Measures of performance

A measure of market performance determines the extent to which the market becomes beneficial to the consumers. That is, such a measure regards the perfectly competitive framework as the benchmark and determines how close is the performance of an industry to that of the benchmark. A higher value of the measure will indicate a lower degree of performance, and it achieves the minimum value when the market is perfectly competitive. Three measures of market performance have been suggested in the literature:the rate of return, the price cost margin and Tobin's (1969, 1980) q.

Rate of return

Rate of return of a firm is its earning as a fraction of total amount of investment. Managers acting in the best interests of the owners would seek to maximize this rate of return. Therefore, it is argued that the rate of return on investment is a correct concept of performance on theoretical grounds (see Hall and Weiss (1967)). A firm may earn just normal profit, the profit that opportunity cost attributes to all of the firm's resources. Opportunity cost values each resource at its most profitable alternative use. Any accounting profit over and above the normal profit is its economic or net profit.

Profit π of a firm is given by

$$\pi = revenues - labor, \ material \ and \ capital \ costs. \qquad (5.1)$$

Measuring revenues, and labor and material costs is easy. The difficulty lies in the measurement of capital costs. These costs are given by the rental costs of capital services, that is, the total amount that the firm could earn by renting them to some other firm. This is simply the opportunity cost to the firm of using its own capital. The rental cost of capital services is a quite appropriate notion of capital cost because by using its own plant and equipment the firm gives up the opportunity cost to earn rental income. If we have well developed capital markets, rental rates become readily available. In case of nonavailability of rental rates, we must employ some procedure to impute the rental rate.

Suppose that a firm can earn an interest rate r by investing in a risk free asset. This interest rate r is the key element in the calculation of the rental cost of capital. If δ denotes the depreciation of the plant and equipment during the period under consideration, then the rental cost of capital is $(r+\delta)$. Depreciation is the rate of decline in economic value of the capital during the period of its use. Finally, if the price of capital goes up at a rate t over the period, than the firm will enjoy a capital gain on the fraction $(1-\delta)$ of its capital stock remaining at the end of the period. This gain in the value of the capital must be subtracted from the rental cost. The cost of capital services that could be purchased for 1 unit of money is given by $[r+\delta-(1-\delta)t]$. That is, $[r+\delta-(1-\delta)t]$ is the rental cost per money unit (e.g. dollar) worth of capital assets. Then the total capital cost turns out to be $kp^k[r+\delta-(1-\delta)t]$, where k stands for the total amount of capital and p^k is its purchase price, that is, kp^k is the value of capital.

To calculate the earned rate of return, we solve for r such that economic profit is zero. Setting $\pi=0$ in (5.1) and solving for r yields

$$r = [revenues - labor\ cost - material\ cost - kp^k\delta + kp^k(1-\delta)t]/kp^k. \quad (5.2)$$

If we define revenues minus labor cost and material cost minus depreciation as net income, then the numerator in (5.2) is net income plus capital gain. The earned rate of return then equals the net income plus capital gain divided by the value of capital. It is easy to see that earning positive economic profit is same as earning excess rate of return (above competitive level). Thus, to calculate the rate of return we look for the rate of return that equates economic profit to zero. We then compare this rate of return with the competitive rate of return. Excess economic profit exists if and only if the rate of return exceeds the competitive rate. Two important points should be noted here. The calculation has taken care of the price appreciation on assets that can arise from inflation. Consequently, the rate of return is a nominal rate of return. If the calculation does not take this into account, then $t=0$ and the rate of return is a real rate of return. Next, capital assets should be valued at replacement cost, which is the cost to purchase an asset of similar quality. Additional problems arise in measuring depreciation. One common calculation assumes that the asset's value decreases in equal annual amount over its lifetime. Clearly, the calculation of rate of return will be sensitive to the accounting concept of depreciation and often we may get biased results. This is particularly true in case of price appreciation. (See Schmalensee (1989) and Carlton and Perloff (1990) for further discussions.)

Price cost margin

Some authors suggested the use of the Lerner index, the ratio between price minus marginal cost and price, as a measure of performance. We know from Chapter 2 (equation (2.6)) that the Lerner index for a monopolist is given by the reciprocal of the absolute value of the elasticity of demand. That is, for a monopolist

$$\frac{p-mc}{p} = \frac{1}{\epsilon}, \quad (5.3)$$

where p = price, mc = marginal cost and ϵ = absolute value of the elasticity of demand. Since it is often difficult to obtain an estimate of marginal cost, the typical measure of cost used to calculate the Lerner index is not marginal cost. Instead, average cost is taken as a substitute of marginal cost. This is same as the requirement that total cost $C(z)$ as a function of output z is a straight line passing through the origin, that is, $C(z) = az$ for some $a > 0$. Equivalently, for given factor prices, the technology is subject to constant returns to scale. This assumption is made on the ground that constant returns to scale are the most common finding in manufacturing industries (see Scherer, Beckenstein, Kaufer and Murphy (1975) for empirical evidence). Now, total cost consists of labor cost, material cost and the rental cost of capital $kp^k(r + \delta - (1-\delta)t) = \mu kp^k$ (say). Substituting the value of average cost in (5.3) and rearranging slightly we get

$$\frac{p - V_1}{p} = \frac{1}{\epsilon} + \mu \frac{kp^k}{pz}, \tag{5.4}$$

where V_1 is the average cost of labor and materials. The profitability measure on the left hand side in (5.4) gives the relative shortfall of the average wage bill and material cost from price. The second term on the right hand side of (5.4) is the capital sales ratio, the rental value of capital as a fraction of revenue.

Since capital earns a normal profit under competition, rates of return on sales will be higher, the more capital intensive the production technologies are. This in turn increases the relative gap between price and average labor and material cost. Thus, we can say that capital sales ratio controls for differences in price cost margins across industries that arise because of capital intensity. The first term on the right hand side of (5.4) is an upper bound on the aggregate market power in an industry. The higher the concentration in the industry, the closer will be the aggregate market power to this upper bound. It should, however, be noted that since in general average cost is not equal to marginal cost, which is the proper cost concept to be used in (5.3), our discussion has a strong limitation.

Measures based on market value of securities

Several measures of performance employ the market value of a firm's securities. These measures are attractive because the difficult problems of estimating rates of return and marginal cost are avoided.

In an early study Stigler (1963) considered the ratio of the market value of a firm's assets or equity to its inflation adjusted book value. The excess value ratio defined as ((market value-book value)/revenue) was considered by Thomadakis (1977) as a measure of ratio of excess profit to sales. Another important measure is Tobin's q (see Tobin (1969, 1980)). It is defined as the ratio of the market value of a firm to the replacement cost of its assets. By market value of a firm we mean the market value of its outstanding stock and debt. The measure q will take on the minimum value 1 if and only if the firm is earning competitive rate of return. If q is greater than 1, then the firm is valued at more than what it would cost to rebuild it. Equivalently, we say that the firm is earning excess profit-its rate of return is higher than that justified by its cost of assets.

Numerical illustrations of all these measures involve the calculation of market value of a firm's assets. This can be done by summing the values of the securities that a firm has issued, such as bonds. For Tobin's q we need to obtain an estimate of the replacement cost of its assets. This will require accurate estimation of the values of used equipments. Further, the firm may possess intangible assets. The estimation of replacement cost of such assets is quite difficult. Researchers usually ignore the replacement cost of intangible assets in their calculation of q.

It is reasonable to inquire whether all the performance measures discussed in this section are highly correlated with one another. In case of high correlation any debate about the relative merits of one measure over another will be meaningless. However, in case of low correlation a great deal matters when we come to the question of selecting one particular measure from a given set. Liebowitz (1982) has reported a low correlation between rates of return and price cost margin. Correlations of rates of return with measures based on market values have also been reported to be low. (See for instance, Ornstein (1972), Martin (1979a), Caves, Porter and Spence (1980), Lindeberg and Ross (1981), Liebowitz (1982), Salinger (1984) and Hirschey (1985).) Libdberg and Ross (1981), however, reported a high correlation between Tobin's q and price cost margin.

Alternative measures of performance and industry structure

Here we present a brief survey on the relationship between industry structure and three performance measures discussed above.

Rate of return

The first empirical study relating rate of return and concentration was carried out by Bain (1951). He studied 335 U.S. firms belonging to 42 industries for the period 1936-40. Rate of return was calculated as the after tax profit divided by the book value of stockholder's equity at the beginning of the year. This was calculated for each firm in each of the years under examination. He then calculated a weighted average of rates of return by industry, using equities of firms as weights.

As a measure of concentration Bain chose the eight-firm concentration ratio for each industry. He found that for industries with a concentration ratio above .7 the average profit rate was 11.8. This rate turned out to be 7.5 for industries with a concentration ratio less than .7. Clearly, Bain's sample confirms his hypothesis regarding the relationship between profit and concentration. According to Bain's hypothesis, profit rates of firms in industries with high concentration should on the average be high. From Bain's study one might be tempted to conclude that it is easier to detect a relation between concentration and profitability for industries above some threshold concentration level than with a continuous regression model. However, Brozen (1971) pointed out that Bain's skewed result might be the consequence of the profit rates of the leading firms rather than the profit rate of the entire industry. Furthermore, the industries considered in Bain's study could be in disequilibrium.

In a later work Bain (1956) argued that concentration alone is not sufficient to guarantee that profits will be above the competitive level. Firms in an industry can earn such profits only if they are protected by entry barriers. He identified four entry barriers:economies of scale, product differentiation advantages, absolute cost advantage and capital requirement.

Bain pointed out three reasons by which product differentiation advantage could retard entry. These are patent control over better quality products, control of better distributive outlets and knowledge of the preference of the buyers for particular products. The first two of these reasons are quite evident. Concerning the third reason we note that in markets with differentiated products consumers usually prefer the existing brands over the unfamiliar brand of an entrant. Therefore, to overcome this preference barrier an entrant would have to offer its product at substantially lower price than the existing firms and/or do heavy advertisement. Such activities lead to higher cost for the new firm and can be analyzed in the same line as the absolute cost advantage barrier. Therefore, a limit price differential is created. A limit price is the highest price which the established firms believe they can charge without persuading entry. That is, in limit pricing, the established firms set their outputs and price such that sufficient demand is not left to support an additional firm. Thus, an incumbent enjoys some advantage because of its existence in the industry. An advantage of this type is called a first mover advantage.

An absolute cost advantage barrier may arise for various reasons. Among them the major ones are:(a) control of supply of vital raw materials by the established firms, (b) lower prices of raw materials because of bulk buying by large established firms or due to prior arrangement with suppliers, (c) control of efficient productive technique by the established firms, (d) lower cost for the established firms due to vertical integration, (e) higher cost for an entrant to attract managerial personnel from the established firms, (f) imposition of risk premium by financial markets on new firms because of the possibility of failure to repay loans. The effect of a premium of this type will be higher, the more capital investment a firm requires for operating a minimum efficient scale (MES) plant. By minimum efficient size of a plant we mean the point at which average cost is minimized. MES plant refers to the minimum level of minimum efficient plant size. Bain referred to the investment needed by a firm to set up an MES plant as an absolute cost disadvantage.

Returns to scale form an important barrier to entry. If an existing firm and an entrant can enjoy the same benefits of economies of scale, then the existing firm may be in an advantageous position for various reasons. For instance, an entrant may have difficulty in raising money for financing large expenditure (required to get advantage of economies of scale). This situation can be analyzed along the same line as the barrier from initial requirements. If a firm cannot come into an industry at MES capacity, it might come in at a smaller scale. But if entering at less than MES capacity involves substantially higher average cost than the existing firms, then entrance would not be feasible. The established firms may then engage themselves in limit pricing. Bain also evaluated economies of multiplant operation and economies of scale in distribution. In the former case a new firm may have to take entrance on a horizontally integrated basis in several geographic markets. In the latter case entrance on a vertically integrated basis in several vertically related markets is feasible. If there is entry on a competitive basis, then investment requirement of the either factor might make entry difficult.

Barrier from initial capital requirement can be analyzed under absolute cost advantage category. To set up a new business one needs an initial capital expenditure. New firms may face difficulty in raising the required initial capital expenditure. If the initial expenditure is substantially large, then it may be quite tough for the entrant to get loan. Even if the entrant can secure the required loan it may have to pay a higher interest rate than the established firms. Therefore, the incumbents have an absolute cost advantage here. Recent contributions argue that entry will be deterred if a large fraction of entry costs is sunk. (See Jacquemin (1987) and Tirole (1988) for extensive discussions.) The relative importance of sunk costs may be correlated with absolute capital requirements (Kessides (1985)).

Bain's sample consisted of 20 U.S. manufacturing industries (in 1947-51) with high concentration levels (as measured by the four-firm concentration ratio). Since the barrier initial capital requirement is dependent on the other three, Bain dropped it in his empirical work. He assessed the heights of the barriers for different industries on the basis of his own evaluation and information received from the industries. The entry barriers were then subdivided into three categories:very important, moderately important and unimportant. (For instance, Bain found that in the industry of gypsum products the absolute cost advantage barrier was very important due to patents and secrecy in know-how, whereas it was substantially important in two industries, copper and steel. In the remaining seventeen industries this barrier was unimportant.) An overall barrier was then expressed as an aggregative function of individual entry barriers, where the weights attached to each type of barrier in the aggregation procedure varied from industry to industry. With respect to overall barriers to entry, Bain divided the industries into three groups. In the high barrier group firms could evaluate price 10 per cent or more above minimal costs while anticipating entry, for firms belonging to the next group (substantial barrier class) the corresponding percentage might range a bit above 7 per cent and for those belonging to moderate to low barrier group the same percentage might be in the range 1 to 4%.

Bain found that large firms in industries with very high barriers generally earned higher rate of return than large firms in industries with substantial or moderate barriers. In his sample high barriers are associated with greater large firm profitability. It was found that among industries with substantial barrier group, the greater is the concentration the greater the large firm profit rate. Bain therefore interpreted his findings confirming his hypothesis:concentration would allow collusion and collusion would allow excess profit for large firms if entry barrier were sufficiently high. Mann (1966) reexamined the relationship between profit and his own subjective estimates of entry barriers over a large sample and later time period. (The sample consisted of 30 U.S. industries in 1950-60.) His examination confirmed Bain's hypothesis.

Orr (1974) using 1964-67 Canadian data estimated a model of the form

$$\Delta n = a(r - r*), \qquad (5.5)$$

where Δn is the gross increase in the number of sellers over the period, a is a positive constant that measures the speed of adjustment, r is the average profit rate and $r*$ is the profit rate at which entry would stop. Orr (1974) substituted for $r*$ a linear function of variables meant to measure the conditions of entry. In a later study, Orr (1974a) used the estimated coefficients of this function to construct a measure of entry barriers for each industry in his sample. His study confirmed the Bain conclusion that high barrier industries are significantly more profitable than other industries.

In the studies of Bain (1956) and Mann (1966) large elements of subjectivity is involved in assessing the ease of entry into the industries considered. However, this is substantially eliminated in the work of Comanor and Wilson (1967), whose empirical analysis is restricted to 41 U.S. consumer good industries in 1954-57. They investigated regression equations of the following form:

$$r = \beta_o + \beta_1(CCN) + \beta_2(E_1) + \ldots + \beta_n(E_{n+1}), \qquad (5.6)$$

where $\beta'_j s$ are unknown coefficients, CCN is a measure of concentration and $E'_j s$ are variables designed to measure the structural determinants of entry barriers. In addition to concentration (four-firm concentration ratio) they used economies of scale, initial capital requirements, product differentiation (effect of advertising) as independent variables. Comanor and Wilson (1967, 1974) and many others have considered the ratio of the output of a plant of MES to the market output as a whole as a measure of importance of scale economies.

The average size of the largest plants accounting for half of the industry output and the size of the smallest of these plants are regarded as common measures of MES. (In their article Comanor and Wilson adopted the former as a measure of MES.) Both these measures are based on the assumption that the size distribution of observed plants relative to MES does not vary systematically from industry to industry (see, however, Weiss (1976), Baldwin and Gorecki (1985) for opposite evidence).

MES measures are also computed using survivorship technique. This method finds MES based upon a concept known as the survival of the fittest. If on looking at the firm size distribution classified by size groups we find that firms are moving into one particular size class over time, then this indicates that in an overall sense the size class which gains contains the MES (Saving (1961), Shepherd (1967), Stigler (1968), Rees (1973)). Thus, for a particular plant size to be efficient, gradually all plants in the industry should approach that size. If the fraction of industry output produced by a particular size class decreases over time, then it must be an inefficient class. A plant that survives for a long time is efficient. If all firms face the same cost function, then survivorship method identifies the efficient plant size as the industry replaces its obsolete plant sizes. On the other hand, if cost functions are different or if there is product diversification, then a survivorship study can reveal only the range of efficient plant sizes, since the optimal scales of firms may vary in such cases. Another method for calculating MES which makes use of inferences based upon observed data was suggested by Lyons (1980). Davies (1980a) demonstrates that the difference between MES measures involving the size distribution of existing plants and those based on survivorship technique or Lyon's approach tend to be positive and to be positively correlated with concentration. (See also Ornstein, Weston, Intriligator and Shrieves (1973) for discussion on MES measures.)

Comanor and Wilson employed two alternative advertising measures to judge the importance of product differentiation as an entry barrier: industry's advertising sales ratio and average advertising expenditure per firm among firms which account for fifty per cent of the industry output. Capital requirements are usually dealt with in the framework given by (5.6) by incorporating among the regressors a variable measuring the capital cost of an MES plant. Comanor and Wilson estimated a large number of equations for explaining profit on equity. Their study reports a strong, positive relation between advertising sales ratio and industry level profitability (measured as the after tax return on equity) for U.S. consumer good industries. This finding has been claimed to be unusually robust. They, however, found that capital requirements have a significant negative coefficient in profitability regression.

Mann (1966) hypothesized that the impact of entry barriers on profitability was independent and additive to that of concentration. He found barriers to be statistically significant under this assumption (Mann (1973)). Mann's hypothesis has been vigorously refuted by Rhoades (1971, 1972). Weiss (1971) argued that Bain's hypothesis called for interactive (concentration × barriers) specifications. Orr (1974a) and Caves, Porter and Spence (1980) could not conclude using Canadian data whether the impact of entry barriers on profitability is better described as additive to rather than interactive with concentration. Salinger (1984) argued that Bain's hypothesis implies that

(5.6) should be replaced by interactive models of the form

$$r = \beta_o + CCN[\beta_1(E_1) + \beta_2(E_2) + \ldots + \beta_n(E_n)] + \beta_{n+1}(G) + \ldots, \quad (5.7)$$

where G is a measure of past sales growth. Equation (5.7) indicates that without barriers to entry there is no reason for market power to arise just because an industry is concentrated. (We talk about Salinger's numerical results later on in this chapter.)

There have been numerous econometric estimates of the relation between rates of return, concentration and a variety of other variables such as those measuring barriers to entry. Econometric studies attempt to measure the effects of variables on rates of return. Such a study can provide not only an estimate of the effect of the variable upon another but can also reveal how reliable the estimate is. When the estimate is statistically insignificant we can say that the data are consistent with the hypothesis that the true effect of the concerned variable is zero. (More precisely, the data will fail to reject the hypothesis that the true effect of the variable is zero.) Mann (1971) found that the effect of concentration on rate of return was significantly greater in the presence of high entry barriers. George (1968) developed Mann's (1966) study in another direction. He used four-firm concentration ratios and included growth of net assets. Barriers to entry were introduced first by means of two dummies, one for very high and another for substantial barriers, and then by multiplying the values of concentration ratios by the values taken by these dummies. George kept 28 industries in his sample. (Mann's sample consisted of 30 industries.) George obtained a coefficient for the concentration ratio significant at 5% level, but low:5×10^{-2}. Growth and the first dummy variable turned out to be significant at 1% level. In the second regression, growth and the variable retaining only concentration ratios of industries with very high barriers to entry were significant at 1% ; the value of the second coefficient was 7×10^{-2}. Weiss (1974) concluded in his survey article that there was definitely some relationship between profits, concentration and barriers to entry. Recent works appear to indicate a weak relationship which is not often statistically significant. For instance, Salinger (1984) estimated an effect which is quite close to being statistically significant for MES in concentrated industries but not for his other entry barriers variables (for example, advertising intensity.) For further discussions, see the works referred to at the extended bibliography.

There are several reasons why the strong positive relation between entry barriers and profit rates may not be detected in empirical investigations based on reported rates of profit. For instance, an industry may record relatively high profit rates without entry barriers if its equity is understated due to omission of intangible capital created by advertising or by research and development. An industry with high entry barriers may not be highly profitable if the rents of many of the scare factors have been capitalized. Similarly, high barriers will imply modest profits if the benefits of monopoly power are reflected in efficiency or nonmonetary benefits. Another factor that might prevent a strong positive relationship between entry barriers and profit rates is limit pricing.

Price cost margins

Quite a few studies along this line have estimated regressions of the form

$$(p - V_1)/p = \alpha_o + \alpha_1 CON + \alpha_2 KSR + \text{ other variables}, \qquad (5.8)$$

where p = price, V_1 = average cost of labor and materials, CON = a measure of concentration (usually the 4-firm concentration ratio) and KSR = capital sales ratio, the (book) value of capital as a fraction of the value of output. Clearly, (5.8) is a version of equation (5.4) when the relationship between market concentration and market power is taken to be linear.

Collins and Preston (1969) estimated an equation of the form (5.8) using a sample of 417 (four digit Standard Industrial Classification) U.S. manufacturing industries for 1963. Their sample consisted of some industries which are regional or local in nature. However, they used the national level concentration ratios computed by the U.S. Bureau of Census. Collins and Preston, therefore, considered a measure of the geographic dispersion of products that will adjust this misspecification. In fact, this is the only variable they used in addition to the four-firm concentration ratio and KSR. Collins and Preston estimated equation (5.8) separately for producer good and consumer good industries. They did not take account of differences in entry conditions across industries. Consequently, only concentration ratios would partially reflect differences in entry conditions. Clearly, this is one shortcoming of this study. Another point that needs to be mentioned is that the price elasticity of demand was not measured on an industry by industry basis. Since market power in an industry is inversely proportional to the price elasticity of demand, use of an inexact elasticity will clearly overestimate or underestimate the aggregate monopoly power.

The Collins-Preston study showed that on an average for consumer good industries, the coefficient of concentration was large and statistically significant, which is unlikely to occur by chance. (The average value of price cost margin for 417 industries was about .25.) Differences in concentration among consumer good industries accounted for a significant portion of the differences in profitability among the industries.

For producer good industries the average effect of concentration on price cost margins was much less significant. While in the case of consumer good industries an increase in concentration by 10% increased price cost margin by 2%, for producer good industries it increased only by .3% for the same change in concentration. However, the coefficient of KSR was smaller for consumer good industries.

Collins and Preston also estimated equation (5.8) for the four largest firms in each industry and for other smaller firms. This type of analysis allows us to investigate whether market power will benefit all firms in the industry or the large firms only. They argued that collusion allowed by concentration of output would benefit only largest firms, particularly when larger firms have cost or/and product differentiation advantage over small firms. Note also that if concentration increases aggregate price cost margin of large firms, then this result reflects market power only. This is another reason for estimating equation (5.8) separately for large and small firms. The analysis showed that for consumer good industries the market concentration increased the price cost margins of large firms, where large firms had higher margins than small firms. This increase in price cost margins of large firms took place because the small firms were at some competitive disadvantage. Product differentiation was an important source of this type of disadvantage. It was also observed that market concentration in such industries did not mean higher margin for smaller firms. For producer good industries the estimated effect of concentration on market power was never precise in a statistical sense (in fact, negative for small firms). (See Miller (1971), Meehan and Duchesneau (1973), Rhoades and Cleaver (1973), Ornstein (1975) and Phillips (1976) for further discussions.)

Using U.S. data, Domowitz, Hubbard and Petersen (1986) estimated equation (5.8) to investigate the behavior of the price cost margin over the period 1958-81. They reported that the differential in price cost margins among industries of high and low concentration decreased over time to large extent. The same feature was observed for the price cost margin differentials for producer and consumer good industries. It was found that for more recent years the coefficient of concentration was much smaller than what it was in 1958. That is, the already small effect of concentration on price in 1958 became even smaller in later periods. The coefficient was becoming statistically insignificant gradually (see also Scott and Pascoe (1986) and Schmalensee (1987)). In general, their study reported that the relationship between price cost margins and concentration was unstable, and in recent times only a quite weak relationship was detected. The study also reported significantly negative estimates of the coefficient of KSR. (See also Ornstein (1975), Liebowitz (1982) and Domowitz, Hubbard and Petersen (1986a).)

Schmalensee (1989) pointed out that most studies of the U.K. have failed to find a positive linear relation between concentration and profitability (see, for example, Hart and Morgan (1977), Hart and Clarke (1980) and Clarke (1984)). Hart and Morgan (1977) noted that the theoretically interesting study of the relationship between the Herfindahl- Hirschman index and profitability by Rader (1972) and Cowling and Waterson (1976) is apparently delicate to changes in the sample of industries considered.

Most of the above studies adopt specifications of the type (5.8). Alternative specifications have also been used. Stigler (1964) claimed better performance of the Herfindahl-Hirschman index than the four-firm concentration ratio. Kwoka (1979, 1981) found that the shares of the two leading firms are more closely related to the aggregate Lerner index than broader concentration ratios (see also Kwoka and Ravenschraft (1986)). Appelbaum (1982) took a quite general route. He considered the share weighted average of the individual Lerner indices in an industry as the degree of oligopoly power. The estimation of the model will yield an estimated value of the conjectural elasticity of total industry output with respect to the output of firm i. This elasticity, which is given by $\theta^i = (\delta X/\delta x_i)(x_i/X)$, will indicate the deviation of the market structure from the two benchmarks of perfect competition and monopoly ($\theta^i = 0$ and $\theta^i = 1$ respectively). It has been assumed that $\theta^i = \theta$ for all i. As we have seen in Chapter 2, the optimality condition for profit maximization of firm i is $p(1 - \theta/\epsilon) = \delta Q_i(w, x_i)/\delta x_i$, where p is price, ϵ is the absolute value of the elasticity of market demand, Q_i is firm i's cost function and w is the vector of factor prices. The cost functions are assumed to satisfy $Q_i(w, x_i) = x_i f(w) + F^i(w)$ for all i. Thus, the firms have linear and parallel expansion paths, so that marginal costs are constant across firms. The industry cost as a function of total output X has been taken to be of generalized Leontief type:

$$Q(w, X) = \sum_i \sum_j b_{ij}(w_i w_j)^{1/2} X + \sum_i b_i w_i, \qquad (5.9)$$

where $b_{ij} = b_{ji}$ and $\sum_i b_i w_i = \sum_i F^i(w)$. Appelbaum assumed that the demand facing the industry has a constant elasticity. He used data from four U.S. manufacturing industries ((i) rubber, (ii) textile, (iii) electrical machinery and (iv) tobacco) in 1947-71. Degree of noncompetitiveness was found to be insignificant in rubber and textile industries but significant in other two industries for all years. The rubber and textile industries had lowest oligopoly powers, but due to low demand elasticities they were much higher than the estimates of θ.

For the electrical machinery industry oligopoly powers were very close to θ due to the fact that demand elasticities were near unity. In the tobacco industry oligopoly powers were highest reflecting a high degree of noncompetitiveness. Appelbaum's approach is quite general, since it does not assume a linear relationship between price cost margin and concentration. But it should be noted that different demand conditions will lead to different oligopoly power measures even if the degree of competition is unchanged.

An interesting dimension of market power analysis will be the comparison of the determinants of profit margins of affiliates of multinational enterprises (MNEs) and local firms (LCEs). Kumar (1990) analyzed 43 Indian manufacturing industries in 1980-81 to examine what explains the superior performance of the MNEs. He assumed that the average profit margins PCM_M of multinational enterprises could be written as

$$PCM_M = a_1 + b_{11}ADS + b_{12}TECH + b_{13}SKIL + c_{11}VAS + c_{12}AKR$$
$$+ c_{13}CCN + c_{14}GROW + c_{15}SIZE_M + c_{16}ERP$$
$$+ c_{17}COR, \qquad (5.10)$$

where ADS = advertising intensity that captures the extent of product differentiation (measured by the proportion of advertisement expenditure in net industry sales, averaged over 1978-79 to 1980-81); TECH = technology intensity which measures the intensity of Research and Development (R and D) and licensing inputs (given by the proportion of in-house R and D expenditure and remittances on account of royalty and technical fees in net sales, averaged over 1978-79 to 1980-81); SKIL = skill intensity that will capture the intensity of the industry in organizational, managerial and technical skills (two alternative measures were considered:(i) proportion of nonproduction workers in total work force in 1978-79, (ii) percentage share of earnings of employees drawing Rs.3000.00 per month or more in total wages and salaries bill, averaged over 1978-79 to 1980-81); VAS = value added to sales ratio which captures the length of production process or the degree of vertical integration necessary to run business (measured by the proportion of value added in net sales in 1980-81); AKR = average capital requirements that proxies initial capital requirement for setting up an average plant (given by average capital employed per firm, averaged over 1978-79 to 1980-81); CCN = four-firm concentration ratio; GROW = growth rate of industry sales (measured by proportionate change in industry sales over 1978-79 to 1980-81); $SIZE_M$ = average firm size which controls for the effect of differential firm size on profitability (given by average net sales per firm); ERF = effective rates of protection that will determine the extent of protection from external competition (source : National Council of Applied Economic Research, New Delhi[1]); and COR = capital output ratio that determinants the opportunity cost of capital (measured by the total capital employed as a proportion of net industry sales, averaged over 1978-79 to 1980-81).

Defining $b_1 = (b_{11}, b_{12}, b_{13})$ and $c_1 = (c_{11}, c_{12}, c_{13}, c_{14}, c_{15}, c_{16}, c_{17})$, we can rewrite (5.10) as

$$PCM_M = a_1 + b_1 Z_1 + c_1 Z_2, \qquad (5.11)$$

where Z_1 is the vector of exogenous variables (ADS, TECH, SKIL)' reflecting entry barriers and Z_2 is the vector (VAS, AKR, CCN, GROW, $SIZE_M$, FRP, COR)', the vector of industry specific factors that are expected to affect profitability of MNEs and LCEs similarly. Therefore, in analogy with (5.11), if we write the average price cost margins of LCEs as

$$PCM_L = a_2 + b_2 Z_1 + c_2 Z_2, \qquad (5.12)$$

then $b_1 \neq b_2$ will mean that entry barriers protect MNEs and LCEs differently.

On the other hand, $a_1 \neq a_2$ will mean that there is ability differential between MNEs and LCEs.

It was observed empirically that MNEs as a group are protected more by entry barriers than their local counterparts. Residual ability differences were not found to be statistically significant for explaining profitability difference. In knowledge intensive industries MNEs were found to enjoy advantages over LCEs both with respect to technology and human skills. This is because being parts of global enterprises, affiliates of MNEs enjoyed advantage over local organizations so far as factors like technological strength, product diversification and reputation are concerned. The higher profit margins of MNEs in knowledge intensive industries can thus be attributed to technical innovation. Effects of both concentration and protection from imports accorded to LCEs were not significant statistically. Operational inefficiency resulting from lack of competition was suspected to nullify the possible favorable effects of these two factors. The advertising intensity also did not appear to play the role as it does in more competitive set ups.

We conclude this discussion by briefly mentioning that several studies have investigated the impact of imports on domestic profitability. Geroski's (1982) study for the United Kingdom, a Taiwan study by Chou (1986), a German study by Neumann, Bobel and Haid (1979, 1985) and studies by Martin (1979) and Marvel (1980) for the United States show negative linear relation between imports/consumption ratio and profitability. These results, in a sense, imply that foreign competition may reduce domestic market power. See also U.S. studies by White (1976), Pugel (1980) and Domowitz, Hubbard and Petersen (1986), a Belgian study by Jacquemin, de Ghellinck and Huveneers (1980), a Canadian study by Caves, Porter and Spence (1980) and a study for Chile by de Melo and Urata (1986) for stronger negative impact of the ratio of imports to domestic consumption on profitability when domestic concentration is high.

Tobin's q

Several empirical studies on structure performance used the q coefficient as a performance measure. Salinger's (1984) study using U.S. data in 1976 can be taken as an illustrative example. He estimated the following equation

$$q = b_1 + b_2(A/k) + b_3(R/k) + (1-b_4U)CCN[b_5M + b_6k + b_7(A/k)] + b_8CCN + b_9G, \tag{5.13}$$

where k = capital; A/k = advertising capital ratio; R/k = Research and Development capital ratio; U = unionization ratio (fraction of workforce unionized); CCN = four-firm concentration ratio; M = minimum efficient scale and G = industry growth rate. Formulation (5.13) is simply the interactive model in (5.7) with q replacing r. As already stated, this formulation means that a relationship between q and concentration, showing market power, should be present only when entry barriers exist. Equation (5.13) also indicates that unions may reduce the strength between market power and the q coefficient. The empirical estimates of b_4, b_5, b_6 and b_7 were not statistically significant. Therefore, the model in (5.13) was not capable of explaining variations in market/book ratios of large U.S. firms in 1976. Hence it did not provide strong support for Bain's interactive hypothesis.

Among other investigations of the relationship between q and industry structure using U.S. data are the studies by Thomadakis (1977), Lindeberg and Ross (1981), Smirlock et al. (1984) and Hirsch and Seaks (1993). Lindeberg and Ross observed that q ratios of firms are stable over time and the firms with high q coefficients tend to have unique products and factors of production. Evidently, these two causes contribute to high degree of market power. They also find that q coefficients are low for competitive industries. An analysis of the Indian motor vehicle industry using q is discussed in the next part of the chapter.

We conclude this part with two general remarks. The first remark is concerning a wide, but by no means exhaustive, list of references to the structure performance literature. Using linear regression, a number of studies found positive relations between (domestic) concentration and profitability. These include studies of Japan (Caves and Uekusa (1976)), Pakistan (White (1974)), France (Jenny and Weber (1976)), Germany (Neumann, Bobel and Haid (1979, 1985)), the United States (Imel, Behr, and Helmberger (1972), Telser (1972), Lustgarten (1975). Peltzman (1977), La France (1979), Marvel (1980) and Masson and Shannan (1982)) and Chile (de Melo and Urata (1986)). But many U.S. studies found statistically insignificant linear relation between (domestic) concentration and profitability. (See for example, Vernon and Nourse (1973), Boyer (1974), Gort and Singamsetti (1976), Cattin and Wittink (1976), Porter (1976), Strickland and Weiss (1976), Martin (1979, 1979a) and Bradburd (1982).) Some U.S. studies reported statistically significant negative coefficient for concentration (see Porter (1976), Grabowski and Mueller (1978), Connolly and Hirschey (1984, 1986)). Non - U.S. studies also failed to detect profitability concentration relationship. (For instance, Phlips (1971) claimed this for French, Belgian and Italian data. His findings were confirmed by Jacquemin, de Ghellinck and Huveneers (1980) for Belgium.) Two excellent survey articles by Caves (1989) and Schamlensee (1989) will provide additional references. Caves (1989) is concerned with non- U.S. empirical studies and Schamlensee (1989) is a general survey on structure performance relationships.

The second remark is concerning the sensitivity of a performance measure to the choice of a concentration index. Kwoka (1981) considered alternative concentration ratios for 314 U.S. manufacturing industries in 1972 and explored their relationships to price cost margins. It was found that the two-firm ratio's relationship to the performance measure is highly significant. The high correlations between all the concentration ratios used (one-firm to ten-firm) do not ensure the emergence of a clear relationship between these alternatives and margins. Thus, high correlations between concentration ratios would be insufficient to draw the conclusion that they are highly correlated with measures of industry performance. Sleuwaegen and Dehandschutter (1986) showed that the choice between the Herfindahl-Hirschman index and k-firm concentration ratio in profit regression may become important when the share of top four firms in the industry is more than half of the market share, that is, for highly concentrated industries. They used rate of return as the performance measure and a large sample of U.S. industries relating to the year 1956 as the data set. A high correlation between two measures of industry structures could as well result from outliers in the distribution. But this need not imply that for explaining the causal effect of a structural measure on a performance index, we can use either of the two measures of structure.

Some additional issues

The cross sectional studies of the relationship between structure and performance across different industries surveyed in this chapter assume that the same structure performance relation holds for all industries. Furthermore, there is implicit assumption that different industries have similar elasticities of demand. Under such assumptions, the estimation of profitability concentration relationship may be biased. Thus, specific industry analysis sometimes may be more accurate.

Further, in any industry there is a trade off between market power and efficiency. This trade off will be in some cases in favor of efficiency and in some cases it will balance out in favor of market power. Therefore, an industry by industry analysis may enable us to understand the structure performance relationship from this perspective also.

Industry level studies

We review three industries under this category:the Indian motor vehicle industry and the U.S. airline and banking industries. The discussion begins with the airline industry. This industry appears to have low entry cost for flying a plane (between city pairs) in airlines already in operation. If necessary planes can be shifted from one route to another. The market for air travel between cities is often used in examples of contestable markets. Baumol, Panzar and Willig (1982) defined a contestable market as one in which (i) entry and exit are perfectly costless, (ii) an entrant will be able to begin servicing before an incumbent can change its price, and (iii) an entrant has the same post-entry costs as incumbents. Loosely speaking, contestability 'replaces price-taking with rapid entry and exit' (Spence (1983, p. 982).

To define equilibrium in a contestable market formally, let us first introduce the notion of feasibility. An industrial configuration with price p and firm outputs $x_1, x_2, \ldots, x_m$ is feasible if (i) the market equates supply and demand:$\sum_{i=1}^{m} x_i = f(p)$, where f is demand function, and (ii) each firm at least covers its production cost, $px_i \geq C(x_i)$, $i = 1, \ldots, m$, with C being the common cost function. A feasible configuration $(p, x_1, x_2, \ldots, x_m)$ is sustainable if it does not offer any profitable entry, that is, $p_e x_e \leq C(x_e)$ for all $p_e \leq p$ and $x_e \leq f(p_e)$. 'In a perfectly contestable market equilibrium can be formed only by a sustainable (and of course feasible) industrial configuration' (Jacquemin (1987, p. 27)).

Under perfect contestability in equilibrium, there will be (a) absence of excessive (monopolistic) prices or profits, (b) absence of inefficiency or waste, (c) absence of predatory pricing and (d) pricing consistent with efficiency in the allocation of economic resources to serve the desires of consumers. To understand these, note that any profit in excess of the competitive rate of return will attract a potential entrant as long as sunk costs are zero. Excessive profits will permit the entrant to undercut the incumbent's excessive prices to a level that still leaves an attractive return to the new enterprise. Next, if a firm incurs costs greater than the lowest permitted by current technology, then a more efficient entrant will benefit in exactly the same manner that excessive profits permit. The point is that excessive prices are always an opportunity for entry, whether attributed to excessive profits or to excessive costs. The prospect of excessive future profits is crucial to predation. Since zero entry cost prevents excessive profits, with impossibility of future excessive profits predation becomes unattractive in a contestable framework. We do not wish to go for a detailed examination of the fourth desirable attribute. (For a full discussion on this, see Baumol, Panzer and Willig (1982).) At equilibrium, in a contestable market price, marginal cost and average cost must be equal. The above arguments show that contestability facilitates the analysis of economic models in many of the ways that perfect competition does.

Hurdle, Johnson, Joskow, Werden and Williams (1989) explored the effect of potential entry on performance in airline markets. They examined the relationship for 867 significant nonstop city pairs in 1985. One of the structural variables used is the number of likely potential entrants (LPEs). 'It is constructed by using data on the characteristics of city-pair routes and of the individual carriers that operate at either of its end points to identify the potential entrants that would be least likely to be deterred from entering by economies of scale and scope' (Hurdle et al. (1989, p. 120)). Economies of scale may deter entry by putting potential entrants into the choice of entry on a scale with significant cost disadvantage. The airline industry may also exhibit economies of scope. The average cost on a city pair decreases as the extent of 'feed' increases (that is, as the extent to which flights deliver passengers to, and receive passengers from, other routes increases.) An entrant may find it difficult to work on a network as an incumbent does. The entry deterring effects of economies of scope should be very high on routes with substantial feed. Now, LEPs can have the same kind effect on competition as incumbents. We refer to such LPEs as other competitors (OCs) to distinguish them from LPEs who can have no effect or insignificant effect on competition.

Clearly, under perfect contestability all LPEs are OCs.

The measure of market performance considered by Hurdle et al. is yield - average revenue on a city pair per mile. Therefore the most important explanatory variables are likely to be those relating to cost. The cost variables considered are distance (DIST), average plane size (APS), load factor (LF) and route density (DEN). Distance was measured by great-circle mileage between airports in the city pair. APS, which indicates the extent to which economies of scale in aircraft size have been achieved, was given by the number of available seats on the city pair divided by the number of departures. On the other hand, LF, which was measured by the number of revenue passengers on the city pair as a fraction of the number of available seats, determines the efficiency of the aircraft. DEN was calculated by the number of revenue passengers flying nonstop on the city pair. It indicates the degree of realization of economies of scale and scope, such as those in advertising and utilization of airport facilities, on a city pair, Hurdle et al. employed some value judgement to define an incumbent and to identify LPEs/OCs.

Two different types of concentration indices were used. One is the incumbent's Herfindahl-Hirschman function I_H and the other is adjusted I_H which also incorporates the number of OCs. This adjusted function is given by $I_{AH} = 1/[(1/I_H) + OC]$. Incumbents' market shares were measured according to their capacities using available seats. Three additional structural variables were used to capture the effects of (a) competition from commuter carriers, (b) competition from carriers offering only connecting service and (c) possible entry deterrence from slot constraints. These variables were interacted with I_H or I_{AH} because they are expected to influence yields when concentration is high. For (a) a dummy variable 'COMM' was used to indicate whether there was at least one commuter on the city pair. For (b), 'proportion of passengers originating and terminating on the city pair that fly on one plane-proportion of single plane (PSP)' was considered. In the case of (c), a dummy variable 'SLOT' taking the value one if either end point of the city pair was slot constrainted has been considered.

Hurdle et al. estimated four linear regressions. We consider the one that contained all the structural variables:

$$\begin{aligned} YIELD \;=\; & \beta_0 + \beta_1 I_H + \beta_2 I_H \times PSP + \beta_3 I_H \times SLOT + \beta_4 I_H \times COMM \\ & + \beta_5 I_{AH} + \beta_6 I_{AH} \times PSP + \beta_7 I_{AH} \times SLOT + \beta_8 I_{AH} \times COMM \\ & + \beta_9 log DIST + \beta_{10} APS + + \beta_{11} LF + \beta_{12} log DEN. \end{aligned} \quad (5.14)$$

We reject contestability if we reject the null hypothesis associated with the regression (5.14) where the null hypothesis states that the effect of structural variables on yields is zero. Contestability has been rejected by the data. The most powerful structural explanatory variable was the modified measure of concentration I_{AH} that incorporates the number and size distribution of incumbents and also the number of potential entrants not significantly deterred by economies of scope or scale. As Hurdle et al. argued these findings focus new light on the policy debate whether threat of entry can be expected to ensure competition to a reasonable extent despite a high degree of incumbent concentration.

Structure and performance in the airline industry have also been studied by Graham, Kaplan and Sibley (1983), Bailey, Graham and Kaplan (1985), Call and Keeler (1985), Moore (1986) and Morrison and Winston (1987). In most of these studies it was observed that there is a modest increase in fares as concentration increases. Borenstein (1985) presents evidence that concentration at a city (rather than on a particular route between two cities) can also lead to modest increase in fares. But threat of entry was considered only by Morrison and Winston (1987). Hurdle et al.'s treatment of this subject is, however, more extensive.

The next industry we consider is the U.S. banking industry. Several studies have attempted to examine the relationship between concentration and measures of performance of banks, such as interest on loans, prices for providing some services (see Gilbert (1984) for a survey). It has been observed in many cases that with increase in market concentration bank performance increases, though the extent of increase in performance is quite small. Amel and Liang (1990) looked at the interesting problem of dynamics of market concentration in U.S. banking. Data for over 2000 U.S. local banking over 1966-86 have been examined. It was found that long run equilibrium market concentration depends significantly on variables measuring the attractiveness of markets for entry. Examples of such variables are market size, measured in bank deposits; market per capita income; population growth in the market; variability in per capita income and geographic location of the market (whether rural or urban). Over longer time periods the equilibrium concentration depends on legal barriers to entry into banking markets. Over twenty years, market structure (concentration) adjusted only 45 to 55 per cent of the distance to its equilibrium level. (See Levy (1985) and Geroski et al. (1987) for similar findings for industrial sector.) Their results demonstrate that entry and other competitive forces tend to decrease above normal profits in local banking markets, but the process is slow.

As mentioned earlier, finally we will be concerned with an analysis of the Indian motor vehicle industry. Employing Tobins q as the performance measure, an analysis of the Indian motor vehicle industry for the period 1966-67 to 1986-87 was done by Agarwal (1991). During this period several policy changes related to this industry took place. Major policy changes were removal of price control, import liberalization, modernization and removal of entry barriers. Due to the nature of the products and different government policy measures, the study was divided into two sectors, viz., the car sector and noncar sector. A linear regression was specified to estimate q using market share, market concentration, sales, advertisement intensity, vertical integration and government policy dummy variables. More precisely,

$$q = \alpha + \beta_1 MS + \beta_2 CCN + \beta_3 logSALES + \beta_4 VI + \beta_5 ADV + \beta_6 RD + \beta_7 I_{75} + \beta_8 I_{82}, \tag{5.15}$$

where due to nonavailability of replacement cost of assets, q was approximated by the ratio between the market value of firms and sales; and MS = market shares of a firm in a particular sector (defined as the ratio of sales of the firm to the aggregate sales in the sector); CCN = Herfindahl-Hirschman concentration index; VI = vertical integration (measured as the ratio of the value added to sales of the firm in the year); ADV = advertisement intensity (defined as the ratio of advertisement expenditures to sales in a year); RD = Research and development expenditure divided by sales in a year; I_{75} = 0 1975 onwards and = 1 during 1967 to 1975; I_{82} = 0 1982 onwards and = 1 during 1967 to 1982. The two dummies I_{75} and I_{82} were introduced to represent government policy measures. I_{75} indicates the government policy of removal of price control on cars and other medium and heavy commercial vehicles and I_{82} indicates the government policy of removal of entry barriers, modernization and import liberalization in the automobile industry.

The coefficients of the two important explanatory variables, viz., sales and the government policy dummy variables turned out to be negative in both sectors. Demand shifting factors like advertisement and RD were found to improve profit in the car sector and in the noncar sector advertising intensity was found to improve profit due to rivalry among leading firms. The government policy in 1980s might have improved profitability but extraneous factors like improved performance of the Indian Railways adversely affected the performance of the motor vehicle industry.

We wind up this discussion by mentioning that several attempts have been made to study profitability concentration relationship at firm level. For instance, Mueller (1986) designed oligopolistic cooperation directly. He assumed that firm i maximizes $\pi_i + \alpha \sum_{j \neq i} \pi_j$, where π_i is the profit of firm i and α is the degree of importance that firm i attaches to the profits of other firms. Data for 551 major U.S. corporations were used to estimate the extent to which cooperation varies with market concentration. He observed that for four-firm concentration ratio above .24 increases in market concentration reduced the degree of cooperation and for concentration below .24 a reverse situation emerged. This gives us a picture of the level of interdependence/rivalry among firms. Martin (1988b) used U.S. data for 1973 to estimate the Lerner indices for firms in the hospital supply and motor vehicle industries. Since these are highly concentrated industries and are characterized by high degree of product differentiation large firms were expected to possess some degree of market power. Martin's empirical analysis provides a clear indication of this. (See also Gale (1972), Shephard (1972), Lindeberg and Ross (1981), Ravenschraft (1983), Harris (1984) and Martin (1988a) for further firm level studies.)

Structure performance relationship: an evaluation from Chicago School's viewpoint

The empirical results presented so far in this chapter indicate that in many cases market concentration and industry profitability are related in a positive monotonic way. In the words of Peltzman (1977, p.229) 'With few exceptions, market concentration and industry profitability are positively correlated'. However, proper interpretation of these results still remains a matter of dispute. In particular, Demsetz (1973a, 1974) and other representatives of the Chicago School[2] began to question the interpretation of these results. They argued that rather than concentration/ market power leading to higher price and profits, the causal direction in fact runs from greater efficiency to both higher profits and incidentally to higher concentration.

The Chicago School does not deny a positive relationship between concentration and profits. Demsetz (1974) argued that '.... some products are more efficiently produced by firms possessing a large share of the market ..... These firms can produce at lower unit costs than smaller firms. They are superior in this respect, and they command an economic rent for achieving primacy. This rent will be measured as profit by accountants' (op cit., pp. 176-177). '..... This supposes that some industries become concentrated because one or more firms have a strong efficiency advantage over their competitors. It is this greater efficiency which leads to the concentration of a large part of the market within the hands of those leading firms and also to greater profitability' (Clarke, Davies and Waterson (1984, p. 436).

On the question of identification of industries that will be concentrated in confirmation with efficiency hypothesis, Demsetz (1973a) argued that an industry can become concentrated under competitive conditions only when 'a differential advantage in expanding output develops in some firms. .... The cost advantage that gives rise to increased concentration may be reflected in scale economies or in downward shifts in positively sloped marginal cost curves, or it may be reflected in better products which satisfy demand at lower costs' (op cit., p. 1). The efficiency interpretation of the positive relationship between market concentration and rate of return now runs as follows. Firms with scale advantages will make higher return per unit because of lower costs. Industry average rate of return will be dominated by large firms' rates of return. Hence industry average rate of return will increase with the degree of concentration[3].

Demsetz (1973a) carried out an empirical test to compare profitability among large and small firms. A general tendency for the rate of return to increase with concentration of large firms was observed. (The concentration index employed for this purpose was the four-firm concentration ratio.) However, no such evidence was observed for small firms. Demsetz interpreted this result as supporting the efficiency hypothesis, arguing that if concentration represents greater efficiency of large firms in contrast to collusion then only large firms will earn higher rates of return in concentrated industries. In the case of concentration representing collusion both small and large firms will earn higher rates of return in concentrated industries. But Bain (1951) noted in his data that '.... the dominant firms in general had earnings rates that were positively influenced by concentration' (op cit., p. 320). This was confirmed by Collins and Preston (1969). Therefore, the Demsetz test depends on a version of the concentration market power hypothesis.

Next, identification of high profits of large firms with efficiency is inappropriate, because their higher efficiency would imply higher profits, but the reverse implication need not hold. This becomes evident if we consider an industry where large firms produce no more cheaply than small firms, but enjoy some nonefficiency oriented advantages (for example, product differentiation or first mover advantages), which allow them to earn higher profits.

The Chicago School regards economies of large scale production and product differentiation advantages of established over potential entrant firms as natural barriers to entry. According to Bork (1978) natural barriers to entry exist 'when existing firms are efficient and possess valuable plants, equipment, knowledge, skill and reputation. (Therefore,) potential entrants will find it correspondingly more difficult to entry the industry, since they must acquire those things' (op cit., p. 310). In this framework these problems to take entry into a market are considered as (natural and) competitive in nature. It views such disadvantages as a form of inefficiency not as a barrier to entry (Bork (1978)).

Clarke, Davies and Waterson (1984) adopted a formulation which is sufficiently general to allow for alternative explanations of a positive concentration profitability correlation. Following Clarke and Davies (1982), they considered an industry of n firms producing a homogeneous good. Assuming that the industry conjectural variation q_i of firm i is of the form $1 + \alpha \sum_{j \neq i}(x_j/x_i)$, the Lerner index of monopoly power of firm i becomes

$$L_i = \frac{\alpha}{\epsilon} + \frac{(1-\alpha)s_i}{\epsilon}, \tag{5.16}$$

where ϵ is the absolute value of the price elasticity of demand and α is the collusive parameter. Then multiplying (5.16) throughout by s_i, the output share of firm i, and summing across firms under the assumption that for each firm marginal and average variable costs coincide, we get:

$$\frac{\pi}{R} = \frac{\alpha}{\epsilon} + \frac{(1-\alpha)}{\epsilon} I_H^m, \tag{5.17}$$

where π/R is the industry profit revenue ratio and I_H^m is the Herfindahl-Hirschman index.

This model will allow us to formalize alternative hypotheses regarding concentration profitability in a simple way. Consider, first the case where industries are free from collusion. This corresponds to the case $\alpha = 0$. It is then evident from (5.17) that industry profitability and concentration are positively related. This is same as what Demsetz predicts. Furthermore, from (5.16) we see that within each industry profitability is directly proportional to output shares. This again supports the Demsetz argument that there are larger profit rates for large firms.

Now, we turn to the alternative view:if concentration facilitates collusion, then higher concentration leads to higher industry profits (small firms as well as large firms should earn higher rates of return in concentrated industries). This view can be accommodated in the above model under the assumption that $0 < \alpha \leq 1$ and $\delta\alpha/\delta\Gamma_H^n > 0$. Since industry profitability is increasing in α, this is also compatible with a positive profitability concentration relationship across industries. In view of equation (5.16), it is still true that larger firms earn higher profits, but the relationship now becomes flatter as the degree of collusion, that is, α increases.

It will now be interesting to look at the impact of product differentiation and scale economies on within industry profitability/output share relation. Clarke, Davies and Waterson (1984) introduced product differentiation by supposing that each of the n firms produces a different brand selling at price p_i. The extent of differentiation is reflected by the value of the parameter k in

$$\frac{\delta p_i}{\delta x_j} = k\frac{\delta p_i}{\delta x_i}, \quad 0 \leq k \leq 1. \tag{5.18}$$

The parameter k represents the degree of closeness in the way consumers regard various brands available in the market. A higher value of k will indicate a higher degree of similarity across brands. Since product prices may now vary across firms, we redefine the market share of firm i as $s_i = p_i x_i / \sum_{j=1}^{n} p_j x_j$. Consequently, the definition of collusive parameter will be modified as :

$$\frac{dx_j}{dx_i} = \alpha\frac{s_j}{s_i}, 0 \leq \alpha \leq 1. \tag{5.19}$$

Firm $i's$ profit and first order condition for profit maximization are, respectively:

$$\pi_i = p_i x_i - c_i x_i \tag{5.20}$$

and

$$\frac{d\pi_i}{dx_i} = p_i + x_i[\frac{\delta p_i}{\delta x_i} + \sum_{j\neq i}\frac{\delta p_j}{\delta x_j}.\frac{dx_j}{dx_i}] = c_i, \tag{5.21}$$

where c_i is its marginal as well as the average variable costs of production. Inserting (5.18) and (5.19) into (5.21), firm i's price cost margin as a proportion its price is

$$\frac{p_i - c_i}{p_i} = \frac{1}{s_i \epsilon_i}[\alpha k + (1 - \alpha)k s_i], \tag{5.22}$$

129

where ϵ_i is the absolute value of firm i's own price elasticity of demand. The weighted average of margins in (5.22), where the weights are market shares of different firms, yields the industry profit revenue ratio as

$$\frac{\pi}{R} = \sum_i \frac{1}{\epsilon_i}[\alpha k + (1-\alpha k)s_i]. \qquad (5.23)$$

Equation (5.23) has some similarity with that in (5.17), instead of αk in the latter we have α in the former. In (5.23) similarity of brands indicates the same signal as collusion. This seems intuitively reasonable, since α is a measure of the extent to which firms' product decisions move together and k measures the degree of closeness among products.

Evidently, from (5.22) we cannot conclude that high market share of a firm will generate high profit for it. Similarly, (5.23) need not imply a positive monotonic relationship between industry profitability and concentration. Without further information on the firm demand curve, no definite conclusion can be drawn regarding the Demsetz effect. We therefore consider a special case where $s_i\epsilon_i$ is same for all firms. The product differentiation assumption (5.18) along with this implies

$$x_i = A_i + B/p_i - k\sum_{j\neq i} x_j, \qquad (5.24)$$

where $s_i\epsilon_i = \sum_j p_j x_j/B = R/B$. In this special case

$$\frac{p_i - c_i}{p_i} = \frac{R}{B}[\alpha k + (1-\alpha k)s_i] \qquad (5.25)$$

and

$$\frac{\pi}{R} = \frac{R}{B}[\alpha k + (1-\alpha k)I_H^n]. \qquad (5.26)$$

From (5.25) and (5.26) we observe that 'within industry variations in profitability still provide qualitatively the same evidence on the market power versus efficiency hypothesis, but quantitatively the relative importance of the market power effect will be understated where differentiation is pronounced (k low)' (Clarke, Davies and Waterson (1984, p. 442)).

On the question of effect of scale economies on efficiency, one might argue following Scherer (1980) that in industries with pronounced scale economies, since large firms are further along the same scale curve, they can be regarded as more efficient and consequently they earn more profits. Loosely speaking, this argument supports a Demsetz view even though the large firms are not on lower cost curves. According to Clarke, Davies and Waterson (1984) if all firms in the industry are able to reach the same scale curve, then a choice of less sensible points by some will provide a manifestation of inefficiency and they argue that this can be represented by different levels of short run costs as in model (5.16).

Using U.K. data, Clarke, Davies and Waterson found no evidence that differences between large and small firm profitability are larger in highly concentrated industries. This finding contrasts some results obtained by Demsetz for the U.S. and is in conflict with the predictions he made had the efficiency explanation been valid. Round (1975) found a positive relation between concentration and differences between profitability of large and small firms in Australia, though Neuman, Bobel and Haid (1979) reported exactly opposite results for Germany. Westbrook and Tybout (1993) used plant level panel data from Chile (1979-86) to address whether efficiency causes plant growth. They could not conclude anything about the presence of the Demsetz effect.

According to Weiss (1974, 1991) the most natural way of discriminating the Bain hypothesis from the Demsetz view was to include both concentration and market share in the same equation. Results using specifications of this type support that in samples of U.S. firms market share is strongly correlated with profitability, the coefficient of concentration is generally negative and insignificant. Examples include Bothwell and Keeler (1976), Gale and Branch (1982), Martin (1983), Ravenschraft (1983), Bothwell, Cooley and Hall (1984), Harris (1984), Smirlock, Gilligan and Marshall (1984), Schmalensee (1985), Smirlock (1985), Mueller (1986), Ross (1986) and Kessides (1987). Shepherd (1974) and Thomadakis (1977) reported positive coefficients for both market share and concentration. However, Neuman, Bobel and Haid (1979) found a positive and significant coefficient for concentration and significant negative coefficient for share for German data.

Many within particular manufacturing industry studies found that profitability is not generally strongly related to market share. Examples include here, Clarke, Davies and Waterson (1984) for the U.K. and Collins and Preston (1969), Comanor and Wilson (1974), Cattin and Wittink (1976), Porter (1979), Caves and Pugel (1980), Daskin (1983) and Schmalensee (1987) for the U.S. These within industry findings suggest that strong correlation between market share and profitability for U.S. firms might be the consequence of dominance of small number of industries with very strong positive relations between share and profitability. (See Schmalensee (1989)).

We conclude this part with a brief discussion on Chicago School's view on deconcentration of industries. Demsetz (1974) argued that in view of deconcentration of an industry 'considerable economies of large scale production or other advantages of large firms would be lost with no compensation in the form of lower prices' (op cit., p. 179). In Bork's (1978) opinion internal growth of a firm occurs because of superior efficiency. Therefore, efficiency loss will take place as a result of dissolution of any such firm. Posner (1979) looked at the practical problem of divestiture of industries. According to Posner 'Any proceeding to deconcentrate an industry by reorganizing the major firms into smaller units would probably be cumbersome, protracted and indeed unmanageable' (op cit., p. 966). The arguments presented above in favor of deconcentration are correct. But it should also be noted that maintenance of dominant positions is a clear indication of the attitude that the large firms be allowed to exercise high market power. We looked at the consequences of this in Chapter 2.

Concluding remarks

We began this chapter with a discussion of different measures of industry performance. We then looked at the links between industrial structure (concentration) and different measures of performance. The empirical studies report mixed results on the relationship between performance and structure. Often it is argued that large firms are large because they are more efficient. This view has been compared with the structure performance paradigm. Arguments have also been put forward in the literature in favor of industry and firm level studies to get a more accurate picture of the performance of organizations. We presented a short discussion on this view also.

A remarkable finding of Bain (1951) which has been discussed in the literature to some extent is the emergence of a critical concentration ratio in the relationship between industry profitability and concentration. It is argued that concentration has an impact on profitability only if it rises above a certain level. A plausible theoretical reasoning behind this argument is that an industry may take a switch from noncooperative to cooperative behavior once the dominance of a few large firms is established. Inserting this hypothesis into an equation like (5.8) will imply that profitability rises with concentration up to some level and then there is a discontinuous jump. Some evidence for a relation of this form has been observed in a number of U.S. studies (see, for example, Rhoades and Cleaver (1973), Dalton and Penn (1976), White (1976) and Kwoka (1979)). In White's specification of the model there is a dummy variable which takes the value zero up to a critical level of four (eight) - firm concentration ratio and and then it becomes one after that level. Dalton and Penn, in addition to introducing the dummy variable, investigated whether a significant change in slope at the critical concentration occurs in the estimated model. Rhoades and Cleaver (1973) have identified a critical ratio after which a systematic positive association of profitability with concentration occurred which did not show up before that level. Bradburd and Over (1982) have identified two critical concentration ratios in the profitability concentration relationship. Geroski (1981) indicated that for U.K. data critical concentration ratio hypothesis does not perform better than the hypothesis of a linear relation.

So far we have mainly discussed whether concentrated industries, on an average, are more profitable than unconcentrated industries. Features other than profitability also distinguish concentrated industries from unconcentrated ones. Some such features are unionization, Research and Development (R and D), capital intensity, prices and cost.

The empirical literature in labor economics has tended to consider the extent of union participation in an industry as being endogenous to market concentration. Focus has been made on those market structure characteristics, such as human capital, market concentration, capital intensity and the size of establishments, which are conductive to participation in unions. Market concentration has been hypothesized to exert a positive influence on union participation. Since organizing workers in concentrated industries involve less costs than organizing workers in unconcentrated industries, concentrated industries become targets for unionization. Furthermore, an incentive exists for organizing a union to capture at least some of the rents that more concentrated industries are able to earn over a fairly long period of time. Weiss (1966) observed that wage rates were positively related to both concentration and unionization in the U.S.A. in 1959. (Phlips (1971) also found positive relation between wages and concentration in Belgium, France and Italy.) Because the demand for labor in concentrated industries is less elastic than that in unconcentrated industries (Hirsch and Addison (1986)), the ability of a union to organize and succeed in obtaining subsequent wage increase is greater in concentrated industries. But it has also been observed that concentrated industries employ more educated and trained workers. Weiss (1966) found that when such differing characteristics between concentrated and unconcentrated industries are added to his regression unionization effect became very weak. Some studies show that there is a significant negative impact of unionization on profits of highly concentrated industries. (See, for example, U.S. studies by Freeman (1983) and Voos and Mishel (1986). Audretsch and Schulenburg (1990) used U.S. data from manufacturing industries to examine the union participation problem in a simultaneous framework and the effect of concentration on unionization was not found to be significant.) However, Domowitz, Hubbard and Petersen (1986a) who used 1958-81 panel data set for U.S. manufacturing found no support for the view that unionization increase has a significant negative impact on profits of highly concentrated industries (see also Clark (1984)). Salinger's (1984) interactive specification found that unions capture all of a firm's monopoly rents. See Ashenfelter and Johnson (1972), Kahn (1972), Haworth and Reuther (1978), Caves, Porter and Spence (1980), Lee (1980), Hirsch and Berger (1984), Miller (1984), Karier (1985), Connolly et al. (1986), Dickens and Katz (1986) and Hirsch and Link (1986) for further discussions.

Another feature through which a concentrated industry can be differentiated from an unconcentrated one is capital intensity. Unconcentrated industries appear to have lower capital output ratios than concentrated industries (Carlton and Perloff (1990)). The precise reason behind this relationship is not well understood. Highly concentrated industries with high capital intensity will adjust more slowly than unconcentrated industries - it is difficult to adjust capital stock than labor force. This has been argued to be one of the reasons that are responsible for the slow rate at which profits rates in concentrated industries are driven to competitive levels (see Stigler (1963), Mueller

(1986)). Since measures of MES derived from the size distribution of plants do not often correctly represent the smallest plant that can operate efficiently, Ornstein, Weston, Intriligator and Shrieves (1973) argued that capital labor ratio is a better indicator of the underlying technology (see also Collins and Preston (1969), Caves and Uekusa (1976)).

A discussion on concentration innovation relationship has been presented in Chapter 1. Additionally, it may be interesting to note that, according to Schumpter (1950) innovative activity is more promoted in markets characterized by imperfect competition, which would enable large firms to capture the economic rents accruing from innovation. In fact, there is no strong support for the Schumpeterian position. Connolly and Hirschey (1984) and Mansfield (1981) found a negative relationship between R and D expenditures and concentration, but Scherer (1965) found that the number of patented inventions is only slightly related to the degree of concentration.

However, the relationship between market concentration and proxy measures of innovation is affected by the technological opportunity class of the industry. In industries characterized by low technology opportunity class (for example, industries producing material inputs and consumer goods), a positive relationship between concentration and R and D intensity generally emerges (Scherer (1967), Globerman (1973), Shrieves (1978)). In contrast, Angelmar (1985) identified a positive relationship between concentration and technical change in high technology opportunity class industries (for example, those producing specialized durable equipment), only when necessary R and D was expensive and there were no barriers to imitation. Several studies have also examined the intensity of R and D on profitability. Despite the contrary results obtained by Martin (1983) some studies (see, for example, Salinger (1984) and Hirschey (1985)) reported that in U.S. manufacturing industries, R and D intensity is positively related to profitability.

Instead of looking at profitability some investigations attempted to analyze primitive components of profitability:prices and costs. The price concentration relationship has been studied in several markets. In general, a positive correlation has been reported in cross sectional comparisons involving markets in the same industry. This relation seems to be more robust than profitability concentration relationship. Some time series studies did not find a positive correlation between changes in concentration and changes in costs. (See Schmalensee (1989) for references to specific case studies.)

We now discuss some general limitations which may be applicable to many of the studies we have reviewed in the chapter. Quite often approximations are made regarding measurement of entry barriers and performance. Such approximations in many cases are unlikely to give the true pictures of the measures. For instance, measurement of entry barriers is often subjective. Since calculation of Tobin's q requires knowledge of market value and replacement cost of a firm's assets, serious measurement problems may arise. Inaccurate calculation of capital cost will generate error in the measurement of rate of return. Knowledge of marginal cost is necessary for calculating the Lerner index and so on. Continuity will give rise to small changes in different measures when observational errors are small. But continuity cannot take care of the errors arising out of approximations.

Sometimes it is argued that concentration in an industry is not the proper variable for explaining industrial performance. We have already demonstrated in Chapter 2 that 'concentration and profitability are jointly determined by the exogenous variables of the system, among which are the expectations adopted by firms concerning their rivals. In this sense indexes of concentration are not measures that allow the prediction of performances on the basis of causal relationship .....' (Jacquemin (1987, p. 62)). This suggests that concentration and performance are interrelated and they need to be explained simultaneously.

Notes

1. This is defined as the increment in value added, made possible by the tariff structure, as a proportion of the free trade value added. Formally, the effective rate of protection is given by $(t - ai)/(1 - a)$, where t is the nominal tariff rate on the final commodity, a is the ratio of the value of the imported input to the value of the final commodity and i is the nominal tariff rate on the imported input. Thus, if under free trade a good which sells at Rs.100 uses imported inputs worth Rs.50, the domestic value added is Rs.50. If a ten per cent tariff is imposed on import of the good, the nominal tariff rate is ten per cent. If the imported inputs remain free of duty, the effective rate of tariff protection will be 20 per cent since the good produced domestically will now sell at Rs.110, which represents an increment of Rs.10 on free trade value added of Rs.50. The effective rate exceeds the nominal rate because the ten per cent rate effectively applies to only half the inputs used in the good, namely those which are supplied domestically . It is possible for the effective protection rate to be negative, if the imported inputs are subject to higher rates of duty than the final good. Though the nominal rate of protections will always be positive, an industry can be 'antiprotected' by the tariff structure and end up with a negative effective rate.

2. Chicago, in the present context, signifies a school of thought, rather than a geographic location. (Important recent work in this tradition took place in Los Angeles, Massachusetts and Chicago.)

3. Jovanovic (1982) has formalized the argument in a dynamic learning model in which firms discover their efficiencies through market experience and eventually expand or exit.

6 The size distribution of firms

We have already noted in Chapters 1 and 5 that economic theories try to explain concentration in terms of mechnisms inherent in the market economy. However, stochastic models take an entirely different view. These models are generated from the perspective that the growth of firms is a purely stochastic phenomenon resulting from the cumulative effect of the chance operations of many factors acting independently. Given specific assumptions about the stochastic model under consideration, a particular distribution explains the size distribution of firms in the sense that it is the limiting outcome of the stochastic process which generates the birth, growth and decline of individual firms. Since such limiting outcomes are usually highly positively skewed, we can say that within a given population of firms there will be an increase in concentration in the limiting situation. The intuitive reasoning behind this is that alllthough initially all firms face the 'same distribution of growth possibilities in proportionate terms' (Curry and Geroge (1983, p. 233)), some firms will have better luck than others. This implies that at the end of the first period these lucky firms will jump ahead of the other firms. At the end of the second period, the already large firms will become larger, again due to chance factors. In this way, in the ultimate situation, a small number of firms will attain dominant positions. Stochastic models, therefore, are capable of explaining the reason for emerging highly skewed distributions. Contributions along this line came from Gibrat (1931), Kalecki (1945), Champernowne (1953), Simon (1955), Hart and Prais (1956), Aitchison and Brown (1957), Simon and Bonini (1958), Hart (1962, 1982), Hymer and Pashigian (1962), Ijiri and Simon (1964, 1971), Archer and Maguire (1965), Samuels (1965), Steindl (1965), Singh and Whittington (1968, 1975), Scherer (1970), Utton (1971), Samuels and Chesher (1972), Hannah and Kay (1977), Chesher (1979), Curry and George (1983), Waterson (1984), Hay and Morris (1991) and many others. The stochastic approaches to the explanation of the size distribution of firms are taken up more explicitly in the next part of this chapter.

From the above discussion it is evident that the stochastic process theories attribute the observed pattern of the size distribution of firms entirely to the operation of the laws of chance. In an interesting paper, Lucas (1978) argued that the size distribution of firms should make use of a hypothesis of some optimizing behavior on the part of the firms. He proposed a new theory which postulates a distribution of persons by managerial talent and then studies the division of persons into managers and employees and the allocation of productive factors in an output maximizing way across managers. We discuss this approach in detail in this chapter.

An alternative approach to generate the distribution of firms is the determination of output distribution across firms that minimizes concentration subject to the constraints that (i) a fixed total output is produced by the industry and (ii) the total cost of producing the output is given (Chakravarty (1989)). The second constraint is adopted to hold the resources available to the industry constant, which is appropriate in a partial equilibrium evaluation. Clearly, the output distribution we determine here is the optimal distribution in a second best framework. This framework is one in which a policy maker has direct control over the distribution of output but not ever resources available to the industry. This approach is elaborated in the present chapter. We conclude the chapter with some remarks.

The stochastic models

The stochastic approaches to the size distribution of firms have been discussed in many places including Hannah and Kay (1977), Curry and George (1983) and Hay and Morris (1991). For completeness of this chapter we briefly explain some of the important results.

Gibrat (1931) was the first to advance the line of thought that the growth of firms might be explained by a stochastic process[1]. He proposed the 'law of proportionate effect', which generates a positively skewed distribution. According to the law of proportionate effect the change in the size measure of a firm at any step is a random proportion of the previous value of its size. That is, if z_t denotes the size measure of a firm at time t, then

$$z_t - z_{t-1} = \epsilon_t z_{t-1}. \tag{6.1}$$

By repeated use of (6.1) we have,

$$log z_t = log z_o + \sum_{j=1}^{t} log(1 + \epsilon_j), \tag{6.2}$$

where z_o is the initial size of the firm. Now, if z_o and the sequence $1 + \epsilon_j$ are assumed to be independent and identically distributed with mean μ and variance σ^2, then for large t, by central limit theorem z_t follows a lognormal distribution (see equation (1.52)).

Letting $U_t = log z_t$ for all $t \geq 0$ and $log(1+\epsilon_j) = \delta_j$ for all $j \geq 1$, we rewrite (6.2) as

$$U_t = U_o + \sum_{j=1}^{t} \delta_j. \qquad (6.3)$$

Under independence and identical distribution assumptions we have $Var(U_t) = Var(U_o) + t\sigma^2$, where Var denotes the variance.

Thus, the outcome of this stochastic process is a variance that rises steadily over time. Therefore, if the variance is regarded as an indicator of concentration, then the model implies rising concentration also. (See Chapter 1 for a discussion on the appropriateness of the variance as a concentration index in the lognormal case.)

A systematic relationship between size and growth can also be analyzed. (See Kalecki (1945). See Also Hart and Prais (1956).) Assume a simple linear relationship between logarithms of growth and logarithms of firm size, so that $U_t = \beta U_{t-1} + (1-\beta)\bar{U} + \delta_t$, where $\bar{U}$ is a constant. Then it can be shown by induction that

$$U_t = \bar{U} + \delta_t + \beta^2 \delta_{t-1} + \beta^t \delta_{t-2} + \ldots \beta^t \delta_o. \qquad (6.4)$$

Thus, U_t remains as the sum of independent and identically distributed random variables $\{\delta_t\}$ and the distribution again tends to lognormality. In this model, under certain assumptions, concentration still increases but at a decreasing rate.

We can also model serial correlation of growth rates. For example, if

$$U_t = U_{t-1} + \alpha(U_{t-1} - U_{t-2}) + \nu_t, \qquad (6.5)$$

then the fraction α indicates the degree of persistence of growth rates between two consecutive periods. In such a case

$$U_t = \nu_t + (1+\alpha)\nu_{t-1} + (1+\alpha+\alpha^2)\nu_{t-2} + \ldots + (1+\alpha+\alpha^2+\ldots+\alpha^t)\nu_o \qquad (6.6)$$

and the outcome will still be a lognormal distribution. The variance of the resulting distribution will depend on α. For $\alpha > 0$, rapid growth in period $(t-1)$ will make rapid growth in period t more likely. Consequently, a more quick increase in concentration is expected.

Champernowne (1953) considered a variant of the law of proportionate effect. He replaces the equal growth assumption by the formulation that the probability that a firm will grow from size class i to size class $(i+j)$ depends on the difference between the relative positions of classes i and $(i+j)$. These two formulations are equivalent if and only if the way in which firms within a particular size class are distributed is the same.

To discuss the Champernowne model more explicitly suppose that the size measure above a certain minimum level z_o is divisible into an infinite number of classes. The ith class given by (z_{i-1}, z_i) satisfies the assumption $z_i = \theta z_{i-1}$. That is, the end points of size classes are equidistant on logarithmic scale.

Let $\rho_t(i,j)$ be the transition probability that a firm belonging to class i at time t will be in class (i+j) at t+1. Then

$$\sum_{j=-(i-1)}^{\infty} \rho_t(i,j) = 1, \qquad (6.7)$$

which means that a firm in class i at time t will be in one of the classes 1,2,3, ..., ∞ with probability 1 (i.e., with certainty). Denote the probability that at time t a firm will be in class i by $\rho_t(i)$. The size distribution $\rho_{t+1}(k)$ at $(t+1)$ will be generated by

$$\rho_{t+1}(k) = \sum_{l=-\infty}^{k-1} \rho_t(k-l)\rho_t(k-l,l). \qquad (6.8)$$

This is referred to as tranisition euqation since it relates the firm size distribution at time $(t+1)$ with the distribution at time t through the transition probabilities $\rho_t(i,j)$.

Champernowne made certain assumptions to derive the equilibrium distribution. These are :
Assumption C.1 The number of firms is constant over time.
Assumption C.2 For each t and i and for some given integer q,

$$\rho_t(i,j) = 0 \qquad (6.9)$$

if $j > 1$ or $j < -q$, and

$$\rho_t(i,j) = a_j > 0 \qquad (6.10)$$

if $-q \leq j \leq 1$ and $j > i$.
Assumption C.3

$$\sum_{j=-q}^{1} j a_j < 0. \qquad (6.11)$$

Assumption C.1 is self explanatory. Equation (6.9) in assumption C.2 means that at any time period a firm cannot move up by more than 1 or down by more than q size classes. Equation (6.10) means that transition probabilities are independent of time and the initial size class i. It depends only the number of size classes (j) a firm can move in a single period. Since size classes are equidistant on a logarithmic scale, any given proportionate change becomes equiprobable at all levels of size measure. Finally, assumption C.3 implies that there should be general long run tendency for existing firms to shrink. Without such a condition the model would have no equilibrium distribution. This assumption technically means that for all size values, initially in any one of the classes $q+1, q+2, q+3, \ldots$, the expected number of classes shifted during the next time period is negative.

Let $\rho_e(k)$ stand for the equilibrium distribution. Then (6.8) along with (6.10) becomes

$$\rho_e(k) = \sum_{j=-q}^{1} \rho_e(k-j) a_j \qquad (6.12)$$

for all $k > 1$ and $\rho_e(1) = \sum_{j=-q}^{o} \rho_e(1-j) h_j$ where $h_j = \sum_{v=-q}^{j} a_v$. Determination of $\rho_e(k)$ will require determination of a solution of (6.12). For this purpose, following Champernowne we substitute $\rho_e(k) = cb^k$ into (6.12) to get

$$g(b) = \sum_{j=-q}^{1} a_j b^{1-j} - b = 0, \qquad (6.13)$$

where g is a polynomial of degree $(q+1)$.

Now, Descartes' rule of sign shows that (6.13) has two real positive roots. One root is unity. For finding the second root, calculate $g'(b)$ from (6.13) at $b=1$ to get $g'(1) = -\sum_{j=-q}^{1} j a_j$, which in view of (6.11) is positive. Since $g(0) = a_1 > 0$, $g(1) = 0$ and $g'(1) > 0$, the second root will lie between zero and unity. Let this root be d. Then

$$\rho_e(k) = c_1 d^k, \qquad (6.14)$$

where the constant c_1 is such that the sum of probabilities becomes unity.

To establish the link between ρ_e in (6.14) and the underlying form of size distribution, let F be the cumulative distribution function. Then

$$\begin{aligned} 1 - F(z_k) &= \sum_{l=k}^{\infty} \rho_e(l) \\ &= c_1 \sum_{l=k}^{\infty} d^l \qquad (6.15) \\ &= c_1 d^k (1-d)^{-1}. \end{aligned}$$

Since $z_i = \theta z_{i-1}$ for all i, we have $z_k = \theta^k z_o$, where z_o is the minimum value of the size measure. We can transform $z_k = \theta^k z_o$ and (6.15) into logarithms to eliminate θ. It then turns out that

$$\log(1 - F(z_k)) = \log \frac{c_1}{1-d} + \alpha \log(\frac{z_o}{z_k}), \qquad (6.16)$$

where $\alpha = --\log d / \log \theta$. Since $0 < d < 1$, α is positive. Equation (6.16) is the Pareto law in its logarithmic form under the assumption that $log(c_1/(1-d)) = 0$ (see equation (1.50)). In fact $log(c_1/(1-d)) = 0$ ensures that the sum of probabilities in (6.14) will be unity.

Simon and Bonini (1958) adopted the assumption that the aggregate of firms in a particular size stratum has an expected percentage growth which is independent of size (see also Simon (1955); Ijiri and Simon (1964, 1971, 1974)). Clearly, this is a variant of the law of proportionate effect. All firms are assumed to possess same chance of disappearing. They deal with the birth of new firms by ensuring that the size of the market increases regularly by 1 'size unit' and with a given probability the additional size constitutes a new firm as opposed to an increase in the size of an existing firm. Similar assumptions are made to deal with the disappearance of firms. These assumptions will lead to the Yule distribution, the upper tail of which can be approximated by the Pareto function. Let $f(z)dz$ be the density function of firm of size z. Then the Yule distribution is given by

$$f(z) = AB(z, \rho + 1), \qquad (6.17)$$

where $A > 0$ is a coefficient of normalization and $B(z, \rho+1) = \int_0^1 t^{z-1}(1-t)^\rho dt$ is the Beta function of z and $\rho + 1$. As $z \to \infty$, $f(z) \to Mz^{-(\rho+1)}$, which is the Pareto function. The reasons for having Pareto distribution in the Champernowne and Simon and Bonini models are that in the case of the former we have a stability condition and in the latter case there are birth and death of firms.

Studies of actual size distributions in many countries concentrated mainly on the Pareto and the lognormal distributions. For the U.K. and the U.S.A. no particular model has been able to describe all industries well. For the U.S.A. in some earlier cases Gibrat's law has been verified but some recent studies report that mean growth rates decrease with firm size (see Schmalensee (1989)). In an earlier study Jacquemin and Saez (1976) showed that as far as the influence of size on the rate of growth is concerned, the myth of the bigger the better is supported neither by the giant Japanese firms, nor by their European counterparts. This, however, does not mean that stochastic attempts do not have any value. They generate size distributions very similar to those found in real world, although not uniformly. (See Waterson (1984), Hay and Morris (1991) for an illuminating discussion on relative merits and demerits of the stochastic approach.)

Managerial efficiency and the size distribution of firms

Lucas (1978) studied an implication of a suggestion of Manne (1965) that the observed size distribution of firms is a solution to the optimization problem : allocate resources over managers of different abilities in an output maximizing way. We briefly discuss the Lucas approach here. It becomes necessary to decide at the outset whether the model will be developed at the industry level or the economy wide level. Recognizing that there is multiproduct nature of many large firms and there may be mobility of managers across industries, it seems more appropriate to do the exercise at the level of the economy. We therefore consider a closed economy with a given workforce W and a given volume K of homogeneous capital, both of which are assumed to be inelastically supplied. Every member of the workforce is endowed with a capability m of managing which will vary over workers. A firm in this economy then consists of one manager and capital and labor under his control.

We consider seperately the production technology and managerial (entrepreneurial) technology. Let $f(l, k)$ be the output produced with l units of labor and k units of capital. Assume that this technology exhibits constant returns to scale so that $f(l, k) = l\phi(r)$, where $r = k/l$ and $\phi : D^1 \to R^1_+$ is increasing and strictly concave. Here D^1 and R^1_+ stand respectively for the positive and nonnegative parts of the set of real numbers R^1. Two elements are involved in managerial technology : variable skill or talent and an element of diminishing returns to scale. For the former we assume that an agent's endowment of managerial talent m is drawn from a fixed distribution $F : R^1_+ \to [0, 1]$. If agent with endowment m (agent m, for short) manages resources l and k, then his firm produces $mg[f(l, k)]$ units of output, where $g : R^1_+ \to R^1_+$ is increasing and strictly concave with $g(0) = 0$. Strict concavity of g ensures that there is diminishing returns to manager's span of control. This in turn implies that a distribution of resources across firms is desirable rather than one manager controlling everything.

Assume that there is a continuum of agents. Let $l(m)$ and $k(m)$ stand for labor and capital managed by agent m. If agent m is an employee, then $l(m) = k(m) = 0$ and for a manager both $l(m)$ and $k(m)$ are positive. Thus, we implicitly assume the existence of a cut off point $m_o > 0$ such that if $m < m_o$, one is an employee and he is a manager otherwise (that is, whenever $m \geq m_o$). By an allocation we then mean a number m_o and a pair of functions $l(m), k(m) : D^1 \to R^1_+$ such that $l(m) = k(m) = 0$ for $m < m_o$ and $l(m), k(m) > 0$ for $m \geq m_o$.

An allocation is feasible if

$$1 - F(m_o) + \int_{m_o}^{\infty} l(m) dF(m) \leq 1 \tag{6.18}$$

and

$$\int_{m_o}^{\infty} k(m) dF(m) \leq K/W. \tag{6.19}$$

Condition (6.18) means that the sum of the fraction of workforce engaged in managing and the fraction engaged as employees should not exceed one. Condition (6.19), on the other hand, means that the total utilization of capital cannot exceed its given volume.

An efficient allocation is one which maximizes average output :

$$\frac{T}{W} = \int_{m_o}^{\infty} mg[f(l(m), k(m)] dF(m) \tag{6.20}$$

with respect to (6.18) and (6.19), where T stands for the total volume of output produceable from K and W. Lucas shows that the efficient allocation will also be competitive equilibrium. Let p_l and p_k be the equilibrium wage rate and rental price of capital respectively. The income of manager m is the residual

$$mg[l(m), k(m)] - p_l l(m) - p_k k(m). \tag{6.21}$$

The first term in (6.21) is the value of output, with output serving as numeraire.

The first order conditions for the above maximization problem include:

$$mg'(f) f_l(l(m), k(m)) = p_l, m \geq m_o, \tag{6.22}$$

$$mg'(f) f_k(l(m), k(m)) = p_k, m \geq m_o, \tag{6.23}$$

where f_j is the partial derivative of f with respect to argument j, $j = l, k$. The above equations show that marginal products of factors are equated across firms. Since $f(l, k) = l\phi(r)$, where $r = k/l$, (6.22) and (6.23) imply

$$\frac{\phi(r) - r\phi'(r)}{\phi'(r)} = \frac{p_l}{p_k}. \tag{6.24}$$

Thus, given ratio of input prices, all firms face a common capital labor ratio $r(p_l/p_k)$. The function r is increasing.

Given r from (6.24), the equilibrium scale $l(m)$ of firm m can be obtained either from (6.22) or (6.23). Using (6.23)

$$mg'[l(m)\phi(r)]\phi'(r) = p_k, \tag{6.25}$$

which determines employment as an implicit function $l(m, p_l, p_k)$. This function is increasing in first two arguments and decreasing in p_k.

Now, to see that the above model predicts a particular relationship between the talent distribution and the size distribution of firms, solve (6.24) for r as a function of p_l/p_k and solve (6.25) for m:

$$m = \frac{p_k}{g'[l\phi(r)]\phi'(r)}. \tag{6.26}$$

Further, to incorporate pattern of growth of individual firms in the model, consider percentage rate of growth of employment in firm m

$$\frac{d}{dt} log[l(m, p_{l(t)}, p_k(t))] \tag{6.27}$$

and of assets

$$\frac{d}{dt} log[r(p_k(t), p_l(t)) l(m, p_l(t), p_k(t))], \tag{6.28}$$

where t denotes time.

As we have stated earlier a well known feature of observed pattern in firm growth is the independence of firm growth and size. This is Gibrat's law or the law of proportionate effect. In the present model Gibrat's law means that the derivatives of expressions (6.27) and (6.28) with respect to m (size) are zero. The two derivatives turn out to be the same. Therefore, without loss of generality we can develop the wage condition only. For this first differentiate (6.25) with respect to p_l and then solve for $l_{p_l}(m, p_l, p_k)$ to get

$$l_{p_l}(m, p_l, p_k) = -r_{p_l}(\frac{p_l}{p_k})\frac{g'(f)\phi''(r) + g''(f)[\phi'(r)]^2 l}{g''(f)\phi(r)\phi'(r)}, \qquad (6.29)$$

where l_{p_l} and r_{p_l} represent the partial derivatives of l and r respectively with respect to p_l. Dividing by $l(m, p_l, p_k)$ and differentiating with respect to m yields

$$\frac{\delta}{\delta m}\frac{l_{p_l}(m, p_l, p_k)}{l(m, p_l, p_k)} = -r_{p_l}(\frac{p_l}{p_k})\frac{\phi''(r)}{\phi(r)\phi'(r)} \cdot \frac{\delta}{\delta m}\frac{g'(f)}{lg''(f)}, \qquad (6.30)$$

recalling that r does not vary with m. Then (6.30) along with $\delta/\delta m$ ($l_{p_l}(m, p_l, p_k)/l(m, p_l, p_k)) = \delta/\delta m(l_{p_k}(m, p_l, p_k)/l(m, p_l, p_k)) = 0$, which follows from the fact that the derivatives of (6.27) and (6.28) with respect to m are zero, give

$$l_m(m, p_l, p_k)[l\phi(r)(g'')^2 - g'g'' - l\phi(r)g^{(3)}] = 0. \qquad (6.31)$$

Since $l_m > 0$ for all $m > m_o$, the bracketed term in (6.31) is zero.

We note that $l\phi(r)$ is just the argument of g and its derivatives. Therefore (6.31) gives the following differential equation

$$v[g''(v)]^2 - g'(v)g''(v) - vg'(v)g^{(3)}(v) = 0. \qquad (6.32)$$

whose solution is $g(v) = \alpha v^\beta$, where $\alpha > 0$ and $0 < \beta < 1$. With this form of g, from (6.25) we get

$$l(m, p_l, p_k) = \frac{1}{\phi(r)}[\frac{p_k}{\alpha\beta m\phi'(r)}]^{1/(\beta-1)}, \qquad (6.33)$$

where r is given by (6.24).

Now insert $l(m, p_l, p_k)$ from (6.33) and $k(m, p_l, p_k) = rl(m, p_l, p_k)$ into the constraints (6.18) and (6.19) to get

$$[\frac{p_k}{\alpha\beta\phi'(r)}]^{1/(\beta-1)}\frac{1}{\phi(r)}H(m_o) = F(m_o) \qquad (6.34)$$

and

$$rF(m_o) = \frac{K}{W}, \qquad (6.35)$$

where
$$H(m_o) = \int_{m_o}^{\infty} z^{1/(1-\beta)} dF(z). \tag{6.36}$$

Using Gibrat's law restriction $g(v) = \alpha v^\beta$ and (6.34), equation (6.26) turns out to be
$$m = \left(\frac{H(m_o)}{F(m_o)}\right)^{(1-\beta)} l^{(1-\beta)}. \tag{6.37}$$

The right hand side of (6.37) (or (6.26)) gives the level of talent m that will manage a firm with l employees at a given talent cut off m_o and per capita capital K/W.

Now, suppose $G(l)$ stands for the probability that randomnly selected firm will have less than l employees. Then under (6.37), $G(l)$ will be the probability that $m < (H/F)^{1-\beta} l^{1-\beta}$, where $m \geq m_o$. That is,
$$G(l) = \frac{F\left[\left(\frac{H(m_o)}{F(m_o)}\right)^{1-\beta} l^{1-\beta}\right] - F(m_o)}{1 - F(m_o)}, \tag{6.38}$$

for $l \geq (H(m_o)/F(m_o))^{1/(1-\beta)}$.

Note that, in view of (6.38), any stochastic approach leading to a particular form of F will have definite implications for G. This means that statistical and economic approaches need not be regarded as alternatives, but can be considered as complementary. Let F be a Pareto type distribution function:
$$F(m) = 1 - B^\rho m^{-\rho}, m \geq B, \tag{6.39}$$

where $B < m_o$. Then (6.38) implies that
$$G(l) = 1 - m_o^\rho \left(\frac{H(m_o)}{F(m_o)}\right)^{-\rho(1-\beta)} l^{-\rho(1-\beta)} \tag{6.40}$$

for $l \geq (F(m_o)/H(m_o)) m_o^{1/(1-\beta)}$. 'An advantage of this combined statistical and economic motivation of a Pareto distribution of firm sizes is that there is a clear motivation for the value of minimal size firm' (Lucas (1978, p. 519)). We note that the arbitrarily selected number B appearing in the talent distribution does not appear in the predicted distribution in (6.40).

An alternative formulation

In this presentation we follow a suggestion put forward by Blackorby, Donaldson and Weymark (1982) to derive 'the most preferred output distribution of all these feasible. In addition to the resource constraint, feasibility will be determined by demand and cost conditions, the behavioral possibilities (reaction functions) of actual and potential firms, and the policy tools available' (op.cit., p. 91). In view of this suggestion the simple optimization problem we consider here is the determination of the size distribution of firms which minimizes concentration subject to the constraint that the total output of the industry is given. In keeping with partial equilibrium evaluation, the industry is assumed to be subject to a fixed cost constraint. Thus, this is a framework in which a policy evaluator has control over the distribution of output across firms in an industry but not over resources available to the industry.

The concentration formula we employ here is the Shannon-Theil (inverse) concentration index $E_1^n(x) = -\sum_{i=1}^n s_i \log s_i$, where $s = (s_1, \ldots, s_n)$ is the output share distribution corresponding to the nominal output vector $x \in D^n$ and $n \geq 1$ is arbitrary. We now consider analogue to the Shannon-Theil index for output distributions defined in the continuum. Let F be the cumulative distribution function. We write f for the density function of the size distribution of firms and λ for the mean output. Let us denote the output of a typical firm by z. Clearly, for this firm $-s_i \log s_i$ becomes $-(z/n\lambda) \log(z/n\lambda)$. Now the total number of firms which produce output between $z - dz/2$ and $z + dz/2$ is $nf(z)\, dz$. If A denotes the set of all firms whose output are at most $\frac{1}{2}dz$ from z, then

$$
\begin{aligned}
-\sum_{i \in A} s_i \log s_i &= -(\frac{z}{n\lambda} \log \frac{z}{n\lambda}) n f(z) dz \\
&= -(\frac{zf(z)}{\lambda} \log \frac{z}{n\lambda}) dz \quad (6.41)\\
&= -(\frac{zf(z)}{\lambda} \log \frac{zf(z)}{\lambda}) dz
\end{aligned}
$$

since, loosely speaking, $f(z)$ denotes the fraction of firms producing output z. Continuous analogue to E_1^n is then found by integrating (6.41) over z:

$$E_1(F) = \int_{z_o}^{\infty} -\frac{zf(z)}{\lambda} \log \frac{zf(z)}{\lambda} dz, \quad (6.42)$$

where, $z_o \geq 0$ is the minimum output level.

With a continuum of firms the feasibility constraints become (i) a given mean output λ for the industry, and (ii) a fixed cost B for producing λ amount of output. Assuming that all the firms in the industry face the same technology, these constraints can be written as

$$\int_{z_o}^{\infty} z f(z) dz = \lambda, \quad (6.43)$$

$$\int_{z_o}^{\infty} C(z) f(z) dz = B, \quad (6.44)$$

where C is the identical cost function for the firms.

Since $E_1(F)$ given by (6.42) is an inverse concentration formula, optimality now requires maximization of (6.42) subject to the constraints (6.43) and (6.44). More precisely, we have

Definition 6.1 : An output distribution will be called optimum if its density function maximizes the objective function (6.42) subject to the constraints (6.43) and (6.44)[2].

Theorem 6.2 : The optimum output distribution is represented by the density function

$$f(z) = \frac{k}{z} e^{-\frac{a\lambda}{z}(C(z)-\frac{b}{a})}, \qquad (6.45)$$

where $k > 0$ and $a \neq 0$, b are constraints such that $\int_{z_o}^{\infty} f(z)dz = 1$.

Proof : We will invoke the Euler-Lagrange Technique[3] to prove the theorem. Let

$$\begin{aligned}
H(f) &= -\int_{z_o}^{\infty} \frac{zf(z)}{\lambda} \log \frac{zf(z)}{\lambda} dz \\
&\quad -\mu_1 [\int_{z_o}^{\infty} zf(z)dz - \lambda] - \mu_2 [\int_{z_o}^{\infty} C(z)f(z)dz - B] \\
&= \log \lambda - \int_{z_o}^{\infty} \frac{zf(z)}{\lambda} \log(zf(z)) dz \\
&\quad -\mu_1 [\int_{z_o}^{\infty} zf(z)dz - \lambda] - \mu_2 [\int_{z_o}^{\infty} C(z)f(z)dz - B],
\end{aligned}$$

where μ_1 amd μ_2 are Lagrange's multipliers.

Let $h : [z_o, \infty] \to R^1$ be any function such that $\int_{z_o}^{\infty} h(z)dz = 0$. For any arbitrary θ denoted $H(f + \theta h)$ by $g(\theta)$. If $E_1(F)$ attains the maximum for some f, then $g(\theta)$ attains the maximum for $\theta = 0$. Now,

$$\begin{aligned}
g(\theta) &= \log \lambda - \frac{1}{\lambda}[\int_{z_o}^{\infty} z(f(z) + \theta h(z)) \log(z(f(z) + \theta h(z))) dz \\
&\quad -\mu_1 [\int_{z_o}^{\infty} z(f(z) + \theta h(z))dz - \lambda] - \mu_2 [\int_{z_o}^{\infty} C(z)(f(z) + \theta h(z))dz - B].
\end{aligned}$$

$$\begin{aligned}
g'(\theta) &= -\frac{1}{\lambda} \int_{z_o}^{\infty} zh(z) \log(z(f(z) + \theta h(z))) dz \\
&\quad -\frac{1}{\lambda} \int_{z_o}^{\infty} z(f(z) + \theta h(z)) \frac{zh(z)}{z(f(z) + \theta h(z))} dz \\
&\quad -\mu_1 \int_{z_o}^{\infty} zh(z)dz - \mu_2 \int_{z_o}^{\infty} C(z)h(z)dz.
\end{aligned}$$

147

Since $g'(0) = 0$, we have

$$-\frac{1}{\lambda}\int_{z_o}^{\infty} zh(z)\log(zf(z))dz - \int_{z_o}^{\infty}(\mu_1 + \frac{1}{\lambda})zh(z)dz - \mu_2\int_{z_o}^{\infty} C(z)h(z)dz = 0. \tag{6.46}$$

We rewrite (6.46) as

$$\int_{z_o}^{\infty}[\frac{z}{\lambda}\log(zf(z)) + (\mu_1 + \frac{1}{\lambda})z + \mu_2 C(z)]h(z)dz = 0. \tag{6.47}$$

Now, (6.47) holds for all h such that $\int_{z_o}^{\infty} h(z)dz = 0$. Therefore, we have

$$\frac{z}{\lambda}\log(zf(z)) + (\mu_1 + \frac{1}{\lambda})z + \mu_2 C(z) = \mu_3, \tag{6.48}$$

where μ_3 is some constant. From (6.48) we get

$$f(z) = \frac{1}{z}e^{-\lambda(\mu_1 + \frac{1}{\lambda}) + \frac{\lambda\mu_3}{z} - \lambda\mu_2 \frac{C(z)}{z}}. \tag{6.49}$$

Clerarly, we can rewrite (6.49) as

$$f(z) = \frac{k}{z}e^{-\frac{a\lambda}{z}(C(z)) - \frac{b}{a}}, \tag{6.50}$$

where $k \neq 0$ and $a \neq 0$ and b are constants such that $\int_{z_o}^{\infty} f(z)dz = 1$.

To ensure that f given by (6.45) maximizes $E_1(F)$ we need to verify the second order condition $g''(0) < 0$. Now,

$$g''(\theta) = -\frac{1}{\lambda}\int_{z_o}^{\infty}\frac{(zh(z))^2}{z(f(z) + \theta h(z))}dz \tag{6.51}$$

which shows that

$$g''(0) = -\frac{1}{\lambda}\int_{z_o}^{\infty}\frac{(zh(z))^2}{z(f(z))}dz < 0. \tag{6.52}$$

Thus, f given by (6.46) is associated with a maximum of $E_1(F)$. This completes the proof of the theorem. □.

It is important to note that the Euler-Lagrange technique provides necessary, and not sufficient, conditions for a solution. Thus, exact identification of the parameters appearing in (6.50) has not been made. The parameters k, a and b are determined by constraints (6.43) and (6.44) and the condition $\int_{z_o}^{\infty} f(z)dz = 1$ as soon as the cost function C(z) is known.

A second feature is that the general formula in (6.50) shows the optimality of a long upper tail although we are maximising an inverse concentration function. That is, the theorem demonstrates that in the optimal situation firms of small as well as of large sizes will exist side by side. To explain this feature, we need to make assumption about the shape of the cost function. Let C_1 and C_2 be two cost functions, where C_1 has a constant average δ and C_2 has a declining average. It is clear that for all $z > \bar{z}$, where $\bar{z}$ is the level of output at which $C_1(z)$ equals $C_2(z)$, C_2 has a smaller marginal that C_1. Thus, if efficient production is to be ensured then the optimal situation should allow existence of more large firms (producing output more than $\bar{z}$ and controlling a reasonable portion of aggregate output) whenever C_2 is adopted against C_1. But by way of doing this we introduce some inequality into the size distribution of firms. Hence the optimal situation should show a trade off between efficiency in production and equity in the size distribution of firms.

A rigorous demonstration of the above argument requires that the optimal density f_2 corresponding to the cost function C_2 should have a thicker upper tail than the optimal density f_1 associated with the cost function C_1. That is, we need to show that $f_1(z) < f_2(z)$ for all $z > \bar{z}$. The optimal density corresponding to the cost function $C_1(z) = \delta z$ is given by

$$f_1(z) = k_1 e^{\frac{\lambda \delta}{z}} z^{-1}, \quad 0 < z_o < z, \tag{6.53}$$

where $k_1 = k e^{-a\lambda\delta} > 0$. Now the inequality $f_1(z) < f_2(z)$ holds if and only if $C(z)/z < \delta$. Since $C_2(z)/z$ is decreasing in z over $(0, \infty)$, for any $z > \bar{z}$, $C_2(z)/z < C_2(\bar{z})/\bar{z} = \delta$. This therefore shows that f_2 has a thicker upper tail than f_1.

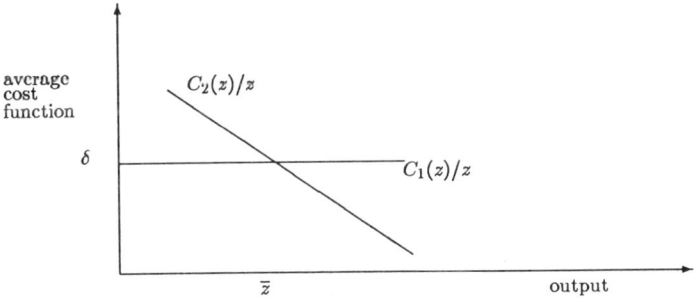

Figure 6.1 Average cost

We may explain this graphically also. In Figure 6.1 the averages of two cost function C_1 and C_2 are plotted. In Figure 6.2 the optimal densities f_1 and f_2 corresponding to C_1 and C_2 are shown. As stated, for all output levels $z > \bar{z}$, $f_1(z) < f_2(z)$.

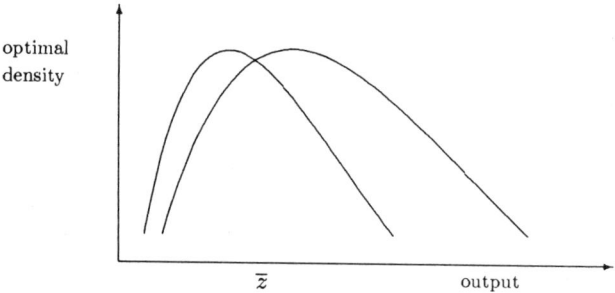

Figure 6.2 Optimal density

We may now illustrate the general formula in (6.50) by an example. Suppose that the cost function is of the form

$$C(z) = \frac{b}{a} + z\log z. \tag{6.54}$$

The marginal associated with C(z) in (6.54) is linear in $\log z$. This marginal, which is an increasing function of z, takes nonnegative values if $z \geq e^{-1}$. It can therefore be said that the threshold parameter z_o for the optimal output distribution corresponding to the cost function in (6.54) is given by e^{-1}. Substituting C(z) given by (6.54) in (6.50), we have

$$f(z) = kz^{-r-1}, \quad e^{-1} \leq z \leq \infty, \tag{6.55}$$

where $r = a\lambda > 0$. Using the fact that $\int_{e^{-1}}^{\infty} f(z)dz = 1$, we can rewrite $f(z)$ in (6.55) as

$$f(z) = re^{-r}z^{-r-1}, \quad z \geq e^{-1} > 0, \tag{6.56}$$

which is the Pareto density function with the threshold parameter $z_o = e^{-1}$. r here becomes the Pareto inequality parameter. It is obvious that the distribution has a finite mean if $r > 1$. Thus, we have a characterization of the Pareto distribution, as the size distribution of firms, without recourse to stochastic foundations.

Concluding remarks

It has been argued in the literature that the size distribution of firms may be generated by a stochastic process in which the size of firms is assumed to be subject to cumulative random shocks over time. Such a formulation depends entirely on the idea that the growth of a firm is a purely random process. We made a brief discussion on this in the present chapter. We then devoted to an analysis of how the distribution of output across firms could be governed by managerial efficiency. Finally, we considered the problem of generating the output distribution that maximizes the Shannon-Theil inverse concentration function subject to a set of feasibility constraints. A special case of this framework establishes the Pareto distribution as the most preferred size distribution of firms.

Notes

1. According to Bork (1978) the size of the firm that is achieved through internal growth is also the most efficient size of the firm.

2. Strictly speaking, in Blackorby et al. (1982) the industry performance evaluation function given by (2.62) has been considered as the objective function. Since in our case total output is given, maximization of (2.62) will essentially mean maximization of an inverse concentration index.

3. See Courant and Hilbert (1953) for a discussion.

Extended bibliography

In order to avoid duplication, the following abbreviations have been used in the extended bibliography :
American Economic Review = AER, Antitrust Bulletin = AB, Bell Journal of Economics = BJE, Canadian Journal of Economics = CJE, Econometrica = ECONM, Economic Journal = EJ, Economica = ECON, Economics Letters = EL, European Economic Review = EER, International Economic Papers = IEP, International Economic Review = IER, International Journal of Industrial Organization = IJIO, Journal of the American Statistical Association = JASA, Journal of Business = JB, Journal of Econometrics = JETS, Journal of Economic Theory = JET, Journal of Economic Literature = JEL, Journal of Industrial Economics = JIE, Journal of Law and Economics = JLE, Journal of Money, Credit and Banking = JMCB, Journal of Political Economy = JPE, Journal of Productivity Analysis = JPA, Journal of the Royal Statistical Society (Series A) = JRSS (A), Oxford Economic Papers = OEP, Quarterly Journal of Economics = QJE, Rand Journal of Economics = RJE, Review of Economic Studies = RES, Review of Economics and Statistics = RESTAT, Scottish Journal of Political Economy = SJPE, Southern Economic Journal = SEJ.

Aaronovitch, S. and Sawyer, M.C. (1975), *Big Business : Theoretical and Empirical Aspects of Concentration and Mergers in the U.K.*, Macmillan, London.

Aczél J. and Daróczy, Z. (1975), *On Measures of Information and Their Characterizations*, Academic Press, London.

Adelman, M.A. (1969), 'Comment on the H concentration measure as a numbers equivalent', *RESTAT*, 51.

Agarwal, R.N. (1991), 'Market structure and profitability relationships in a regulated industry', *Indian Economic Journal*, 39.

Aitchison, J. and Brown, J.A.C. (1957), *The Lognormal Distribution*, Cambridge University Press, London.

Amel, D.F. and Liang, J.N. (1990), 'Dynamics of market concentration in U.S. banking : 1966-86', *IJIO*, 8.

Amey, L.R. (1964), 'Diversified manufacturing business', *JRSS (A)*, 127.

Anderson, O. and Rynning, M.R. (1991), 'An empirical illustration of an alternative approach to measuring the market power and high profits hypothesis', *IJIO*, 19.

Angelmar, R. (1985), 'Market structure and research intensity in high technological opportunity industries', *JIE*, 34.

Apostol, T. (1971), *Mathematical Analysis*, Addison-Wesley, London.

Appelbaum, E. (1982), 'The estimation of the degree of oligopoly power', *JETS*, 19.

Archer, S.H. and Maguire, J. (1965), 'Firm size and probabilities of growth', *Western Economic Journal*, 3.

Arrow, K.J. (1974), *The Limits of Organization*, Norton, New York.

Ashenfelter, O. and Johnson, G.E. (1972), 'Unionism, relative wages and labor duality in US manufacturing industries', *IER*, 13.

Atkinson, A.B. (1970), 'On the measurement of inequality', *JET*, 2.

Audretsch, D.B. and Siegfied, J.B. (eds.) (1992), *Empirical Studies in Industrial Organization*, Kluwer, Boston.

Audretsch, D.B. and von der Schuleenburg, J.M.G. (1990), 'Union participation, innovation and concentration : results from a simultaneous model', *Journal of Institutional and Theoretical Economics*, 146.

Bailey, D. and Boyle, S.E. (1971), 'The optimal measure of concentration', *JASA*, 66.

Bailey, E.E., Graham, D.R. and Kaplan, D.P. (1985), *Deregulating the Airlines*, MIT Press, Cambridge.

Bain, J.S. (1941), 'The profit rate as a measure of monopoly power', *QJE*, 55.

Bain, J.S. (1951), 'Relation of profit rate to industrial concentration : American manufacturing 1936-40', *QJE*, 65.

Bain, J.S. (1956), *Barriers to New Competition*, Harvard University Press, Cambridge.

Baldwin, J.R. and Gorecki, P.K. (1985), 'The determinants of small plant market share in Canadian manufacturing industries in the 1970s', *RESTAT*, 67.

Basu, K. (1993), *Lectures in Industrial Organization Theory*, Blackwell, Oxford.

Baumol, W.J., Panzar, J.C. and Willig, R.D. (1982), *Contestable Markets and The Theory of Industry*, Harcourt Brace, San Diego.

Berge, C. (1961), *Topological Space*, Oliver and Boyd, London.

Berry, C.H. (1971), 'Corporate growth and industrial diversification', *JLE*, 14.

Berry, C.H. (1975), *Corporate Growth and Diversification*, Princeton University Press, New Jersey.

Bertrand, J. (1883), 'Review of Cournot', *Journal des Savants*.

Beutel, P.A. and McBride, M.E. (1992), 'Market power and the North West Republic airline merger : a residual demand approach', *SEJ*, 58.

Blackorby, C., Donaldson, D. and Weymark, J.A. (1982), 'A normative approach to industrial performance evaluation and concentration indices', *EER*, 19.

Blair, J. (1956), 'Statistical measures of concentration in business', *Bulletin of the Oxford Institute of Statistics*, 18.

Blair, J. (1972), *Economic Concentration*, Harcourt Brace, San Diego.

Bol, G. (1986), 'On technical efficiency measures : a remark', *JET*, 38.

Borenstein, S. (1988), 'Hubs and high fares : airport dominance and market power in the U.S. airline industry', University of Michigan.

Bork, R.H. (1978), *The Antitrust Paradox : An Economic Perspective*, Chicago University Press, Chicago.

Bothwell, J.L., Cooley T.F. and Hall T.E. (1984), 'A new view of the market structure - market performance debate', *JIE*, 32.

Bothwell, J.L. and Keeler, T.E. (1976), 'Profits, Market Structure and Portfolio Risk', in Masson, R.T. and Qualls, P.D. (eds.), *Essays in Industrial Organization in honor of J.S. Bain*, Ballinger, Cambridge.

Bowley, A. (1924), *The Mathematical Groundwork of Economics*, Clarendon, Oxford.

Boyer, K. (1974), 'Informative and goodwill advertising', *RESTAT*, 56.

Bradburd, R.M. (1982), 'Price cost margins in producer goods industries and the importance of being unimportant', *RESTAT*, 64.

Bradburd, R.M. and Over, A.M. (1982), 'Organizational costs, sticky equilibria and critical levels of concentration', *RESTAT*, 64.

Bresnahan, T.F. (1989), 'Empirical Studies of Industries with Market Power', in R. Schmalensee, and Willig R.D. (eds.), *Handbook of Industrial Organization*, Vol. II, North Holland, Amsterdam.

Brock, W.A. (1983), 'Contestable market and the theory of industry structure : a review article', *JPE*, 91.

Brozen, Y. (1971), 'Bain's concentration and rates of returns revisited', *JLE*, 14.

Borzen, Y. (1982), *Concentration, Mergers and Public Policy*, Macmillan, London.

Call, G.D. and Keeler T.E. (1983), 'Airline Dergulation, Fares and Market Behavior : Some Empirical Evidence', in Dougherty, A.H. (ed.), *Analytical Studies in Airline Transportation*, Cambridge University Press, London.

Carlsson, B. (1984), 'The development and use of machine tools in historical perspective', *Journal of Economic Behaviour and Organization*, 5.

Carlton, D.W. and Perloff, J.M. (1990) *Modern Industrial Organization*, Scott-Foresman, Illinois.

Casson, M. and Creedy, J. (eds.) (1993), *Industrial Concentration and Economic Inequality, Essays in honor of P. Hart*, Edward Elgar, Aldershot.

Cattin, P. and Wittink, D.R. (1976), 'Industry differences in the relation between advertising and profitability', *Industrial Organization Review*, 4.

Caves, R. (1989), 'International Differences in Industrial Organization', in Schmalensee, R. and Willig, R.D. (eds.), *Handbook of Industrial Organization*, Vol. II, North Holland, Amsterdam.

Caves, R. and Porter, M. (1976), 'Barriers to Exit', in Masson, R.T. and Qualls, P.D. (eds.), *Essays in Industrial Organization in honor of J.S. Bain*, Ballinger, Cambridge.

Caves, R., Porter, M. and Spence M. (1980), *Competition in the Open Economy*, Harvard University Press, Cambridge.

Caves, R. and Pugel, T.A. (1980), *Intraindustry Differences in Conduct and Performance : Viable Strategies in U.S. Manufacturing Industries*, Solomon Brothers Center, New York University, New York.

Caves, R. and Uekusa, M. (1976), *Industrial Organization in Japan*, Brookings Institution, Washington.

Central Statistical Organization (1968), *Standard Industrial Classification*, 3rd edition, London.

Central Statistical Organization (1987), *Revised National Industrial Classification of All Economic Activities : 1987*, New Delhi.

Chakravarty, S.R. (1988), 'On the separable industry performance evaluation function', *EL*, 27.

Chakravarty, S.R. (1989), 'The optimum size distribution of firms', *Mathematical Social Sciences*, 18.

Chakravarty, S.R. (1990), *Ethical Social Index Numbers*, Springer - Verlag, New York.

Chakravarty, S.R. (1992), 'Efficiency and concentration', *JPA*, 3.

Chakravarty, S.R. (1993), 'Oligopolies and Aggregate Market Power', in Diewert, W.E., Spremann, K.D. and Stehling, F. (eds.), *Mathematical Modelling in Economics, Essays in honor of W. Eichhorn*, Springer - Verlag, New York.

Chakravarty, S.R. and Eichhorn, W. (1991), 'An axiomatic characterization of a generalized index of concentration', *JPA*, 2.

Chakravarty, S.R. and Weymark, J.A. (1988), 'Axiomatizations of the Entropy Numbers Equivalent Index of Industrial Concentration', in Eichhorn, W. (ed.), *Measurement in Economics*, Physica-Verlag, New York.

Chamberlin, E. (1956), *The Theory of Monopolistic Competition*, Harvard University Press, Cambridge.

Champernowne, D.G. (1953), 'A model of income distribution', *EJ*, 63.

Chesher, A. (1979), 'Testing the law of proportionate effect', *JIE*, 27.

Chou, T.C. (1986), 'Concentration, profitability and trade in a simultaneous equation analysis : the case of Taiwan', *JIE*, 34.

Clark, K.B. (1984), 'Unionization and firm performance : the impact on profits, growth and productivity', *AER*, 74.

Clarke, R. (1984), 'Profit margins and market concentration in U.K. manufacturing industries', *Applied Economics*, 16.

Clarke, R. and Davies, S.W. (1982), 'Market structure and price cost margins', *ECON*, 49.

Clarke, R. and Davies, S.W. (1983), 'Aggregate concentration, market concentration and diversification', *EJ*, 93.

Clarke, R. and Davies, S.W. (1984), 'On measuring concentration and diversification', *EL*, 15.

Clarke, R., Davies, S.W. and Waterson, M. (1984), 'The profitability concentration relation : market power or efficiency', *JIE*, 32.

Coase, R.H. (1937), 'The nature of the Firm', *ECON*, 4.

Collins, N.R. and Preston, L.E. (1968), *Price Cost Margins in Manufacturing Industries*, University of California Press, Berkeley.

Collins, N.R. and Preston, L.E. (1969), 'Price cost margins and industry structure', *RESTAT*, 51.

Comanor, W.S. (1965), 'Research and technological change in the pharmaceutical industry', *RESTAT*, 47.

Comanor, W.S. and Scherer, F.M. (1969), 'Patent statistics as a measure of technical change', *JPE*, 77.

Comanor, W.S. and White L.J. (1992), 'Market power or efficiency : a review of antitrust standards', *Review of Industrial Organization*, 7.

Comanor, W.S. and Wilson, T.A. (1967), 'Advertising, market structure and performance', *RESTAT*, 49.

Comanor, W.S. and Wilson, T.A. (1974), *Advertising and Market Power*, Harvard University Press, Cambridge.

Connolly, R.A., Hirsch, B.T. and Hirschey, M. (1986), 'Union rent seeking, intangible capital and market value of the firm', *RESTAT*, 68.

Connolly, R.A. and Hirschey M. (1984), 'R and D, market structure and profits : a value-based approach', *RESTAT*, 66.

Corchon, L.C. (1991), 'Oligopolistic competition among groups', *EL*, 36.

Courant, H. and Hilbert, D. (1953), *Methods of Mathematical Physics*, Vol. I, Inter-Science, New York.

Cournot, A. (1897), *Researches into the Mathematical Principles of the Theory of Wealth*, Macmillan, New York.

Cowling, K.G. (1976), 'On the theoretical specification of industrial structure performance relationships', *EER*, 8.

Cowling, K.G. and Waterson, M. (1976), 'Price cost margins and market structure', *ECON*, 43.

Curry, B. and George, K.D. (1983), 'Industrial concentration : a survey', *JIE*, 31.

d'Aspremont, C. and Jacquemin, A. (1985), 'Measuring the power to monopolize : a simple game theoretic approach', *EER*, 27.

d'Aspremont, C., Jacquemin, A. and Mertens, J.F. (1987), 'A measure of aggregate power in organizations', *JET*, 43.

Dalton, J.A. and Penn, J.W. (1976), 'The concentration profitability relations : is there a critical concentration ratio?', *JIE*, 25.

Dansby, R. and Willig, R.D. (1979), 'Industry performance gradient indexes', *AER*, 69.
Dasgupta, P. (1986), 'The Theory of Technological Competition', in Stiglitz, J.E. and Mathewson, G.F. (eds.), *New Developments in the Analysis of Market Structure*, MIT Press, Cambridge.
Dasgupta, P. and Maskin, E. (1986), 'The existence of equilibrium in discontinuous economic games, I : theory and II : applications', *RES*, 53.
Dasgupta, P., Sen, A.K. and Starrett, D. (1973), 'Notes on the measurement of inequality', *JET*, 6.
Dasgupta, P. and Stiglitz, J.E. (1980), 'Industrial structure and innovative activity', *EJ*, 90.
Daskin, A.J. (1983), *Essays on Firm Diversification and Market Concentration*, Ph. D. Dissertation, MIT, Cambridge.
Daughety, A.F. (1990), 'Beneficial concentration', *AER*, 80.
Davies, S.W. (1979), 'Choosing between concentration indices : the isoconcentration curve', *ECON*, 46.
Davies, S.W. (1980), 'Measuring industrial concentration : an alternative approach', *RESTAT*, 62.
Davies, S.W. (1980a), 'Minimum efficient size and seller concentration : an empirical problem', *JIE*, 28.
Davies, S.W. and Lyons, B.R. (1982), 'Seller concentration : the technological explanation and demand uncertainty', *EJ*, 92.
de Melo, J. and Urata, S. (1986), 'The influence of increased foreign competition on industrial concentration and profitability', *IJIO*, 4.
Debreu, G. (1957), 'The coefficient of resource utilisation', *ECONM*, 19.
Defraja, G. and Delbono, F. (1989), 'Alternative strategies of a public enterprises in oligopoly', *OEP*, 41.
Del Monte, A. (ed.) (1992), *Recent Developments in the Theory of Industrial Organization*, Macmillan, London.
Demsetz, H. (1973), *The Market Concentration Doctrine*, American Enterprises Institution, Washington, DC.
Demsetz, H. (1973a), 'Industry structure, market rivalry and public policy', *JLE*, 16.
Demsetz, H. (1974), 'Two Systems of Belief About Monopoly', in Goldschmid, H.J., Mann, H.M. and Weston, J.F. (eds.), *Industrial Concentration : The New Learning*, Little-Brown, Boston.
Demsetz, H. (1990), *Ownership Control and the Firm : The Organization of Economic Activity*, Vol. I, Blackwell, Oxford.
Demsetz, H. (1991), *Efficiency, Competition and Policy : The Organization of Economic Activity*, Vol. II, Blackwell, Oxford.
Dertouzos, J.N. and Trautman, W.B. (1990), 'Economic effects of media concentration : estimation from a model of the newspaper firms', *JIE*, 39.
Devine, P.J., Lee, N., Jones, R.M. and Tyson, W.J. (1979), *An Introduction to Industrial Economics*, 3rd edition, Allen and Unwin, London.

Dickens, W.T. and Katz, L.F. (1986), 'Interindustry Wage Differences and Industry Characteristics', in Lang, K. and Leonard, J. (eds.), *Unemployment and the Structure of Labor Markets*, Blackwell, Oxford.

Dickson, V.A. (1979), 'The Lerner index and measures of concentration', *EL*, 3.

Dickson, V.A. (1982), 'Collusion and price cost margins', *ECON*, 49.

Diewert, W.E. (1982), 'Duality Approaches in Microeconomic Theory', in Arrow, K.J. and Intriligator, M.D. (eds.), *Handbook of Mathematical Economics*, Vol. II, North Holland, Amsterdam.

Diewert, W.E. and Parkan, C. (1983), 'Linear Programming Tests of Regularity Conditions for Production Functions', in Eichhorn, W. et. al. (eds.), *Quantitative Studies on Production and Prices*, Springer-Verlag, Vienna.

Dixit, A. (1986), 'Comparative statics for oligopoly', *IER*, 27.

Dixit, A. and Stern, N. (1982), 'Oligopoly and welfare', *EER*, 19.

Doi, N. (1991), 'Aggregate export concentration in Japan', *JIE*, 39.

Domowitz, I., Hubbard, R.G. and Petersen, B.C. (1986), 'Business cycles and the relationship between concentration and price cost margins', *RJE*, 17.

Domowitz, I., Hubbard, R.G. and Petersen, B.C. (1986a), 'The intertemporal stability of the concentration margins relationship', *JIE*, 35.

Donaldson, D. and Weymark, J.A. (1980), 'A single parameter generalization of the Gini indices of inequality', *JET*, 22.

Donsimoni, M.P., Geroski, P.A. and Jacquemin, A. (1984), 'Concentration indices and market power : two views', *JIE*, 32.

Dorfman, R. and Steiner P. (1954), 'Optimal advertising and optimal quality', *AER*, 44.

Downie, J. (1958), *The Competitive Process*, Duckworth, London.

Edgeworth, F.Y. (1925), *The Pure Theory of Monopoly*, Macmillan, London.

Eichhorn, W. (1978), *Functional Equations in Economics*, Addison - Wesley, London.

Encaoua, D. and Jacquemin, A. (1980), 'Degree of monopoly, indices of concentration and threat of entry', *IER*, 21.

Encaoua, D., Jacquemin, A. and Moreaux, M. (1986), 'Global market power and diversification', *EJ*, 96.

Engels, F. (1887), *Note Inserted into Volume 3 of Marx's (1887) Capital*.

Evans, W.N. and Kessides, I.N. (1993), 'Localised market power in U.S. airline industry', *RESTAT*, 75.

Fairbanks, J.A. and Kay, J.A. (eds.) (1989), *Mergers and Mergers Policy*, Oxford University Press, London.

Färe, R. (1986), 'Addition and efficiency', *QJE*, 101.

Färe, R. and Grosskopf, S. (1983), 'Measuring congestion in production', *Zeitschrift Fuer Nationaloekonomie*, 43.

Färe, R., Grosskopf, S. and Loveall, C.A.K. (1985), *The Measurement of Efficiency of Production*, Kluwer, Boston.

Färe, R., Grosskopf, S. and Lovell, C.A.K. (1993), *Production Frontiers*, Cambridge University Press, London.

Färe, R., and Lovell, C.A.K. (1978), 'Measuring the technical efficiency of production', *JET*, 19.

Farrell, J. and Shapiro, C. (1990), 'Horizontal mergers : an equilibrium analysis', *AER*, 80.

Farrell, M. (1957), 'The Measurement of productive efficiency', *JRSS(A)*, 120.

Federal Trade Commission (1967), *Industry Classification and Concentration*, Washington, DC.

Finkelstein, M. and Friedberg, R. (1967), 'The application of entropy theory of concentration to the Clayton Act', *Yale Law Journal*, 76.

Freeman, R.B. (1983), *'Unionism, price cost margins and the return on capital'*, NBER working paper No. 1164, Princeton.

Friedman, J. (1986), *Game Theory with Application to Economics*, Oxford University Press, London.

Frisch, R. (1951), 'Monopoly and polypoly : the concept of force in economy', *IEP*, 1.

Galbraith, J.K. (1967), *The New Industrial State*, André Deutsch, London.

Gale, B.T. (1972), 'Market share and rate of return', *RESTAT*, 34.

Gale, B.T. and Branch, B.S. (1982), 'Concentration vs. market share : which determines performance and why does it matter?', *AB*, 27.

Gehrig, W. (1983), 'On a characterization of the shannon concentration measure', *Utilitas Mathematica*, 24.

Gehrig, W. (1988) 'On the Shannon - Theil Concentration Measure and Its Characterizations', in Eichhorn, W. (ed.), *Measurement in Economics*, Physica-Verlag, New York.

George, K.D. (1986), 'A note on concentration, barriers to entry and rate of return', *RESTAT*, 50.

George, K.D. and Jacquemin, A. (1992), 'Dominant firms and mergers', *EJ*, 102.

George, K.D., Lynk, E.L. and Joll, C. (1992), *Industrial Organization : Comptetion, Growth and Structural Change*, 4th edition, Routledge, London.

Geroski, P.A. (1981), 'Specification and testing the profits concentration relationships : some exeriments for the UK', *ECON*, 48.

Geroski, P.A. (1982), 'Simultaneous equations models of the structure performance paradigm', *EER*, 19.

Geroski, P.A., Masson, R.T. and Shaanan, J. (1987), 'The dynamics of market structure', *IJIO*, 5.

Geroski, P.A. and Pomroy, R. (1990), 'Innovation and the evolution of market structure', *JIE*, 38.

Gerrard, B. (1990), 'Industrial economics : a survey of textbooks', *Bulletin of Economic Research*, 42.

Gibrat, R. (1931), *Les Inégalités Économiques*, Sirley, Paris.

Gilbert, R.A. (1984), 'Bank market structure and competition : a survey', *JMCB*, 16.
Globerman, S. (1973), 'Market structure and R and D in Canadian manufacturing industries', *Quarterely Review of Economics and Business*, 13.
Gorecki, P.K. (1974), 'The measurement of enterprise diversification', *RESTAT*, 56.
Gorecki, P.K. (1975), 'An interindustry analysis of diversification in the U.K. manufacturing sector', *JIE*, 24.
Gort, M. (1962), *Diversification and Integration in American Industry*, Princeton University Press, New Jersey.
Gort, M. and Singamsetti, R. (1976), 'Concentration and profit rates : new evidence on an old issue', *Explorations in Economic Research*, 3.
Grabowski, H.G. and Muller, D.C. (1978), 'Industrial research and development, intangible capital stocks and firm profit rates', *BJE*, 9.
Graham, D.R., Kaplan, D.P. and Sibley, D.S. (1983), 'Efficiency and concentration in the airline industry', *BJE*, 14.
Grant, R.M. (1974), 'On the theory of diversification', *SJPE*, 21.
Hall, M. and Tideman, N. (1967), 'Measures of concentration', *JASA*, 62.
Hall, M. and Weiss, L.W. (1967), 'Firm size and profitability', *RESTAT*, 49.
Hannah, L. (1974), 'Managerial innovation and the rise of the large scale company in interwar Britain', *Economic History Review (Second Series)*, 27.
Hannah, L. and Kay, J.A. (1977), *Concentration in Modern Industry : Theory, Measurement and the U.K. Experience*, Macmillan, London.
Hannah, L. and Kay, J.A. (1981), 'The contribution of mergers to concentration growth : a reply to Prof. Hart', *JIE*, 29.
Hanoch, G. and Rothschild, M. (1972), 'Testing the assumptions of production theory : a nonparametric approach', *JPE*, 80.
Harris, F.H. deB (1984), 'Growth expectations, excess value and the risk adjusted return to market power', *SEJ*, 51.
Hart, P.E. (1962), 'The size and growth of firms', *ECON*, 29.
Hart, P.E. (1971), 'Entropy and other measures of concentration', *JRSS(A)*, 134.
Hart, P.E. (1975), 'Moment distribution in economics : an exposition', *JRSS(A)*, 138.
Hart, P.E. (1979), 'On bias and concentration', *JIE*, 27.
Hart, P.E. and Clarke, R. (1980), *Concentration in British Industry : 1935-75*, Cambridge University Press, London.
Hart, P.E. and Morgan, E. (1977), 'Market structure and economic performance in the U.K.', *JIE*, 25.
Hart, P.E. and Prais, S.J. (1956), 'The analysis of business concentration : a statistical approach', *JRSS(A)*, 119.
Hassid, J. (1973), 'Recent evidence on conglomerate diversification in UK manufacturing industry', *Manchester School*, 43.

Hause, J.C. (1977), 'The measurement of concentrated industrial structure and the size distribution of firms', *Annals of Economic and Social Measurement*, 6.

Haworth, C.T. and Reuther, C. (1978), 'Industry concentration and intra-industry wage discrimination', *RESTAT*, 60.

Hay, D.A. and Morris, D.J. (1991), *Industrial Economics and Organization : Theory and Evidence*, Oxford University Press, London.

Hay, G.A. and Werden, G.J. (1993), 'Horizontal mergers : law, policy and economics', *AER*, 83.

Herfindahl, O.C. (1950), *Concentration in the U.S. Steel Industry, Doctoral Dissertation*, Columbia University, New York.

Hilferding, R. (1910), *Finance Capital.* (An English language edition has been published by Routledge, London, 1981.)

Hilke, J.C. and Nelson, P.B. (1988), 'Diversification and predation', *JIE*, 37.

Hirsch, B.T. and Addison, J.C. (1986), *The Economic Analysis of Unions*, Allen and Unwin, London.

Hirsch, B.T. and Berger, M.C. (1984), 'Union membership determination and industry characteristics', *SEJ*, 50.

Hirsch, B.T. and Link, A.L. (1986), 'Labor union effects on innovative activity', University of North Carolina.

Hirsch, B.T. and Seaks, T.G. (1993), 'Functional form in regression models of Tobin's q', *RESTAT*, 75.

Hirschey, M. (1985), 'Market structure and market value', *JB*, 58.

Hirschman, A.O. (1945), *National Power and the Structure of Foreign Trade*, University of California Press, Berkeley.

Horowitz, A. (1972), 'A suggestion for a comprehensive measure of concentration : a comment', *SEJ*, 38.

Horowitz, A. and Horowitz, I. (1968), 'Entropy, Markov process and competition in the brewing industry', *JIE*, 16.

Horowitz, I (1970), 'Employment concentration in the common market : an entropy approach', *JRSS(A)*, 133.

Horvath, J. (1970), 'A suggestion for a comprehensive measure of concentration', *SEJ*, 36.

Hurdle, G.J., Johnson, R.L., Joskow, A.S., Werden, G.J. and Williams, M.A. (1989), 'Concentration, potential entry and performance in the airline industry', *JIE*, 38.

Hymer, S. and Pashigian, P. (1962), 'Firm size and rate of growth', *JPE*, 70.

Ijiri, Y. and Simon, H.A. (1964), 'Business firms : growth and size', *AER*, 54. (Reprinted in Ijiri and Simon (1977)).

Ijiri, Y. and Simon, H.A. (1971), 'Effects of mergers and acuisitions on business firm concentration', *JPE*, 79. (Reprinted in Ijiri and Simon (1977)).

Ijiri, Y. and Simon, H.A. (1974), 'Interpretations of departures from the Pareto curve firm size distributions', *JPE*, 82. (Reprinted in Ijiri and Simon (1977)).

Ijiri, Y. and Simon, H.A. (1977), *Skewed Distribution and the Size of Business Firms*, North Holland, Amsterdam.

Imel, B., Behr, M.R. and Helmberger, P.G. (1972), *Market Structure and Performance*, Lexington Books, Lexington.

Jacquemin, A. (1987), *The New Industrial Organization*, Clarendon, Oxford.

Jacquemin, A. and Berry, C.H. (1979), 'Entropy measure of diversification and corporate growth', *JIE*, 27.

Jacquemin, A. and de Jong, H.W. (1977), *European Industrial Organization*, Wiley, New York.

Jacquemin, A., de Ghellinck, E. and Huveneers, C. (1980), 'Concentration and profitability in a small open economy', *JIE*, 29.

Jacquein, A. and de Lichtbuer, M.C. (1973), 'Size structure, stability and performance of the largest British and EEC Firms', *EER*, 4.

Jacquemin, A. and Kumps, A.M. (1971), 'Changes in the size structure of the largest european firms : an entropy measure', *JIE*, 20.

Jacquemin, A. and Saez, W. (1976), 'A comparison of the largest European and Japanese firms', *OEP*, 28.

Jacquemin, A. and Slade, M.E. (1989), 'Cartels, Collusions and Horizontal Mergers', in Schmalensee, R. and Willig, R.D. (eds.), *Handbook of Industrial Organization*, Vol. I, North Holland, Amsterdam.

Jacquemin, A. and Thisse, J. (1972), 'Strategy of the Firm and Market Structure : An Application of Optimal Control Theory', in Cowling, K.G., (ed.), *Market Structure and Corporate Behaviour*, Gray Mills, London.

Jenny, R. and A.P., Weber, (1976), 'Profit rates and structural variables in French manufacturing industries', *EER*, 7.

Jovanovic, B. (1982), 'Selection and the evolution of industry', *ECONM*, 50.

Kahn, L.M. (1979), 'Unionism and relative wages : direct and indirect effects', *Journal of Industrial and Labor Relations Review*, 32.

Kakwani, N.C. (1980), *Income Inequality and Poverty : Methods of Estimation and Policy Applications*, Oxford University Press, London.

Kalecki, M. (1945), 'On the Gibrat distribution', *ECONM*, 13.

Kamien, M.I. and Schwartz, N.L. (1975), 'Market structure and innovation : a survey', *JEL*, 13.

Kamien, M.I. and Schwartz, N.L. (1983), 'Conjectural variations', *CJE*, 16.

Karier, T. (1985), 'Unions and monopoly profits', *RESTAT*, 67.

Kay, J. and King, M. (1978), *The British Tax System*, Oxford University Press, London.

Kelly, Jr. W.A. (1981), 'A generalised interpretation of the Herfindahl index', *SEJ*, 48.

Kessides, I.N. (1986), 'Advertising, sunk costs and barriers to entry', *RESTAT*, 68.

Kessides, I.N. (1987), 'Do firms differ much? some additional evidence', University of Maryland.

Kessides, I.N. (1990), 'Market concentration, contestability and sunk cost', *RESTAT*, 72.

Kilpatrick, H.W. (1967), 'The choice among alternative measures of industrial concentration', *RESTAT*, 49.

Kolm, S.C. (1969), 'The Optimal Production of Social Justice', in Margolis, J. and Guitton, H. (eds.), *Public Economics*, Macmillan, London.

Koopmans, T.C. (ed.) (1951), *Activity Analysis of Production and Allocation*, Wiley, New York.

Kopp, R.J. and Diewert, W.E. (1982), 'The decomposition of frontier cost function deviations into measures of technical and allocative efficiency', *JETS*, 19.

Kreps, D.A. (1990), *A Course in Microeconomic Theory*, Princeton University Press, New Jersey.

Krouse, C.G. (1990), *Theory of Industrial Economics*, Blackwell, London.

Kumar, N. (1990), 'Mobility barriers and profitability of multinational and local enterprises in Indian manufacturing', *JIE*, 38.

Kwoka, Jr. J.E. (1979), 'The effect of market share distribution on industry performance', *RESTAT*, 59.

Kwoka, Jr. J.E. (1981), 'Does the choice of concentration measure really matter', *JIE*, 29.

Kwoka, Jr. J.E. (1985), 'The Herfindahl index in theory and practice', *AB*, 30.

Kwoka, Jr. J.E. and Ravenschraft, D. (1986), 'Cooperation vs. rivalry : price-cost margins by line of business', *ECON*, 53.

La France, V.A. (1979), 'The impact of buyer concentration - an extention', *RESTAT*, 59.

Lee, L.F. (1980), 'Racial differentials in union relative wage effects - a simultaneous equation approach', *Journal of Labor Research*, 1.

Lerner, A.P. (1934), 'The concept of monopoly and the measurement of monopoly power', *RES*, 1.

Levy, D. (1985), 'Specifying the dynamics of industry concentration', *JIE*, 34.

Liebowitz, S.J. (1982), 'What do census price cost margins measure?' *JIE*, 25.

Linda, R. (1976), *Methodology of Concentration Analysis Applied to the Study of Industries and Markets*, Commission of EEC, Brussels.

Lindeberg, E.B. and Ross, S.A. (1981), 'Tobin's q ratio and industrial organization', *JB*, 54.

Lucas, R. (1978), 'On the size distribution of business firms', *BJE*, 9.

Luce, R.D. and Raiffa, H. (1957), *Games and Decisions*, Wiley, New York.

Lustgarten, S. (1975), 'The impact of buyer concentration in manufacturing industries', *RESTAT*, 57.

Lyons, B.R. (1980), 'A new measure of minimum efficient plant size in U.K. manufacturing industry', *ECON*, 47.

Malmquist, S. (1951), 'Index number and indifference surfaces', *Trabajo de Estatistica*, 3.

Mann, H.M. (1966), 'Seller concentration, barriers to entry and rates of return in 30 industries', *RESTAT*, 48.
Mann, H.M. (1971), 'The interaction of barriers and concentration : a reply', *JIE*, 19.
Mann, H.M. (1973), 'Concentration, barriers to entry and rates of return revisited : a reply', *JIE*, 21.
Manne, H.G. (1965), 'Mergers and the market for corporate control', *JPE*, 73.
Mansfield, E. (1981), 'Composition of R and D expenditure : relationship to size of firm, concentration and innovative output', *RESTAT*, 63.
Mansfield, E. (1984), 'R and D and Innovation : Some Empirical Findings', in Giriliches, V (ed.), *R and D, Patents and Productivity*, Chicago University Press, Chicago.
Mansfield, E. et. al. (1971), *Research and Innovation in the Modern Corporation*, Norton, New York.
Masson, R.T. and Shannan, J. (1982), 'Stochastic dynamic limit pricing : an empirical test', *RESTAT*, 64.
Martin, S. (1979), 'Advertisiting, concentration and profitability : the simultaneity problem', *BJE*, 10.
Martin, S. (1979a), 'Entry barriers, concentration and profit', *SEJ*, 46.
Martin, S. (1983), *Market, Firm and Economic Performance : An Empirical Analysis*, New York University Press, New York.
Martin, S. (1988), *Industrial Economics*, Macmillan, London.
Martin, S. (1988a), 'Market power and/or efficiency', *RESTAT*, 70.
Martin, S. (1988b), 'The measurement of profitability and the diagnosis of market power', *IJIO*, 6.
Martin, S. (1993), *Advanced Industrial Economics*, Blackwell, Oxford.
Marvel, H.P. (1988), 'Foreign trade and domestic competition', *Economic Inquiry*, 18.
Marx, K. (1887), *Capital*, Sonnenschein, London.
Meade, J.E. (1968), 'Is the new industrial state inevitable', *EJ*, 78.
Meehan, J. and Duchesneau, T.D. (1973), 'The critical level of concentration : an empirical analysis', *JIE*, 22.
Miller, B. (1984), 'Industrial structure and unionization : evidence from U.S. manufacturing sectors', San Antonio, Texas.
Miller, R.A. (1967), 'Marginal concentration ratios and industry profit rates : some empirical results', *SEJ*, 34.
Miller, R.A. (1971), 'Marginal concentration ratios as market structure variables', *RESTAT*, 53.
Modigliani, F. (1958), 'New development on the oliogoply front', *JPE*, 66.
Moore, M. (1972), 'Stigler on inflexible prices', *CJE*, 5.
Morrison, S.A. and Winston, C. (1987), 'Empirical implications of the contestability hypothesis', *JLE*, 30.
Mueller, D.C. (1986), *Profits in the Long Run*, Cambridge University Press, London.

Muller, J. (1967), 'The impact of mergers on concentration : a study of eleven West German inudstries', *JIE*, 25.

Nash, J.F. (1951), 'Non-cooperative games', *Annals of Mathematics*, 45.

Nash, J.F. (1953), 'Two-person cooperative games', *ECONM*, 21.

Nelson, R.L. (1963), *Concentration in the Manufacturing Industries of the United States*, Yale University Press, New Haven.

Neumann, M., Bobel, I. and Haid, A. (1979), 'Profitability, risk and market structure in West German industries', *JIE*, 25.

Neuman, M., Bobel, I. and Haid, A. (1985), 'Domestic concentration, foreign trade and economic performance', *IJIO*, 3.

Niehans, J. (1958), 'An index of the size of industrial establishments', *IEP*, 8.

Novshek, W. (1980), 'Nash-Cournot equilibrium with entry', *RES*, 47.

Ornstein, S.I. (1972), 'Concentration and profits', *JB*, 45.

Ornstein, S.I. (1975), 'Empirical uses of price cost margins', *JIE*, 24.

Ornstein, S.I. (1976), 'The advertising - concentration controversy', *SEJ*, 26.

Ornstein, S.I., Weston, J.F., Intriligator, M.D. and Shrives, R.E. (1973), 'Determinants of market structure', *SEJ*, 39.

Orr, D. (1974), 'An index of entry barriers and its application to the market structure performance relationship', *JIE*, 23.

Orr, D. (1974a), 'The determinants of entry : a study of the Canadian manufacturing industries', *RESTAT*, 56.

Peltzmann, S. (1977), 'The gains and losses from industrial concentration', *JIE*, 20.

Penrose, E.T. (1959), *The Theory of the Growth of the Firms*, Blackwell, London.

Perry, M.K. (1984), 'Scale economies, imperfect competition and public policy', *JIE*, 32.

Perry, M.K. and Porter, R.H. (1985), 'Oligopoly and the incentive for horizontal merger', *AER*, 75.

Phillips, A. (1976), 'A critique of empirical studies of relations between market structure and profitability', *JIE*, 24.

Phlips, L. (1971), *Effects of Industrial Concentration*, North Holland, Amsterdam.

Porter, M.E. (1976), *Interbrand Choice, Strategy and Bilateral Market Power*, Harvard University Press, Cambridge.

Porter, R.H. (1991), 'A review essay on Handbook of Industrial Organization', *JEL*, 29.

Posner, R.A. (1979), 'The Chicago School of antitrust analysis', *University of Pennsylvania Law Review*, 127.

Prais, S.J. (1981), 'The contribution of mergers to industrial concentration : what do we know ?', *JIE*, 29.

Prais, S.J. (1981a), *The Evolution of Giant Firms in Britain*, 2nd edition, Cambridge University Press, London.

Pugel, T.A. (1980), 'Profitiablity, concentration and the interindustry variation in wages', *RESTAT*, 62.

Quandt, R.E. (1966), 'On the size distribution of firms', *AER*, 56.

Rader, T. (1972), *Theory of Microeconomics*, Academic Press, New York.

Ravenscraft, D.J. (1983), 'Structure profit relationships at the line of business and industry level', *RESTAT*, 65.

Rényi, A. (1961), 'On Measures of Entropy and Information', in Neyman, J. (ed.), *Proceedings of the 4th Berkley Symposium on Mathematical Statistics and Probability*, Vol.1, University of California Press, Berkeley.

Rees, R.D. (1973), 'Optimum plant Size in UK industries : some survivor estimates', *ECON*, 40.

Rhoades, S. (1971), 'Concentration, barrier and rates of return : a note', *JIE*, 19.

Rhoades, S. (1972), 'Concentration, barriers to entry and rates of return revisited', *JIE*, 20.

Rhoades, S. (1973), 'The effect of diversification on industry profit performance in 241 manufacturing industries', *RESTAT*, 55.

Rhoades, S. (1974), 'A further evaluation of the effects of diversification on industry profit performance', *RESTAT*, 56.

Rhoades, S. and Cleaver, J. (1973), 'The nature of the concentration price/cost margin relationship for 352 manufacturing industries : 1967', *SEJ*, 39.

Rhodes, G.F. Jr. (ed.) (1991), *Econometric Methods and Models of Industrial Organizations, Advances in Econometrics*, Vol.9, JAI Press, Connecticut.

Rosenbluth, G. (1955), 'Measures of Concentration, in Stigler, G. (ed.), *Business Concentration and Price Policy*, Princeton University Press, New Jersey.

Ross, D.R. (1986), 'Do markets differ much : comment-markets differ by stage of processing', Williams College.

Round, D.K. (1975), 'Industry structure, market rivalry and public policy : some australian evidence', *JLE*, 18.

Russell, R.R. (1985), 'Measures of technical efficiency', *JET*, 35.

Russell, R.R. (1988), 'On the Axiomatic Approach to the Measurement of Technical Efficiency', in Eichhorn, W. (ed.), *Measurement in Economics*, Physica-Verlag, New York.

Salant, S., Switzer, S. and Reynolds, R. (1983), 'Losses due to mergers : the effects of an exogenous change in industry structure on Cournot-Nash equilibrium', *QJE*, 98.

Salinger, M.A. (1984), 'Tobin's q, unionization and the concentration profits relationship', *RJE*, 15.

Salit, S.S. and Sankar, U. (1977), 'The measurement of firm size', *RESTAT*, 59.

Samuels, J.M. (1965), 'Size and the growth of firms', *RES*, 32.

Samuels, J.M. and Chesher, A.D., (1972), 'Growth, Survival and the Size of Companies, 1960-69', in Cowling, K.G. (ed.), *Market Structure and Corporate Behaviour*, Gray Mills, London.

Samuels, J.M. and Smyth, D.J. (1968), 'Profits, variability and firm size', *ECONM*, 35.

Saving, T.R. (1961), 'Estimation of optimum size of plant by the survivor technique', *QJE*, 75.

Saving, T.R. (1970), 'Concentration ratios and the degree of monopoly', *IER*, 11.

Scherer, F.M. (1967), 'Market structure and the employment of scientists and engineers', *AER*, 57.

Scherer, F.M. (1970), 'The causes and consequences of rising industrial concentration', *JIE*, 22.

Scherer, F.M. (1980), *Industrial Market Structure and Economic Performance*, 2nd edition, Rand McNally, Chicago.

Scherer, F.M. (1986), 'On the Current State of Knowledge in Industrial Organization', in de Jong, H.W. and Shephard, W.G. (eds.), *Mainstreans in Industrial Organization*, Vol.I, Kluwer, Boston.

Scherer, F.M., Bekenstein, A., Kaufer, E. and Murphy, R.D. (1975), *The Economics of Multi-Plant Operation*, Harvard University Press, Cambridge.

Schmalensee, R. (1977), 'Using the H-index of concentration with published data', *RESTAT*, 59.

Schmalensee, R. (1983), 'The New Industrial Organization and the Economic Analysis of Modern Markets', in Hildenbrand, W. (ed.), *Advances in Economic Theory*, Cambridge University Press, London.

Schmalensee, R. (1985), 'Do markets differ much?', *AER*, 75.

Schmalensee, R. (1987), 'Collusion versus differential efficiency : testing alternative hypotheses', *JIE*, 35.

Schmalensee, R. (1989), 'Inter-Industry Studies of Structure and Performance', in Schmalensee, R. and Willig, R.D. (eds.), *Handbook of Industrial Organization*, Vol.II, North Holland, Amsterdam.

Schmalensee, R. (1992), 'Sunk cost and market structure : a review article', *JIE*, 40.

Schumpeter, J.A. (1950), *Capitalism, Socialism and Democracy*, Harper, New York.

Scitovsky, T. (1955), 'Economic Theory and the Measurement of Concentration', in Stigler, G. (ed.), *Business Concentration and Price Policy*, Princeton University Press, New Jersy.

Scott, J.T. and Pascoe, G. (1986), 'Beyond firm and industry effects on profitability in imperfect markets', *RESTAT*, 68.

Selten, R. (1975), 'Reexamination of the perfectness concept for equilibrium points in extensive games', *International Journal of Game Theory*, 4.

Shannon, C.E. (1948), 'A mathematical theory of communication', *Bell System Technical Journal*, 27.

Shapiro, C. (1989), 'Theories of Oligopoly Behavior', in Schmalensee, R. and Willig, R.D. (eds.), *Handbook of Industrial Organization*, Vol.1, North Holland, Amsterdam.

Shapley, L.S. (1953), *A Value for n-Person Games*, Annals of Mathematics Study 28, Princeton University Press, New Jersey.

Shapley, L.S. and Shubik, M. (1954), 'A method for evaluating the distribution of power in a committee system', *American Political Science Review*, 48.

Sharkey, W. (1982), *The Theory of Natural Monopoly*, Cambridge University Press, London.

Shephard, R.W. (1970), *Theory of Cost and Production Functions*, Princeton University Press, New Jersey.

Shepherd, W.G. (1967), 'What does the survivor technique show about economies of scale', *SEJ*, 34.

Shepherd, W.G. (1972), 'Elements of market structure : an interindustry analysis', *SEJ*, April.

Shepherd, W.G. (1974), *The Treatment of Market Power*, Columbia University Press, New York.

Shepherd, W.G. (1986), 'The Economics of Industrial Organization', in de Jong, H.W. and Shepherd, W.G. (eds.), *Mainstreams in Industrial Organization*, Vol.I, Kluwer, Boston.

Shrieves, R.M. (1978), 'Market structure and innovation : a new perspective', *JIE*, 26.

Silber, J. (1989), 'Factor components, population subgroups and the computation of the Gini index of inequality', *RESTAT*, 71.

Simon, H.A. (1955), 'On a class of skew distribution functions', *Biometrica*, 42. (Reprinted in Ijiri and Simon (1977).)

Simon, H.A. and Bonini, C.P. (1958), 'The size distribution of business firms',*AER*, 48. (Reprinted in Ijiri and Simon (1977).)

Singh, A. and Whittington, G. (1975), 'The size and growth of firms', *RES*, 42.

Sleuwaegen, L. and Dehandschutter, W. (1986), 'The critical choice between the concentration ratio and the H-index in assessing industry performance', *JIE*, 35.

Smirlock, M. (1985), 'Evidence on the (non) relationship between concentration and profitability in banking', *JMCB*, 17.

Smirlock, M., Gilligan, T. and Marshall, W. (1984), 'Tobin's q and the structure-performance relationship', *AER*, 74.

Smyth, D.J., Boyes, W.J. and Pessan, D.E. (1975), 'The measurement of firm size : theory and evidence for the U.S. and U.K.', *RESTAT*, 42.

Spence, A.M. (1983), 'Concentestable markets and the theory of industry structure : a review article', *JEL*, 21.

Stackelberg, von H. (1934), *Market Form Und Gleichgewicht*, Julius Springer, Viena.

Steindl, J. (1965), *Random Process and the Growth of Firms*, Hafner, New York.

Stigler, G.J. (1950), 'Monopoly and oligopoly by merger', *AER*, 40.

Stigler, G.J. (1963), *Capital and Rates of Return in Manufacturing Industries*, Princeton University Press, New Jersey.

Stigler, G.J. (1964), 'A theory of oligopoly', *JPE*, 72.

Stigler, G.J. (1968), *The Organization of Industry*, Richard D. Irwin, Illinois.

Strickland, A.D. and Weiss, L.W. (1976), 'Advertising, concentration and price-cost margins', *JPE*, 84.

Sutton, J. (1991), *Sunk Costs and Market Structure : Price Competition, Advertising and the Evolution of Concentration*, MIT Press, Cambridge.

Sutton, J.C. (1973), 'Management behaviour and a theory of diversification', *SJPE*, 20.

Sweezy, P.M. (1942), *The Theory of Capitalist Development*, Monthly Review Press, New York.

Telser, L.G. (1972), *Competition, Collusion and Game Theory*, Aldine, Chicago.

Theil, H. (1967), *Economics and Information Theory*. North Holland, Amsterdam.

Thomadakis, S.B. (1977), 'A value based test of profitability and market structure', *RESTAT*, 59.

Thompson, R.S. (1984), 'Structure and conduct in local advertising markets', *JIE*, 33.

Tirole, J. (1988), *The Theory of Industrial Organization*, MIT Press, Cambridge.

Tirole, J. (1993), 'Collusion and the Theory of Organization', in Laffont, J.J. (ed.), *Advances in Economic Theory II*, Cambridge University Press, London.

Tobin, J. (1969), 'A general equilibrium approach to monetary theory', *JMCB*, 1.

Tobin, J. (1980), *Asset Accumulation and Economic Activity*, Chicago University Press, Chicago.

US Bureau of the Budget (1967), *Standard Industrial Classification Manuel*, Washington, DC.

Utton, M.A. (1971), 'The effects of mergers on concentration : U.K. manufacturing industry, 1954-65', *JIE*, 20.

Utton, M.A. (1977), 'Large firm diversification in british manufacturing industry', *EJ*, 87.

Utton, M.A. (1979), *Diversification and Competition*, Cambridge University Press, London.

Varian, H.R. (1984), *Microeconomic Analysis*, 2nd edition, Norton, New York.

Varian, H.R. (1992), *Microeconomic Analysis*, 3rd edition, Norton, New York.

Vernon, J.M. and Nourse, R.E.M. (1973), 'Profit rates and market structure of advertising intensive firms', *JIE*, 22.

Voos, P.B. and Mishel, L.R. (1986), 'The union impact on profits in the supermarket industry', *RESTAT*, 68.

Waterson, M. (1983), 'Economies of scope within market frameworks', *IJIO*, 1.

Waterson, M. (1984), *Economic Theory of the Industry*, Cambridge University Press, London.

Weiss, L.W. (1966), 'Concentration and labour earnings', *AER*, 56.

Weiss, L.W. (1971), 'Quantitative Studies of Industrial Organization', in Intriligator, M.D. (ed.), *Frontiers of Quantitative Economics*, North Holland, Amsterdam.

Weiss, L.W. (1971a), 'The effects of mergers on concentration : UK manufacturing industries 1954-65', *JIE*, 26.

Weiss, L.W. (1974), 'The Concentration Profits Relationship and Antitrust', in Goldschmid, H.J., Mann, H.M. and Weston, F.J. (eds.), *Industrial Concentration : The New Learning*, Little - Brown, Boston.

Weiss, L.W. (1976), 'Optimal Plant Size and the Extent of Sub-optimal Capacity', in Masson, R.T. and Qualls, P.D. (eds.), *Essays in Industrial Organization in honor of J.S. Bain*, Ballinger, Cambridge.

Weiss, L.W. (ed.) (1989), *Concentration and Price*, MIT Press, Cambridge.

Westbrook, M.D. and Tybout, J.R. (1993), 'Estimating returns to scale with large imperfect panels : an application to Chilean manufacturing industries', *The World Bank Economic Review*, 7.

White, L.J. (1974), *Industrial Concentration and Economic Power in Pakistan*, Princeton University Press, New Jersey.

White, L.J. (1976), 'Searching for the Critical Industrial Concentration : An Application of the Switching of Regimes Technique', in Goldfeld, S.M. and Quandt, R.E. (eds.), *Studies in Non-Linear Estimation*, Ballinger, Cambridge.

White, L.J. (1987), 'Antitrust and merger policy : a review and critique', *Journal of Economic Perspectives*, 1.

Williamson, O.E. (1968), 'Economics as an antitrust defence : the welfare trade-offs', *AER*, 58.

Williamson, O.E. (ed.) (1990), *Industrial Organization : An Elgar Reference Collection*, Edward Elgar, Aldershot.

Zieschang, K.D. (1983), 'A Note on the decomposition of cost efficiency into technical and allocative components', *JETS*, 23.

Zieschang, K.D. (1984), 'An extended Farrell technical efficiency measure', *JET*, 33.

Index

ability differential 120
absolute
   concentration 20
   cost advantage 112
additive decomposability 18
additivity 64
advertising intensity 119
allocative efficiency 85
anonymity 63-4
Antimonopoly Law 1947 100
antitrust authorities 62
   law 101
Australia 131
average marginal revenue 27

bariers to entry, see entry barriers
   to exit 30
   to imitation 134
behavioral policy 72
Belgium 121, 133
Berry diversification index 22
Bertrand
   conjecture 74
   equilibrium 74
best instantaneous rate 68
Beta function 141
boundedness 47, 64
British firms 19
Business Standard 8

capital gain 108
   recquirement 111
cartel 45
Cauchy - Schwartz inequality 69
central limit theorem 137
Central Statistical Organization 4
characteristic function 60
Chile 120,121,131
Clarke - Davies diversification index 24
Clayton Act 100
closed set 48
coalition
   losing 61
   minimal winning 61
   winning 61
Cobb - Dougls function 71
coefficient of variation 20
collusive parameter 129
commensurability principle 81
commuter carriers 124
compact set 49
competitive fringe 43
complete concentration 10
comprehensive concentration index 17
concave function 36
concentration curve 10
               dominance 11
conglomerate merger 8

conjectural variation 40
consistent conjectural equilibrium 74
Consolidated Coffee 92
consumers' surplus 66-7
consumption efficiency 41
contestabilty 122
continuity 9
convex
   function 36
   set 57
core 60
cost function 39
Cournot equilibrium 43
critical concentration ratio 132
cumulative distribution function 35

deadweigent loss 67
Debreu-Farrell efficiency measure 82
deconcentration 131
demand side substitute 4
density function 35
depriciation 107
Descartes' rule 140
diversification
   curve 22
   index 22
dominant
   cartel 45
   firms 43
   group 45
   strategy 58
duopoly 42
dynamic learning 135

economic efficiency 83
Economic Times 90
economies of scale 111
   of scope 56
effective rates of protection 119
efficiency hypothesis 128
efficient input vectors 78

elasticity of innovation possibility 33
entry barriers 30, 106
envelope theorem 69
Euler - Lagrange Technique 147
European Economic Community 19
excess value ratio 110
expansion paths 84
external welfare effect 102

Färe - Lovell efficiency index 87
feasible configuration 123
first best 106
   mover advantage 111
folk theorem 60
France 121,133
free disposability 79
frontier function 76

game
   cooperative 57
   extensive form 57
   monotonic 61
   multiperiod 59
   noncooperative 57
   repeated 59
   simple 61
   single period 59
   strategic form 57
   weighted majority 61
   voting 61
generalized Leontief cost function 118
German law 62
Germany 15,121,131
giant Japanese firms 141
Gibrat's law 144
Gini coefficient 20
global efficiency 85
Godrej Soaps 92

Herfindahl-Hirschman index 16, 17
Hindustan

Aluminum Company 91
Lever 92
homogenity 6
horizontal merger 8

India 4,8,21,90,92,100
Indian manufacturing industries 118
   motor vehicle industry 125
   Railways 126
   Tobacco Company 21
industry performance gradient index 68
innovational oppurtunity 33
input correspondence 77
   isoquant 78-9
   requirement set 77
interactive specifications 114
isoconcentration curves 19
isocost line 84
isoprofit curve 44
Italy 45,133

Japan 100,121

k-firm concentration ratio 15

law of proportionate effect 137
Lerner index 39
limit price 111
limited capacity 74
Linda index 16
load factor 124
local firms 119
lognormal distribution 35
Lorenz curve 12
   dominantion 12

Malmquist - Shephard distance function 78
managerial talent 142
marginal concentration ratio 36
market criterion 3
market value of a firm 109
maxium efficiency principle 80
mercury cartel 45

merger principle 8
minimal concentration 10
minimum efficient scale 111
   list heading 4
mining of iron ore 4
mixed oligopoly 71
   strategy 59
mobility 30
Monopolies and Restrictive Practices (Inquiry and Control) Act 1948 100
Monopolies and Restrictive Trade Practices Act 1969 90
monopolistic competition 52
monopoly 41
   movement 90
multinational enterprises 118
multiplicative decomposability 21

Nash equilibrium 57
   subgame perfect 60
   with free legal entry 32
National Council of Applied Economic Research, New Delhi 119
natural monopoly 94
New Bank 8
normalization 6, 47
null player condition 64
numbers equivalent 17

oligopoly 42
   movement 90
operational inefficiency 120
opportunity cost 107
optimal density 149-50
optimum output distribution 147
output transfers principle 7
overall barriers 112

Pakistan 121
Pareto distribution 35
partial equilibrium 137
patent rights 30

payoff function 57
perfect competition 40
perfectly competitive equilibrium 41
power set 77
predation 22
price correlation 4
price leadership oligopoly 44-6
    collusive 45
    noncollusinve 45
prisoner's dilemma 58
private firm 71
Procter and Gamble 92
producers' surplus 66-7
profit
    economic 108
    normal 75
proportion of single plane 124
pseudo concentration curve 29
public firm 71
    policy 67
Punjab National Bank 8
pure strategy 59, 75

quasiconcave function 58
quasilinear economic function 48
quasiordering 11

rate of return
    earned 108
    excess 108
    nominal 108
    real 108
rational expectation 45
reaction function 43
Reliance
    Industry 91
    Petrochemicals 91
Renusagar Power Supply 91
Rényi entropy formula 18
replication principle 6
representative market power 48
Research and Development 31
residual demand 45

Rosenbluth index 16
route density 124
Russell efficiency index 87

S - convex 13
second best 137
secret price discount 26
shadow price 85
Shannon entropy function 18
Shapley value 63
Sherman Act 90, 100
single - parameter genralized Gini 20
skill intensity 119
slot constraints 124
small - firms property 7
Spain 45
Stackelberg equilibrium 44
standard deviation 20
Standard Industrial Classification 4
strategy space 57
structural optimum 72-3
    policy 72
subadditivity 93
sunk cost 30
superadditivity 61
supergame 60
supply side substitute 4
survivorship technique 114
sustainable configuration 123
symmetry 7
synergies 91

Taiwan 120
talent distribution 143
Tata
    Oil Mill Company 92
    Tea 92
technological criterion 3
    opportunity class 134
theory of intervention 67
Tobin's q 109-10
transition equation 139

probability 139

U.K. 4,15,21,28,33,90,100,117,131,133
U.S. airline industry 122
    banking industry 122
    Bureau of Census 116
    consumer good industries 116
    manufacturing industries 116
    producer good industries 116
    Steel 90
U.S.A. 4,21,28,90,133
unionization 132

value 60
variance 20
vertical merger 8

weak maximum efficiency principle 81
    monotonicity 81
welfare 66
world petroleum market 44

Yule distribution 141

zero output independence 8
Zieschang efficiency index 88

DATE DUE

Feb 7 2660	